Communities AROUND Us

Silver Burdett Ginn
Parsippany, NJ • Needham, MA
Atlanta, GA   Deerfield, IL   Irving, TX   Santa Clara, CA

PROGRAM AUTHORS

Juan R. García
Associate Professor of History and Associate Dean
  of the College of Social and Behavioral Sciences
University of Arizona
Tucson, AZ

Daniel J. Gelo
Associate Professor of Anthropology, Division of
  Behavioral and Cultural Sciences
University of Texas at San Antonio
San Antonio, TX

Linda L. Greenow
Associate Professor and Acting Chair, Department of Geography
S.U.N.Y. at New Paltz
New Paltz, NY

James B. Kracht
Professor of Geography and Educational
  Curriculum and Instruction
Texas A&M University
College Station, TX

Deborah Gray White
Professor of History
Rutgers University
New Brunswick, NJ

Silver Burdett Ginn
A Division of Simon & Schuster
299 Jefferson Road, P.O. Box 480
Parsippany, NJ 07054-0480

CONTENTS

Theme 3 Communities Yesterday and Today **158**

Reference 318

Maps

Atlas Maps

Map Adventures

Time Lines

Graphs, Tables, and Diagrams

x

Skills

Songs, Pledge

Literature

The following books are recommended for optional reading.

Map Handbook
CONTENTS

ARCTIC OCEAN

NORTH AMERICA

EUROPE

ASIA

ATLANTIC OCEAN

AFRICA

PACIFIC OCEAN

SOUTH AMERICA

INDIAN OCEAN

AUSTRALIA

World

N W E S

ANTARCTICA

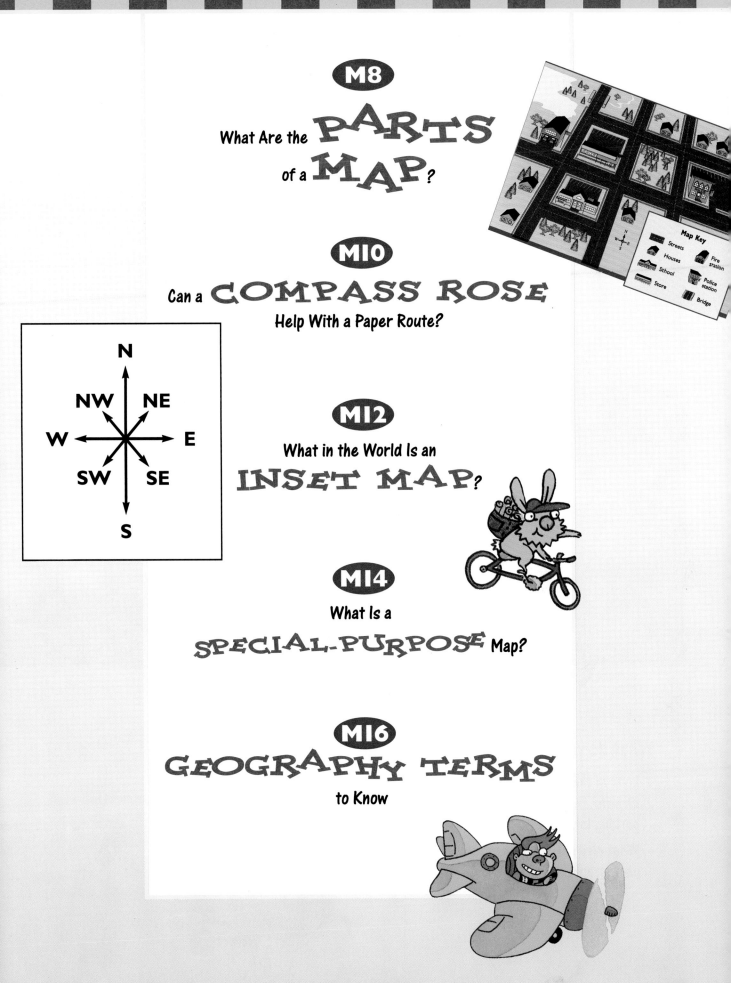

How Does a MAP Show Our WORLD?

What does a place look like if you see it from above? The photograph below was taken from an airplane. The same area is shown on the **map** on page M3. A map is a drawing that shows what a place looks like from above.

What do you see?

- Look at the photograph. Find the streets, the buildings, and a parking lot.
- What else can you find in the photograph?

The map below has a special part called the **key**. The key shows what **symbols**, or signs, are used in the map. Sometimes, colors are used as symbols. Always look at the key to find out what real places and things the symbols stand for.

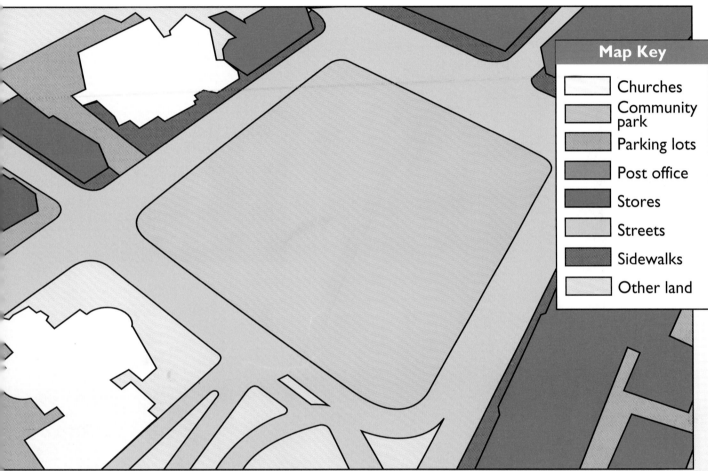

Map Key

- Churches
- Community park
- Parking lots
- Post office
- Stores
- Streets
- Sidewalks
- Other land

Use the map key.

- Find a park in the photograph. What color in the map key stands for the park? Now find the park on the map.

- Find the streets and the buildings. Do the photograph and the map show these in the same places?

Now Try This!

Find a photograph in this book that shows an outdoor scene. How would it look from above?

- **Use the photo as a guide. Then draw a map of the place.**

- **Add a key to your map. Use different colors or make up symbols to show its important features.**

M3

What Will You Find on a GLOBE?

This year you will learn about many places on Earth. One way to learn about Earth is to look at a **model**. A model is a small copy of a real thing. A **globe** is a model of Earth. The bottom picture below shows how Earth looks from space. In the top picture, the globe shows the same part of Earth.

Which is which?

- Which photograph shows the real Earth?
- What does the other photograph show?

Earth or globe?

How are the photograph of Earth from space and the globe alike? How are they different?

The map below shows Earth divided into two parts. Between the halves, find the line that is called the **equator**. The equator divides Earth into the **Northern Hemisphere** and the **Southern Hemisphere**. People who live in the United States live in the Northern Hemisphere.

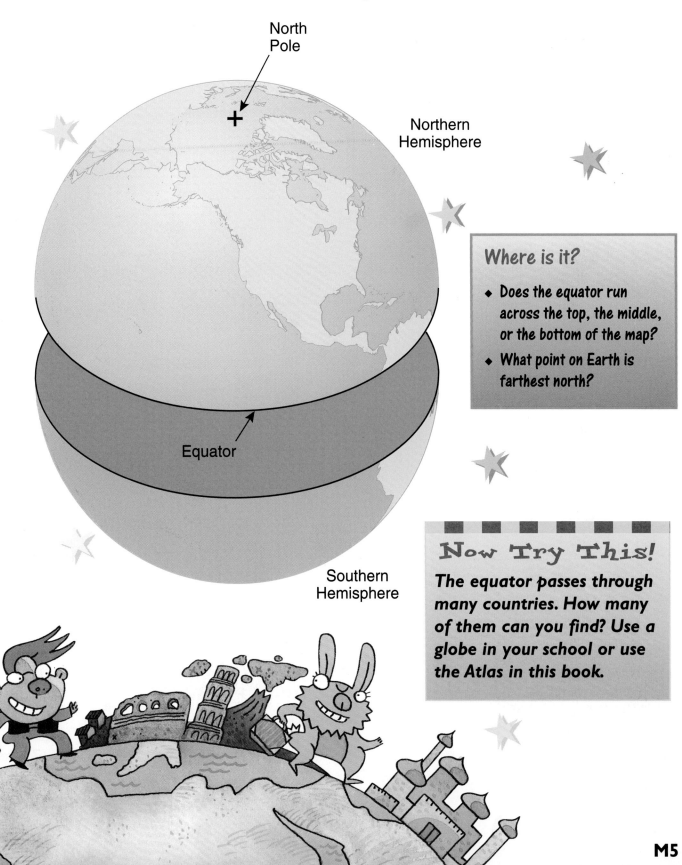

North Pole

Northern Hemisphere

Equator

Southern Hemisphere

Where is it?

♦ Does the equator run across the top, the middle, or the bottom of the map?

♦ What point on Earth is farthest north?

Now Try This!

The equator passes through many countries. How many of them can you find? Use a globe in your school or use the Atlas in this book.

What on Earth Are OCEANS and CONTINENTS?

If you traveled around Earth in a spaceship, you would see a huge ball made of water and land. You would see that almost three fourths of Earth is covered by water. Much of that water is in the **oceans**. The four oceans are the biggest bodies of water on Earth.

The rest of Earth's surface is made up of land. These large land areas are called **continents**.

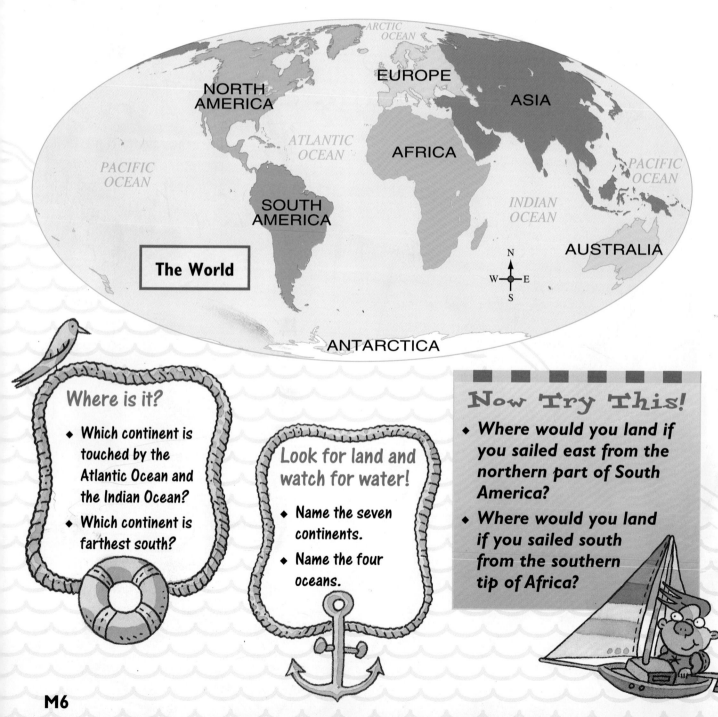

The World

Where is it?

- Which continent is touched by the Atlantic Ocean and the Indian Ocean?
- Which continent is farthest south?

Look for land and watch for water!

- Name the seven continents.
- Name the four oceans.

Now Try This!

- Where would you land if you sailed east from the northern part of South America?
- Where would you land if you sailed south from the southern tip of Africa?

What Are MAP SYMBOLS?

A map can show where places are found. It can show natural things, like land, mountains, or rivers. Maps can also show things that people have put on the land. Roads, bridges, and cities are things made by people.

Maps use **symbols** to stand for real places and things. When you read a map, you have to know what the symbols stand for. That's why a map has a **key**, or **legend**. A map key may contain several symbols.

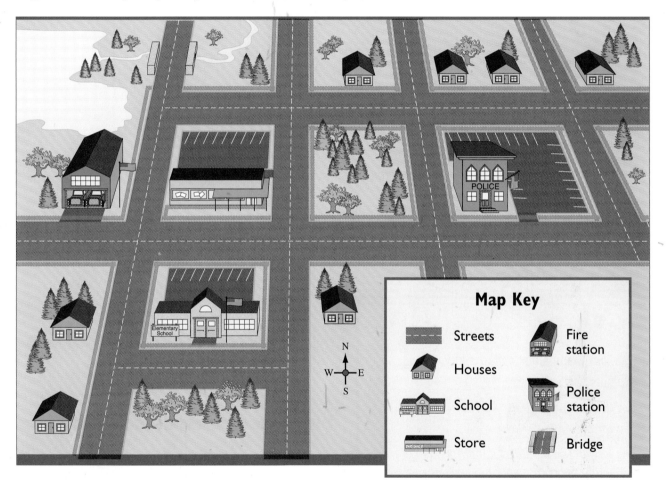

Map Key

Streets		Fire station	
Houses		Police station	
School		Bridge	
Store			

Look at the map key.

- Tell what each symbol stands for.
- Find the places and things on the map.

Now Try This!

Try drawing some map symbols of your own. Next to each symbol, explain what it stands for. If you need some ideas, look at the maps in this book.

What Are the PARTS of a MAP?

There are many maps in this book. Some of them are large and some are small. Some show all of Earth. Some show only a small part of it.

You only need to know a few things to read any map in this book. Those things are explained in the boxes below.

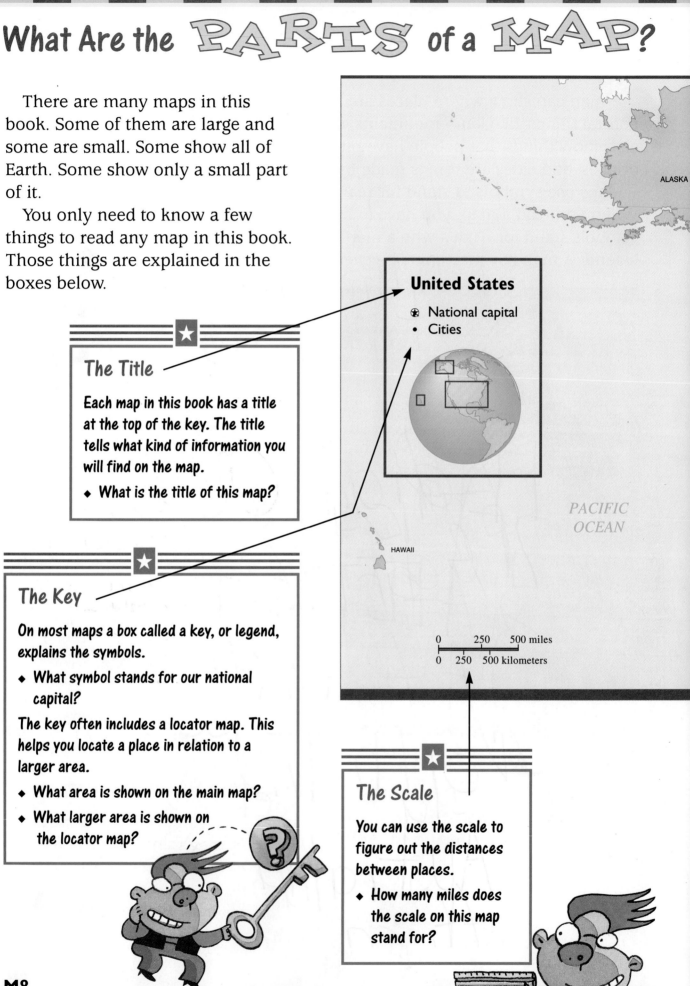

ALASKA

United States

⊛ National capital
• Cities

PACIFIC
OCEAN

HAWAII

0   250   500 miles
0   250   500 kilometers

⭐ The Title

Each map in this book has a title at the top of the key. The title tells what kind of information you will find on the map.

◆ What is the title of this map?

⭐ The Key

On most maps a box called a key, or legend, explains the symbols.

◆ What symbol stands for our national capital?

The key often includes a locator map. This helps you locate a place in relation to a larger area.

◆ What area is shown on the main map?

◆ What larger area is shown on the locator map?

⭐ The Scale

You can use the scale to figure out the distances between places.

◆ How many miles does the scale on this map stand for?

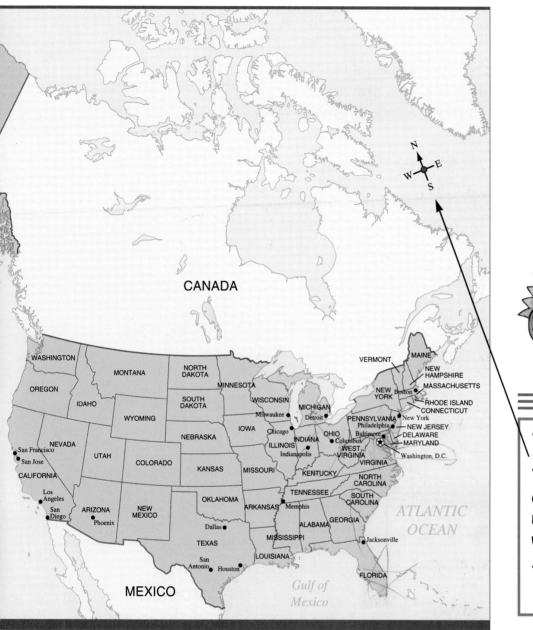

WASHINGTON
OREGON
IDAHO
MONTANA
NORTH DAKOTA
SOUTH DAKOTA
WYOMING
NEVADA
UTAH
COLORADO
CALIFORNIA
San Francisco
San Jose
Los Angeles
San Diego
ARIZONA
NEW MEXICO
Phoenix
MINNESOTA
WISCONSIN
Milwaukee
IOWA
NEBRASKA
KANSAS
MICHIGAN
Detroit
Chicago
ILLINOIS
INDIANA
Indianapolis
OHIO
Columbus
WEST VIRGINIA
MISSOURI
KENTUCKY
OKLAHOMA
ARKANSAS
Memphis
TENNESSEE
NORTH CAROLINA
SOUTH CAROLINA
TEXAS
Dallas
San Antonio Houston
LOUISIANA
MISSISSIPPI
ALABAMA
GEORGIA
Jacksonville
FLORIDA

VERMONT
MAINE
NEW HAMPSHIRE
MASSACHUSETTS
NEW YORK
Boston
RHODE ISLAND
CONNECTICUT
New York
PENNSYLVANIA
Philadelphia
NEW JERSEY
Baltimore
DELAWARE
MARYLAND
VIRGINIA
Washington, D.C.

CANADA

MEXICO

Gulf of Mexico

ATLANTIC OCEAN

N
W E
S

★

The Compass Rose

The compass rose is a drawing that tells where north, south, east, and west are on the map.

◆ Is Milwaukee north or south of Chicago?

Now Try This!

First draw a rough map of your community. Draw in the major streets, then put in the major places of interest. Put in your school and your home and any other places you like to visit.

Can a COMPASS ROSE
Help With a Paper Route?

A **compass rose** is a drawing that helps you find directions on a map. Look at the first drawing of a compass rose below. The letters N, S, E, and W stand for north, south, east, and west.

The second drawing of a compass rose gives even more information. It shows the in-between directions. A place that lies between the north arrow and the east arrow is between north and east. In other words, it is in the northeast, an in-between direction.

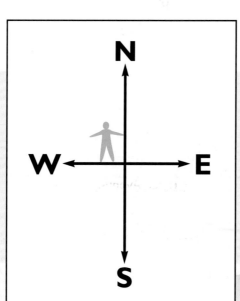

What way is it?

Look at the map on page M11.

- Which house is furthest east, the Sanford house or the Jones house?
- Is the Smith house north or south of the Robinson house?

Places between two arrows

The letters NE on the compass rose stand for the in-between direction northeast.

- What do the letters SE, SW, and NW stand for?
- What direction is between south and west?
- What direction is between west and north?

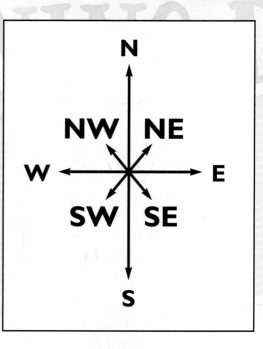

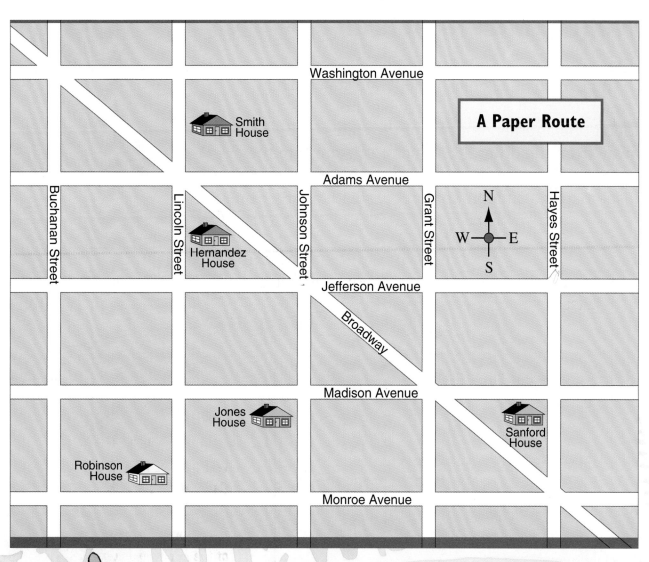

A Paper Route

Deliver the papers.

From the Robinson house, go to the Sanford's.

◆ In what direction should you travel on Monroe Avenue? In what direction do you turn on Hayes Street?

◆ In what direction should you go now to get to the Hernandez house?

Now Try This!

Find your state on the map on pages M8–M9.

◆ In what main or in-between direction are these states from your state?

Minnesota
New York
Texas
California

What in the World Is an INSET MAP?

The United States has 50 separate states. They stretch over a huge area. Forty-eight of the states touch one another, but two of the states are located far away from the other 48. Which two states are they?

The map on these pages has two **inset maps**. An inset map is a small map that goes with a larger one.

Inset Maps

One of the inset maps shows the state of Hawaii.

◆ What state does the other inset map show?

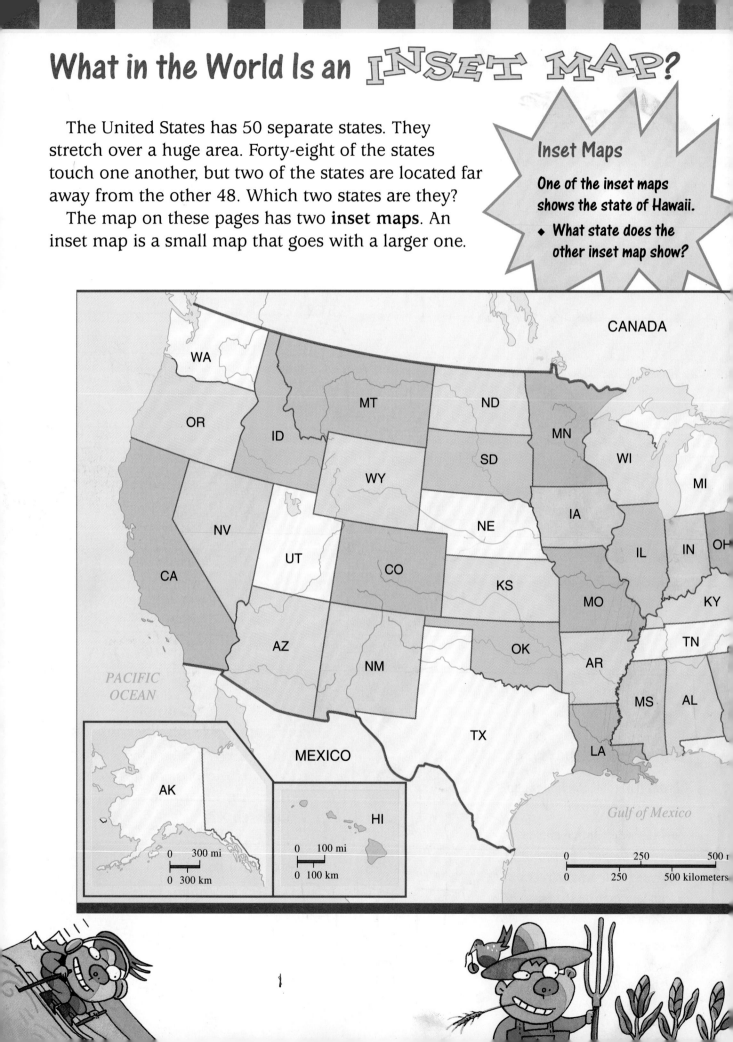

CANADA

WA

OR

MT

ND

MN

WI

MI

ID

WY

SD

NE

IA

IL

IN

OH

NV

UT

CO

KS

MO

KY

CA

AZ

NM

OK

AR

TN

MS

AL

KY

PACIFIC OCEAN

TX

LA

MEXICO

Gulf of Mexico

AK

0 300 mi

0 300 km

HI

0 100 mi

0 100 km

0 250 500 r

0 250 500 kilometers

An **abbreviation** is a shortened form of a word. Look at the map of the United States. Because there are so many states, mapmakers often use abbreviations for state names. The name of each state is shown with just two letters. Sometimes the first two letters of the state are used.

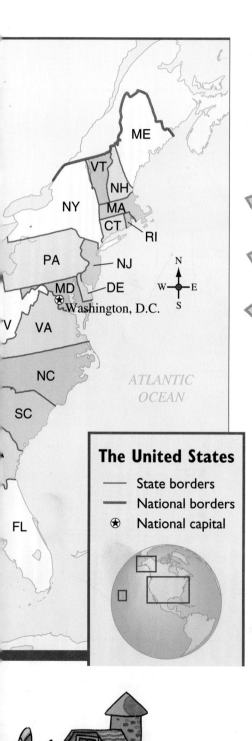

The United States

— State borders
— National borders
⊛ National capital

Look for patterns.

Find at least five abbreviations for each pattern.

♦ the first two letters of the name of the state
♦ the first and last letter of the name of the state
♦ the first letter of two words

Now Try This!

♦ Make a list of the abbreviations for ten state names.
♦ Trade papers with a partner.
♦ Write the full name of each state next to its abbreviation.

Did you and your partner choose any of the same abbreviations? Did you both choose the name of the state where you live?

Alabama	AL
Alaska	AK
Arizona	AZ
Arkansas	AR
California	CA
Colorado	CO
Connecticut	CT
Delaware	DE
Florida	FL
Georgia	GA
Hawaii	HI
Idaho	ID
Illinois	IL
Indiana	IN
Iowa	IA
Kansas	KS
Kentucky	KY
Louisiana	LA
Maine	ME
Maryland	MD
Massachusetts	MA
Michigan	MI
Minnesota	MN
Mississippi	MS
Missouri	MO
Montana	MT
Nebraska	NE
Nevada	NV
New Hampshire	NH
New Jersey	NJ
New Mexico	NM
New York	NY
North Carolina	NC
North Dakota	ND
Ohio	OH
Oklahoma	OK
Oregon	OR
Pennsylvania	PA
Rhode Island	RI
South Carolina	SC
South Dakota	SD
Tennessee	TN
Texas	TX
Utah	UT
Vermont	VT
Virginia	VA
Washington	WA
West Virginia	WV
Wisconsin	WI
Wyoming	WY

What Is a SPECIAL-PURPOSE Map?

Maps can show many things. They can show where places are, and they can show the distance between places.

The map on these pages shows about how much rain falls in the United States in any one year. We call this kind of map a **special-purpose map**. That's because it has a special purpose–to show rainfall.

On the rainfall map, color is used to show which places get more rain and which places get less rain.

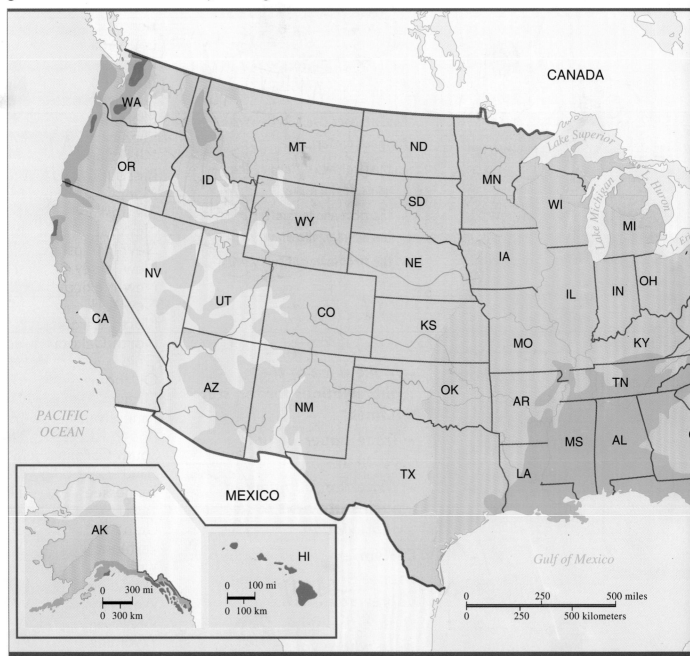

Read a rainfall map.

Match the color on the map with the map key.

- What color is used for the state of Virginia? Find that color in the map key.
- How much rain does Illinois get in an average year?

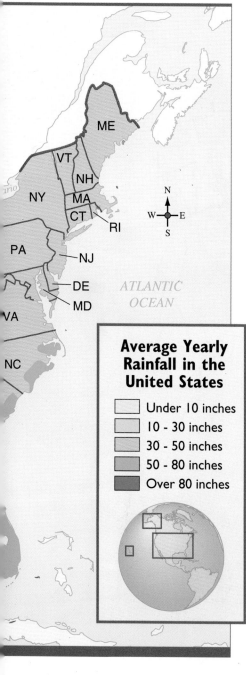

Average Yearly Rainfall in the United States

- ☐ Under 10 inches
- ☐ 10 - 30 inches
- ☐ 30 - 50 inches
- ☐ 50 - 80 inches
- ☐ Over 80 inches

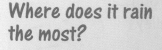

Where does it rain the most?

- Which state receives more rain, Nevada or New York?
- Which gets more rain, Alaska or Hawaii?

Now Try This!

Make up a quiz for a partner. Write three questions about the rainfall map. Then trade papers and write answers to your partner's questions.

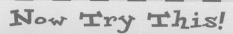

GEOGRAPHY TERMS to Know

The land and the water on Earth have many different shapes. Some important forms of land and water are described on these pages. To see what a certain form looks like, check the number next to its description. Then find it on the drawing.

1 canyon A canyon is a deep, narrow valley with steep sides.

2 coast A coast is land that borders on the sea or ocean.

3 forest A forest is a heavy growth of trees that covers a large area.

4 harbor A harbor is a sheltered area of water where ships can anchor safely.

5 hill A hill is raised land that is lower and more rounded than a mountain.

6 island An island is an area of land that is surrounded by water.

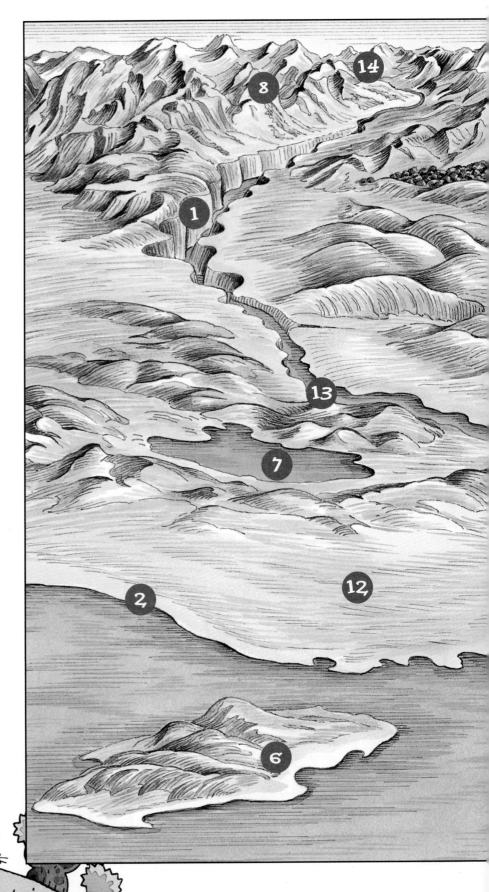

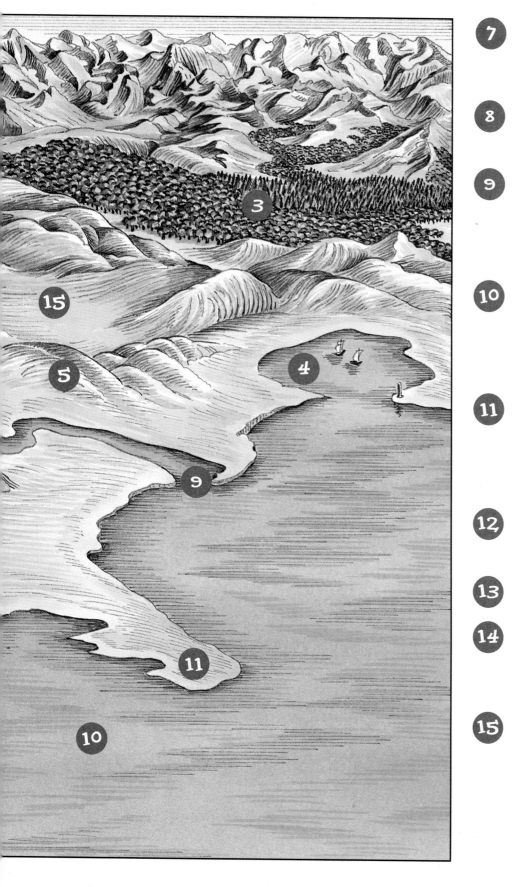

7 **lake** A lake is a body of water that is sometimes completely surrounded by land.

8 **mountain** A mountain is a steep, high land area.

9 **mouth of a river** A river mouth is the place where a river flows into a larger body of water.

10 **ocean** The oceans are the entire body of salt water that covers almost three fourths of Earth's surface.

11 **peninsula** A peninsula is a piece of land that is surrounded by water on three sides.

12 **plain** A plain is a broad stretch of level, or nearly level, land.

13 **river** A river is a flowing body of water.

14 **source of a river** A river source is the place where a river begins.

15 **valley** A valley is a long, low area of land, usually between mountains or hills.

Learning About Communities

A community is a place that's big
like a country, state, or town.
Or it's small like your own classroom
with friendship all around.

A community is a place to meet,
to work and play and care.
A community is a feeling
that all of us can share.

Chapter 1

Our

In this chapter you'll discover many different kinds of communities and some ways the people who live in them depend upon each other.

▼ Where are baseball bats made? Find out on page 19.

CONTENTS

Communities

You can learn special things about communities from these books. Read one that interests you and fill out a book-review form.

READ AND RESEARCH

Round and Round the Money Goes: What Money Is and How We Use It by **Melvin and Gilda Berger, illustrated by Jane McCreary** (Ideals Publishing Corporation, 1993)
People in communities earn, spend, and save money. Do you know what people used for money before coins and dollar bills were invented? Find out what you can do with money you earn or are given. *(nonfiction)*
• *You can read a selection from this book on page 20.*

Where Do I Live? by **Neil Chesanow, illustrated by Ann Iosa** (Barron's Educational Series, 1995)
Can you name all the places where you live? From your small room to a huge universe, you will discover the many places that are a part of you and your home. *(nonfiction)*

Riddle City, USA! A Book of Geography Riddles by **Marco and Giulio Maestro** (HarperCollins Children's Books, 1994)
There's a riddle in this book for each of our fifty states. Can you find the one about your own state? You'll have fun learning about our country's cities, mountains, rivers, and lots more. *(humor)*

Knowing how to use a map of the United States can help you locate each state by its name and shape.

UNDERSTAND IT
A map of the United States, like the one below, shows the location of the 50 states. You can find each state by knowing its name and the states that border it.

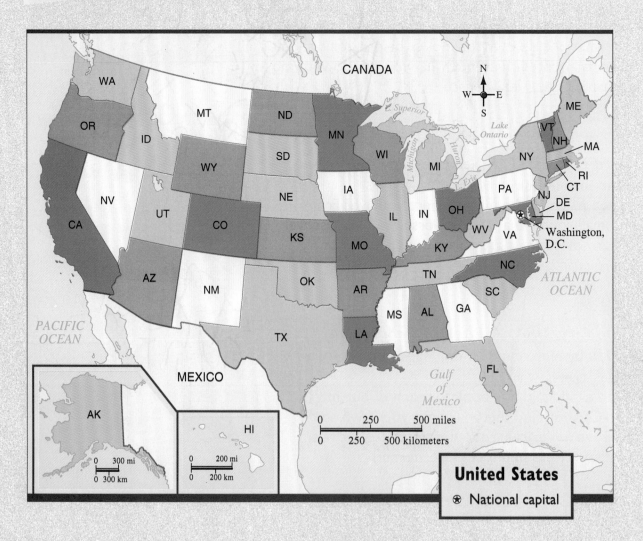

United States
⊛ National capital

4

OUR FIFTY STATES

EXPLORE IT

The name of each state is shown with just two letters. Look at page M13 in the Map Handbook to see a list of the state names and their abbreviations. What's the abbreviation for your state? Some states border, or touch, other states, bodies of water, or other countries.

A map of the United States also needs inset maps to show two states that are located far away from the other states. What are the names of these two states? Look in the Atlas on page 324 to see the actual location of these states.

TRY IT

Which states can you identify on the map on page 4? With a partner, try naming the states by playing this game.

Take turns. Close your eyes and point to a spot on the map. If your finger isn't on a state, try again. Your partner can help direct you.

When you touch a state, say its name. Use the state's abbreviation, its location, or its shape to help you. Your partner can give you hints.

SKILL POWER SEARCH *Look at each map in this chapter, and see how quickly you can locate states by recognizing their names and shapes.*

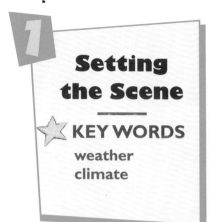

What Is a

FOCUS *People live in communities that are alike and different in many ways.*

Living in Communities

Everyone lives in a community. A community is a group of people who share a place. We call the place a community, too.

People live in many kinds of communities. In farming communities, small numbers of people might live far away from one another. In cities, large numbers of people might live close together.

Look at the map. It shows some communities in the United States. In this book you will learn about these communities and many more. Find the community on the map that is closest to the place where you live.

OR

CA

7

PACIFIC
OCEAN

AK

Community?

CANADA

MEXICO

Communities Around Us

⊛ National capital
★ State capitals
1 Americus, GA
2 Chicago, IL
3 Denver, CO
4 Fremont, NE
5 Houston, TX
6 Levittown, NY
7 Los Angeles, CA
8 Madison, WI
9 New York, NY
10 Phoenix, AZ
11 Plymouth, MA
12 St. Louis, MO
13 Topeka, KS
14 Washington, D.C.

Kinds of Places

Communities are located in many kinds of places. The land around communities may be flat or hilly. Communities may be located near oceans, lakes, or rivers. Describe the places shown in the photos at left and below.

Weather and Climate

A community has a certain kind of **weather**. The weather might be sunny or cloudy, cold or hot, wet or dry, at a particular time. What can you tell about the weather in the photograph below?

Climate is the kind of weather a place usually has. Climate affects the way people live. For example, people who live in a cold, snowy climate often wear warm clothes and boots. For fun, they might ski and sled.

weather The condition of the air at a certain time
climate The kind of weather a place has over a long period of time

9

Communities Are Everywhere

Communities all over the world are alike in some ways. In every community, people come together to meet their needs. They help each other by sharing the work and caring for one another.

1 SAANEN, SWITZERLAND
A town in the Swiss Alps

2 SITKA, U.S.
A fishing and lumbering center in Alaska

3 RIO DE JANEIRO, BRAZIL
A city known for its scenery, including Sugar Loaf Mountain

4 NAIROBI, KENYA
A street scene in Kenya's largest city

Communities are different in some ways, too. Look carefully at the photographs, and you will see some ways that communities are alike and different.

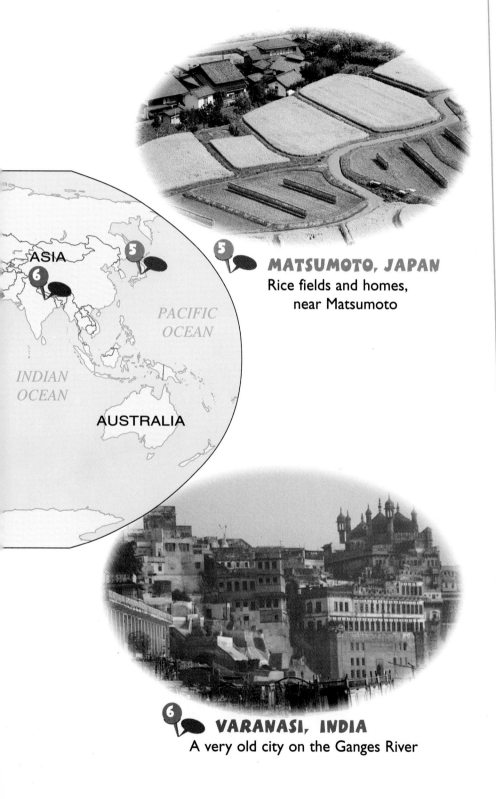

5 MATSUMOTO, JAPAN
Rice fields and homes, near Matsumoto

6 VARANASI, INDIA
A very old city on the Ganges River

ASIA

PACIFIC OCEAN

INDIAN OCEAN

AUSTRALIA

SHOW WHAT YOU KNOW!

REFOCUS

1. What is a community?

2. How are communities alike and different?

THINK ABOUT IT

How does the climate where you live affect the ways in which people work and play?

COMMUNITY CHECK

Whenever you see the drawing above, you will find activities to help you learn about your own community.

Draw a picture to show what the land around your community would look like if you were to take a photo of it.

Belonging to

FOCUS *People belong to many different communities at the same time.*

Different Communities

Do you know that you are a member of different communities? If you are a member of a club or a sports team, you are part of that community. You are also part of your school community.

These are only some of the communities you can belong to. Can you think of others?

Many Communities

How You Belong

When you belong to a community, you share some interests with the people in that community. You **participate**, or take part in, community activities. As you look at the photographs on these pages, you will see people who enjoy doing certain activities together.

⭐ **participate** To take part in something with other people

Our Many Communities

Karen wanted to show the communities where she belongs. She put a photo of herself in the center of a large paper plate. Then she drew several larger and larger circles around her photo. Inside each circle she wrote the name of a community. She drew pictures next to the names to illustrate her communities.

Like Karen, you are a member of many communities. Your school, neighborhood, town or city, and country are just some of your communities. You can even think of the whole world as your biggest community of all.

SHOW WHAT YOU KNOW!

REFOCUS

1. What are some of the communities that people belong to?

2. How do people show that they belong to a community?

THINK ABOUT IT

If you were to draw the communities to which you belong, what would you draw in the first circle around your photo?

COMMUNITY CHECK

Find some communities that people in your city or town belong to because they share certain interests. For each community, tell what interest people share.

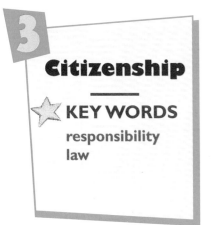
Communities Have Rules and Laws

FOCUS *Rules and laws help people in communities live together.*

Rules We Follow

Every community has rules that help people live together. These rules can be stated in writing or spoken in words. For example, your coach might tell you to be on time for practice—an unwritten rule. What are the written and unwritten rules being followed in the photo below?

Think of the communities you belong to. What rules do your communities have?

15

Girl Scout Troop 10

The next meeting is on September 21.

Tasks		Who's Responsible
Help new scouts get to know the other girls		Jeanne, Maria
Serve snack and juice		Isabel, Makeda, Carolyn
Wipe off tables		Jessica, Marta, Inez
Put craft supplies away		Emily, Joanna

Our Responsibilities

As a member of a community, you have **responsibilities**. Look at the list of responsibilities the Girl Scout troop has made to prepare for its next meeting. Think of what might happen if one of the girls forgets to do the job she has signed up to do.

Knowing what responsibilities you have in a community can make you feel comfortable and part of that group. When others can count on you to do what you are expected to do, they feel good, too.

⭐ **responsibility** Something a person is expected to do or take care of

Laws for Everyone

Like your teams, clubs, and school, the place you live has rules, too. The rules that everyone must follow are called **laws**. Does your pet dog or cat ever have to get a rabies shot? If so, that may be because your town or city has a law that requires this.

States make laws, too. Your state has a law that tells how many days you must attend school each year.

Countries also make laws. In the United States, special laws help protect you by making sure that new toys and bikes are safe to use.

⭐ **law** A written rule that everyone must follow

REFOCUS

1. What is the difference between a responsibility and a law?

2. What communities make laws?

THINK ABOUT IT

How do the responsibilities you have as a student help your school to work well?

COMMUNITY CHECK

Find out about the laws in your city or town that protect people from fire. Make a list of other important laws that protect your city or town.

Spotlight

⭐ **KEY WORDS**

factory
goods
services

FOCUS *People in communities make goods and provide services. They also use goods and services.*

Places Where People Work

People in communities have many kinds of jobs and work in many kinds of places. Some people work in places outside the home, and others work at home. The drawing below shows some of the places where people work. Find the **factory** which is on the edge of town.

⭐ **factory** A building where products are made, especially by people using machines

[Illustration of a town showing: Gas station, Rx Drug store, Lake Avenue, Diner, Movies, Valley Road, Avenue, Main Street, Hospital, Ridge Road, Bank, Hardware, School, Big Buy, Post Office, Open Book, Bakery, Market, Hillside Avenue, Pleasant Street, and a factory on the hillside]

18

Communities

Making Goods

Some workers make **goods**, or products. Think of all the goods you use each day. Your clothes, toys, and books are all goods that someone made. Some goods, such as baseball bats, are made in a factory. Other goods are made in small shops or at home.

Providing Services

Some workers provide **services**, or work that helps people in some way. At a store a clerk helps you. Teachers help you learn at school. Scientists, trash collectors, plumbers, and the police are just a few of the workers that provide services.

⭐ **goods** Products that can be bought and sold
services Work that is done for others

Round and Round the Money Goes:

What Money Is and How We Use It

by Melvin and Gilda Berger, Illustrated by Jane McCreary

How could you earn money by providing a service? What are some good ways to use the money you earn? Read on for some helpful answers to these questions.

Round and Round the Money Goes
What Money Is and How We Use It

By Melvin and Gilda Berger
Illustrated by Jane McCreary

Suppose you want to earn some money.

You can mow lawns, shovel snow, or baby sit.

You can walk dogs, weed gardens, or deliver
    bundles.

You can sell old, used toys, games, or books.

Can you think of other ways to earn money?

It's fun to spend money you earn.

You can buy something you need.

But always ask a grownup first.

Or you can give money to charity.

Charities help people who are in need.

They may be very old
or homeless.
They may be children who
are poor or sick.

You can also give money to
—churches or temples
—hospitals or animal shelters
—orchestras or museums
—and lots of other groups.

It's also fun to save your money. You can save for something special. You might want
—a new CD or video
—a bike or ice skates
—a book or computer game
—or a jacket or sneakers.

Start saving your money at home.
Find a good, safe place to keep it.

After awhile, bring your money
to a bank.

To find out more about money, check this book out of your school or public library.

REFOCUS

1. Where are goods made?

2. What choices can people make about the money they earn?

THINK ABOUT IT

What are some of the services that your family buys from other people?

How do these services help meet your needs?

COMMUNITY CHECK

List some jobs in your community. Next to the name of each job, write an *S* if that job provides a service or a *G* if it is a job that produces goods.

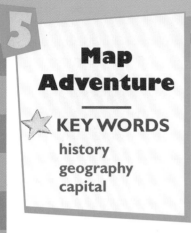

Map Adventure

⭐ **KEY WORDS**

history
geography
capital

The United

FOCUS *Knowing about our country is an important part of being a member of the United States community.*

One Big Community

The United States of America is a community—one with more than 250 million people. You are a member of this community. So is everyone else from each of our 50 states.

States Community

Learning About Our Country

As members of the United States community, we have a responsibility. We should know about our country, its people, its laws, its **history**, and its **geography**. The more we know about our country, the more we can help make it a better place to live.

You can begin to learn more about our country by playing the map game that follows. You'll have fun as you learn about some rivers and mountains as well as the 50 states and their **capitals**.

⭐ **history** The story of the past
geography The study of the earth and the ways in which people use it

⭐ **capital** A city where laws and plans for a state or a nation are made

U.S. Facts and Figures

- Alaska, the largest state, has 656,424 square miles.
- Rhode Island, the smallest state, has 1,545 square miles.
- Mount McKinley, in Alaska, is the highest mountain.
- Stampede Pass, Washington, is the snowiest town, with a record snowfall of about 431 inches.
- Mount Waialeale, Hawaii, gets the most rain, about 460 inches a year.

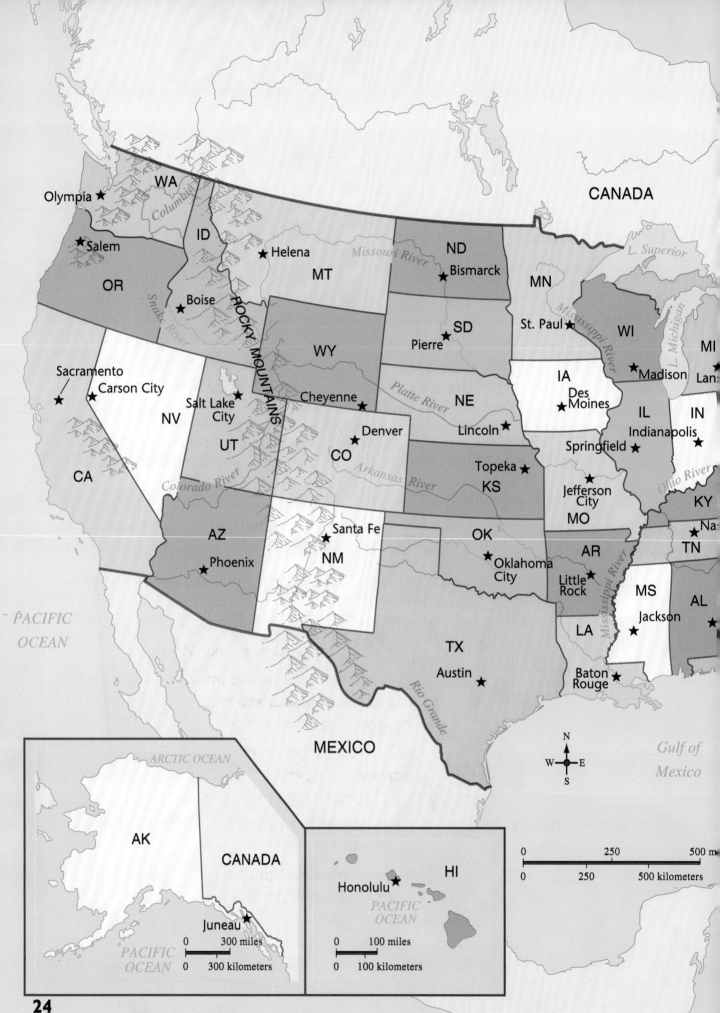

Olympia ★

WA

Salem ★

OR

Columbia River

CANADA

Helena ★

MT

Missouri River

ND
Bismarck ★

L. Superior

MN

St. Paul ★

Mississippi River

WI
Madison ★

L. Michigan

MI
Lan★

Boise ★

ID

Snake River

ROCKY MOUNTAINS

WY

Cheyenne ★

SD
Pierre ★

Platte River

NE

Lincoln ★

IA
Des ★
Moines

IL
Springfield ★

Indianapolis ★

IN

Sacramento ★
Carson City ★

NV

Salt Lake
City ★

UT

Denver ★

CO

Arkansas River

Topeka ★

KS

Jefferson ★
City

MO

Ohio River

KY
Na★

TN

CA

Colorado River

AZ

Phoenix ★

Santa Fe ★

NM

OK

Oklahoma ★
City

AR

Little ★
Rock

MS
Jackson ★

AL
★

LA

Mississippi River

TX

Austin ★

Baton ★
Rouge

PACIFIC
OCEAN

MEXICO

Rio Grande

N
W ◆ E
S

Gulf of

Mexico

ARCTIC OCEAN

AK

CANADA

Juneau ★

PACIFIC
OCEAN

0   300 miles

0   300 kilometers

HI

Honolulu ★

PACIFIC
OCEAN

0   100 miles

0   100 kilometers

0   250   500 m

0   250   500 kilometers

ME
VT
Augusta ★
NH
Lake Ontario
Montpelier ★
Concord ★
NY
Boston ★
Albany ★
MA
Providence ★
L. Erie
Hartford ★
RI
CT
PA
NJ
Harrisburg ★
★ Trenton
Columbus
Annapolis
Dover ★
DE
APPALACHIAN MOUNTAINS
WV
⊗ ★ ★
MD
ton ★
Richmond ★
Washington, D.C.
ort
VA
★ Raleigh
NC
SC
Columbia ★
ATLANTIC
lanta
OCEAN
GA
mery
Tallahassee
FL

REFOCUS

1. How many states make up the United States community?

2. What is one responsibility of a member of the United States community?

MAP IT

Play "What's My Name?" by using the map at left and the clues below to help you.

1. The abbreviation for my state name is ME. What's my name? What's the name of my capital?

2. I am a state that is southwest of North Dakota. I contain a large lake. What is my name?

3. Trace my route on the map. I am the river that begins in Minnesota and empties into the Gulf of Mexico. What's my name?

4. Put your finger on the state of Montana. Now move your finger to the north. I am the country that is your northern neighbor. What's my name?

EXPLORE IT

Now take turns with a classmate, making up clues and finding the answers on the map.

25

1 DO YOU REMEMBER...
COMPREHENSION

1. What's the difference between weather and climate?

2. What can make you feel you belong to a community?

3. Why is it important to meet your responsibilities?

4. Describe some services that workers provide.

5. What are some things we need to know about our country?

3 WHAT DO YOU THINK?
CRITICAL THINKING

1. How might it be easier to live in a dry climate than in a rainy one?

2. "To be a member of a community, you must participate in all its activities." Explain why you agree or disagree with this statement.

3. Why do communities have "no littering" laws?

4. Name some service workers in your school.

5. How might knowing our country's laws make you a helpful member of the United States community?

2 SKILL POWER
LOCATING OUR FIFTY STATES

Work in a small group. Choose ten states and make a chart with four columns that shows the states, countries, and oceans that border each state. Label the first column *State*, the second column *Bordering States*, the third *Bordering Countries*, and the fourth *Bordering Oceans*. Use the map on page 4 to find the information you need.

4 SAY IT, WRITE IT, USE IT
VOCABULARY

Choose five of the words below. Describe what each word means by giving two examples. For instance, hot and cold describe kinds of weather.

capital	law
climate	participate
factory	responsibility
geography	services
goods	weather
history	

5 GEOGRAPHY AND YOU
MAP STUDY

Use the maps in the chapter to answer the questions below.

1. Which states share a border with Lake Superior?

2. What river forms the eastern border of Arkansas?

3. Name two states that are northeast of our nation's capital.

4. Name the states that share a border with Mexico.

6 TAKE ACTION
CITIZENSHIP

What events have you enjoyed within your school community? Maybe you've gone to a spring fair or attended plays and concerts. Many people work hard to make these events happen. Talk to a parent or teacher and find out what is done to organize one of these events. Ask how students can help in the future.

7 GET CREATIVE
SCIENCE CONNECTION

Keep a record of your community's weather for one week. Listen to weather reports on the radio, watch weather reports on TV, or check the weather page of a newspaper. Record information on temperatures, sunshine, clouds, rain, and snow. After a week, write a report on the weather in your community.

LOOKING AHEAD

Discover in the next chapter what landforms are found in different communities.

Chapter 2

Communities are located in many different kinds of places. Learn why the location of a community is so important.

▼ Where did this boy's pet lizard come from? Find out on page 36.

CONTENTS

and Communities

These books are all about land, water, and communities. Read one that interests you and fill out a book-review form.

READ AND RESEARCH

If You're Not From the Prairie . . .
by David Bouchard, illustrated by Henry Ripplinger

(Simon & Schuster, 1995)
Let the words of a Canadian poet describe the prairie sun, wind, and sky. Let the artist's drawings show you the prairie's beauty. *(poetry)*
• *You can read a selection from this book on page 52.*

A River Ran Wild **by Lynne Cherry**

(Harcourt Brace & Co., 1992)
Thousands of years ago, people chose to settle on the shores of the clear, sparkling Nashua River. Find out how life along the river has changed and learn how one caring woman worked to save the river. *(nonfiction)*

A First Atlas **edited by Sue Hook**

(Scholastic, 1995)
You will learn about different regions of the world in this colorful atlas. Find out why people in the United States built their communities near certain bodies of water and on certain kinds of landforms. *(reference)*

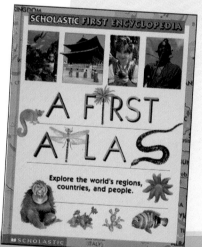

SKILL POWER COMPARING

Comparing and contrasting can help you understand how things are alike and different.

UNDERSTAND IT

How is your backpack different from your friend's? How are the backpacks alike? Think about the colors, the sizes, and the materials they are made from.

• When you describe how two things are alike and different, you are comparing and contrasting.

• To compare is to show how things are alike. To contrast is to show how things are different.

EXPLORE IT

Some places have football teams. Others have soccer teams. How are these sports alike? How are they different?

Football   **Soccer**

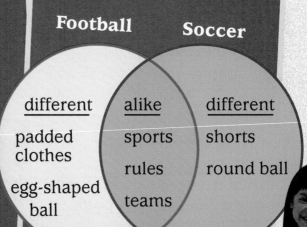

different	alike	different
padded clothes	sports	shorts
egg-shaped ball	rules	round ball
	teams	

The Venn diagram above compares and contrasts the two sports. The words in the middle tell how the sports are alike. The words on the outside tell how they're different.

AND CONTRASTING

TRY IT

Working with a partner, try comparing and contrasting two pets you have or would like to have. Then draw pictures of the two animals you and your partner have chosen. Have fun making the pictures! As you draw, talk about how the animals are alike and how they are different.

On a large piece of paper, make a Venn diagram about your silly pets. In the middle, write how the animals are alike. On the outside, write the differences. Include your diagram in a class "Guide to Pets" bulletin-board display.

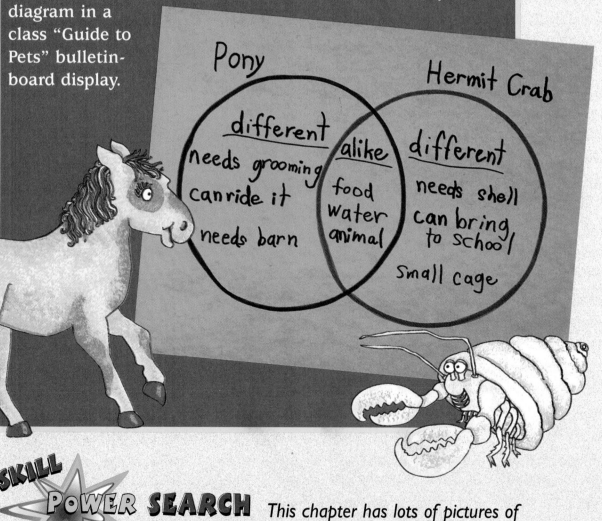

Pony

Hermit Crab

different
needs grooming
can ride it
needs barn

alike
food
water
animal

different
needs shell
can bring to school
small cage

SKILL

POWER SEARCH *This chapter has lots of pictures of places in the United States. Use a Venn diagram to help you compare and contrast two of them.*

Landforms

FOCUS *Landforms, bodies of water, and natural resources are important to communities.*

The Great Outdoors

Do you ever go camping? Before going, you need to make some decisions. Do you want to camp near an ocean, a lake, or a mountain? Later in the trip, you need to decide where to put your tent. This will bring up other questions. Is there drinking water nearby? Is there protection from bad weather?

Throughout history, people have been asking these same questions. When people decided to start a new community, they made choices about where to build it. Some people considered the different landforms, or shapes of land, before building. They thought about what natural resources, or useful materials, each area offered.

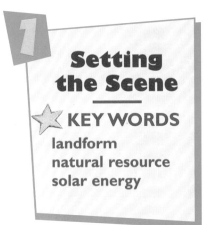

⭐ **landform** The shape of the land's surface
natural resource Something found in nature that is useful to people

32

and Water

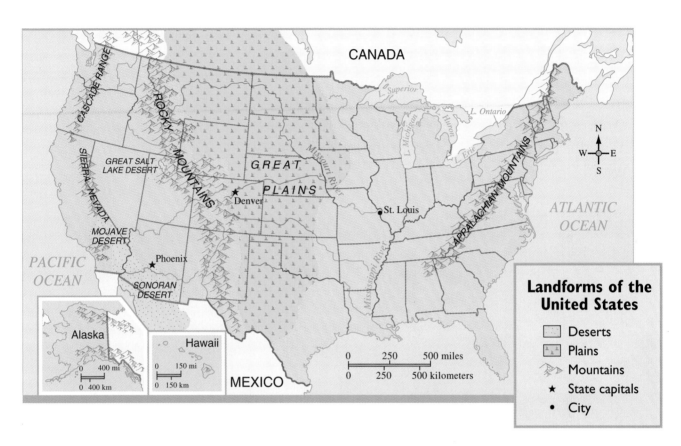

Landforms of the United States

- Deserts
- Plains
- Mountains
- ★ State capitals
- • City

CANADA

CASCADE RANGE
ROCKY MOUNTAINS
SIERRA NEVADA
GREAT SALT LAKE DESERT
GREAT PLAINS
Denver
MOJAVE DESERT
Phoenix
SONORAN DESERT
PACIFIC OCEAN
Superior
L. Ontario
L. Michigan
L. Huron
L. Erie
Missouri River
St. Louis
Mississippi River
APPALACHIAN MOUNTAINS
ATLANTIC OCEAN

N
W — E
S

Alaska
0 400 mi
0 400 km

Hawaii
0 150 mi
0 150 km

MEXICO

0   250   500 miles
0   250   500 kilometers

Types of Land and Water

A mountain is a landform that is much higher than other land. A plain is another kind of landform. It is a flat area with grass or trees. A desert is a dry area where very little rain falls and few kinds of plants can grow. Some deserts are very hot and others are quite cool, especially at night.

Bodies of water have different sizes and shapes. Lakes have land all around them. Rivers are long, flowing streams of water. Oceans are the largest bodies of water on Earth.

Choosing a Place to Live

The map above shows some of the major types of land and water in the United States. To early settlers who came to build their new communities, some places looked easier to live in than others. Many early communities were built near rivers because rivers offered natural resources such as fish to eat and fresh water to drink. Many people also used rivers to travel by boat or canoe. Today there are communities in all kinds of places.

Bodies of Water

The different bodies of water have many natural resources that people need. The lakes and rivers in the United States provide millions of pounds of fish every year. Many rivers have been used as important travel routes to move goods and people.

There are lots of natural resources found in the salty waters of the Atlantic, Pacific, Indian, and Arctic oceans. Oceans have a huge variety of fish and plant life. And oceans are the biggest water routes—they connect the United States to other countries around the world.

▲ Rivers are home to many different plants and animals, such as this great blue heron.

The Mountains

There are three main mountain ranges in the United States. Find the Appalachians, (ap uh LAY chunz), the Rockies, and the Sierra Nevada on the map on page 33.

Mountains offer many natural resources. They have lots of trees and animals. Many mountains also contain other useful materials. For example, gold, silver, and copper have all been found in the Rockies.

Mountains are also great places for outdoor activities. You can hike, bike, ski, or watch for birds and other wild animals.

▲ Melting snow from mountaintops can turn into powerful rivers.

▼ Wheat is one of the crops grown on the plains.

The Plains

The Great Plains stretch across a big part of the center of our country. Huge amounts of wheat, corn, and other crops are grown here. These grains are used to make bread and other food products.

The grasses that grow on the plains can feed cows, sheep, and goats. So the plains can also supply meat and dairy products. Wildlife is common on the plains. If you visited the plains, you might see rattlesnakes, opossums, buffaloes, or a prairie dog like the one shown here.

▲ They may be hard to find, but many animals, such as this collared lizard, live in deserts.

The Deserts

In the southwestern United States, you'll find the Mojave (moh HAH vee), the Sonoran, and the Great Salt Lake deserts. Do these hot, dry places have any natural resources? Yes! You just have to look closely. Deserts may look empty, but they are really full of life. You can find lizards, spiders, and snakes here. Cactus and sagebrush are among the plants that grow in deserts. Some of these plants produce fruits or flowers.

In deserts the sun itself is a valuable resource. Its strong rays can bake clay pots and bricks. People today also know how to trap and store energy from the sun. This **solar energy** is an important resource.

⭐ **solar energy** Energy that comes from the sun

Building Successful Communities

The United States has many different landforms and bodies of water. Our land and water offer us a wide range of natural resources. But resources alone are not enough. It is important to figure out the best way to protect and use these natural resources. A community that does is more likely to succeed.

DID YOU KNOW . . . The largest desert in the United States, the Mojave Desert in California, covers 25,000 square miles.

Mount McKinley, in Alaska, is the highest mountain in the United States.

The Mississippi River, one of the longest rivers in the United States, starts as a small stream in Minnesota.

Three Communities

You're about to take a look at three communities. Each one is a different kind of place. St. Louis, Missouri, sits right next to the Mississippi River. Denver, Colorado, is a Rocky Mountain community. And Phoenix, Arizona, lies in the Sonoran Desert. Each of these places has made the most of its natural resources and each has become a strong community.

SHOW WHAT YOU KNOW!

REFOCUS

1. What are some natural resources that mountains and deserts provide?

2. What kinds of natural resources do bodies of water provide?

THINK ABOUT IT

What might happen to a community with few natural resources?

COMMUNITY CHECK

Make a list of types of land and natural resources near your community.

FOCUS *River communities often become centers of trade and transportation.*

The Mighty Mississippi

The Mississippi River is 2,340 miles long and cuts through the middle of the United States. It provides a travel route from Minnesota to the Gulf of Mexico. On the map, find other rivers, such as the Missouri and Ohio rivers, that feed into the Mississippi.

Throughout history, people have carried goods up and down the Mississippi. In the past they used steamboats for transportation. Now people mostly use **barges**. A barge is a large flat boat often pushed or pulled by a smaller boat called a tugboat. The present-day photo below shows a barge on the Mississippi in New Orleans.

⭐ **barge** A large flat boat used for carrying goods along a river

▲ This picture from 1906 shows a Mississippi steamboat being loaded.

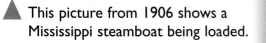

Communities

The Mississippi River

★ State capital
● City

Towns by the River

Long ago, people moving up and down the river needed places to stop. They needed meeting places where their products could be bought and sold. This is why towns sprang up along the Mississippi River.

Some of these towns became quite big. They had large waterfronts, or areas of land along the river. Boats carrying goods such as wheat, coal, and factory products could be loaded and unloaded here.

Boats carried these goods to be sold at other places all over the United States. Trade, or the buying and selling of products, also worked the other way. Boats from other places brought many items up and down the Mississippi to the towns along the river.

⭐ **trade** The buying and selling of products

Gateway to the West

St. Louis, Missouri, is one Mississippi River city that grew into a major center of trade. St. Louis lies near the spot where the Mississippi and Missouri rivers meet, so people from many different places brought goods here. As trade grew, St. Louis grew.

By the 1840s, St. Louis was more than just a city on a river. It had become the "Gateway to the West." From here, people left to explore and settle the West. Many travelers stopped in St. Louis to buy supplies.

St. Louis Today

Today the Mississippi River remains a major trade route. And St. Louis continues to be a busy and important river city. Many boats arrive at its waterfront each day. These boats carry millions of tons of products through St. Louis each year. Of course, a boat is no longer the only way to move large amounts of goods. Planes, trains, and trucks also carry products from place to place. St. Louis has 12 railroad lines and a major airport. Millions of people pass through St. Louis each year.

▼ The Gateway Arch was built in St. Louis in 1965 to remind everyone of the city's days as the Gateway to the West.

Living in St. Louis

The people of St. Louis take great pride in their city. St. Louis has universities, a zoo, sports teams, and lots of museums. Many people in St. Louis take advantage of the activities held in Forest Park, such as an Earth Day parade and a yearly hot-air balloon festival. St. Louis is a successful river community. It has made the most of its location on the great Mississippi River.

SHOW WHAT YOU KNOW!

REFOCUS

1. Why have many cities developed along the Mississippi River?

2. Why is St. Louis called the Gateway to the West?

THINK ABOUT IT

What are some of the advantages and disadvantages of living in a river community?

WRITE ABOUT IT

Draw a picture and write a paragraph describing the different types of transportation you might find in a river city.

Mountain

Then and Now

⭐ **KEY WORDS**

mine

boom town

FOCUS *Mountains have natural resources that can help communities develop.*

The Rocky Mountains

The Rocky Mountains are the longest mountain chain in North America. The Rockies cover more than 3,000 miles. They stretch from Alaska southward through Canada and many western states.

Each year, the Rockies receive tons of snow. As some of this snow melts, it runs down the mountains and turns into rivers. Big rivers such as the Colorado and the Rio Grande start high in the Rockies.

CANADA

WA

Helena ★ MT

ND

OR

Boise ★ ID

SD

WY

ROCKY MOUNTAINS

★ Cheyenne

Salt Lake City ★

★ Denver

NV

UT

CO

Colorado River

CA

AZ

★ Santa Fe

NM

Rio Grande

TX

MEXICO

The Rocky Mountains

★ State capitals

0	200	400 miles
0	200	400 kilometers

Communities

Natural Resources

The water found in mountain streams is a good natural resource. The Rockies also offer lots of other resources. The pine forests of the Rockies are one example. The wood from these pine trees is used in many ways.

The rocks themselves have many natural resources. Gold, silver, copper, and coal can all be found in the Rockies.

The Rockies are also filled with wildlife. Bears, deer, hawks, minks, and mountain lions are just a few of the animals that live in the forests. Many other creatures, such as goats and bighorn sheep, live higher up where trees don't grow.

A Hard Place to Live

Even though mountains like the Rockies are full of natural resources, living in the mountains can be hard. Traveling can be difficult and food can be hard to grow. The weather can also change quickly in the mountains. One day it might be very warm and the next day it could snow.

A long time ago, Native American groups such as the Utes (yoots) and the Shoshones (shoh-SHOH neez) figured out how to live successfully in the Rockies. But by the early 1800s, few other people lived here. To most people, life in the Rockies just looked too hard.

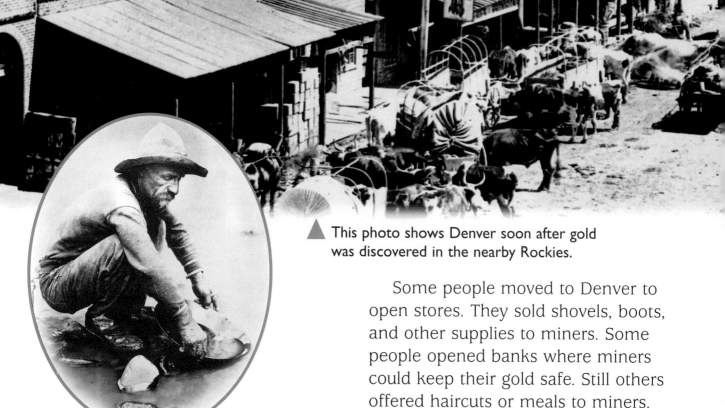

This photo shows Denver soon after gold was discovered in the nearby Rockies.

Some people moved to Denver to open stores. They sold shovels, boots, and other supplies to miners. Some people opened banks where miners could keep their gold safe. Still others offered haircuts or meals to miners.

Denver today is a large, busy city.

Gold-Rush Days

In 1858 something happened that brought people rushing to the Rockies. Gold was discovered. People built **mines** to dig gold out of the rocks. Many people, like the miner shown above, hoped to strike it rich. Towns that sprang up near the mines were called **boom towns** because they grew with a "boom," or sudden burst. One such town was Denver, Colorado.

mine A hole dug in the earth to dig out natural resources, such as gold
boom town A town that starts suddenly

Developing New Resources

Then the gold started to run out. Denver needed to find new resources. People began to dig other metals, such as silver, out of the rocks. A railroad line was built, and cattle and sheep ranches were set up. People even built a tunnel straight through the mountains to connect their community to places farther west.

Denver Today

People in Denver have continued to discover all sorts of ways to make use of the area's resources. Lumber companies as well as ranching and mining companies are all important businesses now.

Recreation is another use for the mountains. People enjoy the outdoors in many different ways. Many tourists come here to ski, hike, or watch for mountain wildlife. Some people attend the Outward Bound school to learn how to survive in the mountains.

Denver started out as a community that served miners. But today it is a strong, modern city that serves all kinds of people.

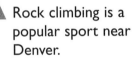

Rock climbing is a popular sport near Denver.

SHOW WHAT YOU KNOW!

REFOCUS

1. What are some natural resources in the Rockies?

2. Why was Denver called a boom town?

THINK ABOUT IT

Other boom towns disappeared after the gold ran out. How did Denver keep growing?

WRITE ABOUT IT

Make a Venn diagram to compare Denver during the gold rush with Denver today.

Desert

FOCUS *People living in the desert must face many challenges to meet their needs.*

The Sonoran Desert

If you were trying to walk across the Sonoran Desert in Arizona, you'd feel the sun beating down on your head and burning your skin. You'd need to bring lots of water to drink because there would be no water in sight. The ground would be dry. You'd see cactuses and rocks of all different shapes and sizes.

You might think that no community could be built in such a place. But you'd be wrong! Phoenix, Arizona, is located here. Phoenix receives only about seven inches of rain each year and temperatures often hit 100°F. Yet more than 2 million people live here.

The Sonoran Desert Area

★ State capital
• Cities
▢ Desert

46

Communities

Living in the Desert

How do desert communities such as Phoenix survive in this hot, dry climate? Well, first the people have to figure out how to get enough water and how to stay cool in the desert heat.

Once those problems are solved, people can then enjoy the special beauty of the desert plants and animals. These plants include many kinds of cactuses. Desert animals include coyotes, owls, rabbits, skunks, tarantulas, and lizards.

Getting Water

Hundreds of years ago, the Hohokam (huh HOH kum) Indians lived in the Arizona desert. They built ditches to carry water onto land from the Gila and Salt rivers. This allowed them to grow crops such as corn, cotton, and squash. In museums in Phoenix today, you can see Hohokam items like the one shown above.

The Roosevelt Dam helps Phoenix get needed water.

Solving Problems

When **explorers** came to Phoenix in the 1860s, they survived by learning from what the Hohokam left behind. They used Hohokam ditches for water, and they planted crops. Then in 1911 the Roosevelt Dam was built. The **dam** creates a lake where water is stored and released when needed.

explorer A person who travels to unknown places
dam A wall built to hold back the flow of water

Then in the 1950s air conditioning came into widespread use. This invention helped to solve Phoenix's other problem—desert heat.

A Modern City

Phoenix has grown into a large desert city. Its dry, sunny climate has attracted many people from states with cold winters. People also have come to Phoenix to find jobs. They work in one of the many businesses that have moved here.

Many people come to Phoenix on vacation. If you visit Phoenix today, you'll see a big modern city. It is a place where you can enjoy many activities. You might visit the zoo or walk through one of the 138 parks. Phoenix also has a famous desert museum.

The people of Phoenix have solved many of the problems of living in the desert. And they have found ways to enjoy the natural resources around them.

SHOW WHAT YOU KNOW!

REFOCUS

1. What is the climate of a desert?

2. What is a dam?

THINK ABOUT IT

What are some of the challenges of living in the desert?

WRITE ABOUT IT

Write a story about what it would be like to live in a desert.

Sharing the

FOCUS *People in both the United States and Canada use the natural resources of the Great Plains.*

The Great Plains

How "great" is the Great Plains region? Well, it's 3,000 miles from north to south and up to 700 miles east to west. As the map shows, the region covers parts of many states, from Colorado to Texas to North Dakota. This vast area stretches north into Canada, reaching parts of Alberta, Saskatchewan (sas KACH uh wahn), and Manitoba.

Summers in the Great Plains are hot. The winters are cold. There's not a lot of rainfall, but some places here get two to three times more rain than the Arizona desert does. The soil here is dark and rich—a good place to grow wheat.

And as you can see on the table on page 51, both the United States and Canada grow large amounts of wheat. By sharing the Great Plains, both countries benefit from this landform.

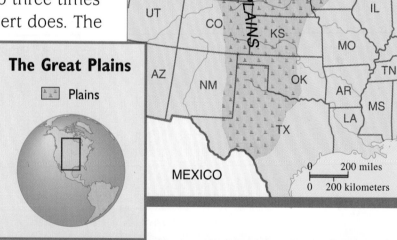

The Great Plains

Plains

50

Plains

Growing the Wheat

If you visited the Great Plains, you'd see many prairies, or large grassy areas. You'd also see many wheat fields. In spring you'd see machines out in these fields, planting seeds in long ditches. In summer you'd see the sun shining on tall stalks of wheat. In fall you could watch the wheat **harvest**, when the wheat is cut by **combines**.

If you can't visit the Great Plains region, you can always look at your family's breakfast table. The bread, cereal, and muffins you see there were probably made with flour from wheat grown on these plains.

In Canada and the United States, wheat farmers often own many large fields. Each farmer may live miles from his or her nearest neighbor. Yet these farm families form strong communities. They help each other out in times of sickness or trouble. Together they share the job of providing food for millions of people.

⭐ **harvest** A gathering of ripe crops from the land where they were grown

combine A machine used to harvest grain

LEADING WHEAT-GROWING AREAS IN THE U.S. AND CANADA

Area	Bushels of Wheat Grown in a Year
Saskatchewan	🌾🌾🌾🌾🌾
Kansas	🌾🌾🌾🌾
North Dakota	🌾🌾🌾
Alberta	🌾🌾🌾

🌾 stands for 100 million bushels

If you're not from the prairie...

by David Bouchard, illustrated by Henry Ripplinger

Read about what it's like to live on the plains in Canada.

If you're not from the prairie,
You don't know what's flat,
You've *never* seen flat.

When travellers pass through across our great plain,
They all view our home, they all say the same:
"It's simple and flat!" They've not learned to see,
The particular beauty that's now part of me.

If you're not from the prairie,
You *don't* know what's flat.

52

SHOW WHAT YOU KNOW!

REFOCUS

1. What is the climate like in the Great Plains?

2. What is a combine used for?

THINK ABOUT IT

How could families who live far apart on the plains still be part of the same community?

WRITE ABOUT IT

Write a poem, song, or paragraph that describes the land in your community.

If you're not from the prairie,
You've not heard the grass,
You've never *heard* grass.

In strong summer winds, the grains and grass bend
And sway to a dance that seems never to end.
It whispers its secrets—they tell of this land
And the rhythm of life played by nature's own hand.

If you're not from the prairie,
You've never *heard* grass.

You can find out more about life on the plains by checking this book out of your school or public library.

SUMMING UP

1 DO YOU REMEMBER . . .
COMPREHENSION

1. What natural resources can be found on the land and in bodies of water?

2. How are products moved to and from St. Louis today?

3. Explain why it can be difficult to live in the Rockies.

4. What plants and animals live in the Sonoran Desert?

5. What important crop is grown in the Great Plains region?

2 SKILL POWER
COMPARING AND CONTRASTING

Choose two types of land that were described in this chapter. Then make a Venn diagram to show how they are alike and different. You may want to draw or paste illustrations around your diagram. Use pictures of the natural resources found in the land. When you are finished, share your diagram by making a "Land of the United States" display.

3 WHAT DO YOU THINK?
CRITICAL THINKING

1. If you were an early settler, what kind of place would you build a community near? Explain.

2. Why do you think people use river barges to carry products?

3. Would people have ever moved to the Rockies if gold had not been discovered there?

4. Why can it be hard to live in the desert?

5. What does wheat need to grow well?

4 SAY IT, WRITE IT, USE IT
VOCABULARY

Use five of the words below to write a story about different kinds of places.

barge	landform
boom town	mine
combine	natural resource
dam	solar energy
explorer	trade
harvest	

CHAPTER 2

5 GEOGRAPHY AND YOU
MAP STUDY

Use the maps in the chapter to answer the following questions.

1. In what state does the Mississippi River start?
2. What part of Utah do the Rocky Mountains go through?
3. What rivers can you find in the Sonoran Desert?

6 TAKE ACTION
CITIZENSHIP

With a small group of classmates, choose one type of land mentioned in this chapter. Then discuss how it is sometimes damaged, polluted, or misused. Find out about groups of people who are trying to protect the land you have chosen. Tell the class what you find out. Use pictures to illustrate your talk.

7 GET CREATIVE
COMPUTER CONNECTION

Use a computer to write and publish a travel brochure about the land and water near your community. Illustrate the brochure with computer graphics or your own drawings.

LOOKING AHEAD

Read the next chapter to discover what life is like in rural communities.

Different Kinds of Places

If we lived on a ranch, what would we see?
  We'd see herds of cattle and sheep roaming free.
If we lived in a city, what would we do?
  We'd ride on a subway to visit the zoo.
If we lived in a suburb, where would we go?
  We'd shop at the mall with people we know.
There are all kinds of places, now don't you agree?
  But which ones are in your community?

Chapter 3

Rural

▼ Where do all these fruits and vegetables grow? You can find out on page 69.

Rural areas are good places to live and important sources of food and other farm products. Learn how people in rural communities live and work.

CONTENTS

Communities

These books tell about life in different rural areas. Read one that interests you and fill out a book-review form.

READ AND RESEARCH

Family Farm by **Thomas Locker** (Penguin USA, 1994)
If you've ever wondered what life on a farm is like, read this book. You will see in the beautiful paintings why farm families hate to give up farming, even during tough times. *(fiction)*
• *You can read a selection from this book on page 74.*

Back Home by **Gloria Jean Pinkney,**
pictures by Jerry Pinkney (Penguin USA, 1992)
Join Ernestine as she travels to North Carolina for a visit to the farm where she was born. You will enjoy meeting her aunt and uncle and especially her cousin Jack. *(fiction)*

Lobster Boat by **Brenda Z. Guiberson,**
illustrated by Megan Lloyd (Henry Holt & Co., 1993)
Spend a day with Tommy and Uncle Russ on their lobster boat, the *Nellie Jean.* You'll learn that catching those tasty lobsters takes lots of hard work. *(fiction)*

SKILL POWER

READING

Knowing how to use a flowchart can help you understand how something works or how something is done.

UNDERSTAND IT

How would you put together this model dinosaur? Should the legs or head go on first? Would you paint the pieces before or after you glue them together? Model kits usually come with a flowchart that shows how to put the model together.

Flowcharts let you see the steps of a process. Arrows and numbers help you follow the steps in order.

EXPLORE IT

Have you had oat cereal for breakfast? This flowchart shows the steps it takes to make this cereal.

FROM OATS TO CEREAL

1. The oat seeds are planted.

2. When the oat plants are grown, they are cut down.

3. The oats are taken to a factory and made into cereal.

4. Best Oats Cereal is brought to a store near you.

FOOD STORE

Tyrannosaurus Rex

A FLOWCHART

TRY IT

Do you have a favorite food—a salad, sandwich, or dessert? Show how to make your favorite food by making a flowchart like the one on this page. Use numbers and arrows to show the order of the steps. When you are finished, share your flowchart with your classmates. You could make a class cookbook of flowchart recipes.

How to Make a Peanut Butter and Jelly Sandwich

1. Get what you need.

2. Spread peanut butter on a slice of bread.

3. Spread jelly on another slice of bread.

4. Put bread slices together and enjoy!

SKILL POWER SEARCH You'll find more flowcharts in this chapter. Can you find other places in the chapter where flowcharts would be useful?

Setting the Scene

⭐ **KEY WORDS**

rural area
hatchery
pie graph
technology

Living in a

FOCUS *Some people in rural areas work to provide many of the basic goods that all people need to live.*

What Are Rural Areas?

Jeff Miller lives in a **rural area**, where towns are far apart and surrounded by open land. People live in rural areas for many reasons. Some may enjoy the peace and quiet of their surroundings. Other people live in rural areas because their jobs are there. Jeff's parents are farmers. Farming is one of the most important activities in the United States. Our food and many other products come from the crops and livestock raised on farms.

⭐ **rural area** An uncrowded place where towns are far apart and surrounded by fields, other open lands and forests

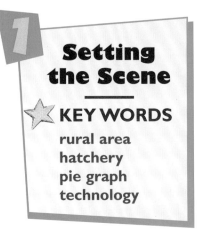

Rural Area

Modern Communications

In the United States, farm families may live quite far away from their neighbors. But farm families are like other families in the United States in that they talk on the telephone, send messages by computer, and watch the news on TV.

These communication devices also help Jeff's family run a successful farm. For example, one telephone call will tell them about crop prices. The TV brings news about the weather. A computer modem connects Jeff's family to information about raising crops that produce greater quantities.

People in rural areas are also connected to each other by the towns located near them. These towns provide the people of the surrounding area with services and products. They also help give people a sense of belonging—a sense of community.

Rural Towns

The town nearest the Miller farm is very important to the family. It has several stores, a post office, a bank, a library, and a hospital.

Jeff goes to school in town, and his mom is a teacher there. On Saturdays, Jeff's family often travels into town to run errands and shop. Later, the family might eat in a restaurant and rent a video to watch at home.

Community Life

In town, families have a chance to visit with other neighbors. In fact, the bank in town might be thought of as the town's "living room," because people often meet and talk there. Many people also meet at the town's houses of worship. All these experiences help people in rural areas feel part of a community.

Many special events, such as the parade shown below, happen in town. Tonight Jeff's family will go to a basketball game, where Jeff's sister Linda will play center for her team. But to Jeff the most exciting local event is the 4-H fair.

In 4-H, a national club for young people, members complete special projects. Jeff is raising a pig for his 4-H project. After a year, Jeff will take his pig to the 4-H fair. If the pig is big and healthy, Jeff could win a ribbon or even a trophy.

Making a Living

There are many different ways to make a living in a rural area. Some people have the same kinds of jobs as those who live in cities. Many farmers, like Jeff's mom, have two jobs, one on the farm and one in town.

There are also different kinds of farming in rural areas. Did you know that fish can be a farm crop? People still fish the waters of the United States, but many waters have been overfished and some are polluted, or dirty. So fish farmers raise fish in unpolluted lakes, ponds, and large **hatcheries**, or places where eggs are hatched.

The number of fish farms is growing. Mississippi leads the nation in catfish farming. Fish farms in the United States also produce oysters, salmon, and trout.

Many catfish are raised in big hatcheries and removed when they are the right size to eat.

hatchery A place for hatching eggs

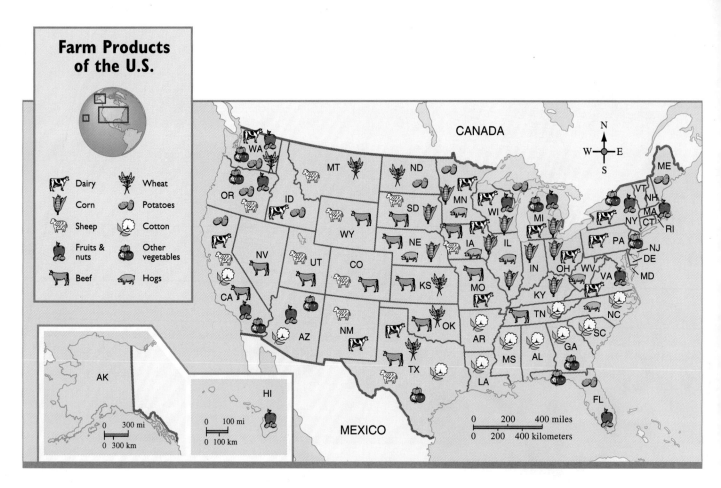

Farm Products of the U.S.

Legend:
- Dairy
- Corn
- Sheep
- Fruits & nuts
- Beef
- Wheat
- Potatoes
- Cotton
- Other vegetables
- Hogs

Farm Products

The next time you're at the supermarket, look closely at the food products. Almost everything you see comes from a farm. The meat comes from animals raised on farms. The fruits and vegetables come from farms, too.

Look at the map and find the states that have the cotton symbol. This cotton symbol appears only in the states considered cotton producers.

The weather, climate, and soil of an area affect where a crop grows best. For example, cotton grows best in places with rich soil. Cotton plants also need plenty of rain, warm temperatures, and a long growing season. Most southern states have all these conditions, which is one reason that the United States is a world leader in cotton production.

Unlike cotton, wheat needs a fairly dry, cool climate. Wheat grows best in states such as Kansas and Oklahoma.

Corn grows best in flat lands with rich soil. Look at the map. Which states produce lots of corn?

A combine cuts down the corn stalks, removes the corn from the cobs, and loads the corn into a truck.

Farm Work Today

Today, there are fewer farm jobs than in the past. Look at the **pie graphs** for the years 1900 and 1992. A pie graph shows how much of one thing there is in a whole. On each pie graph shown, the whole pie stands for all jobs. Find the slice of each pie that stands for farm jobs. Which pie shows fewer farm jobs?

Farming has changed because of **technology**—the use of science to make work easier. Technology has produced farm machines that quickly do several jobs at one time. So fewer people are now needed to do the work on a farm.

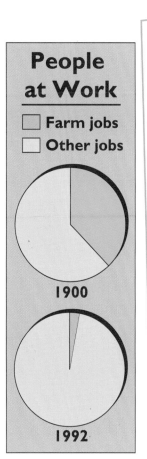

People at Work

☐ Farm jobs
☐ Other jobs

1900

1992

⭐ **pie graph** A kind of graph drawn in the shape of a pie
technology The use of science to make tasks easier in industry and everyday life

REFOCUS

1. Why are rural areas important?

2. How would you describe a rural area?

THINK ABOUT IT

When you visit a supermarket, make a list of some products and tell what farming areas in the United States they might come from.

COMMUNITY CHECK

Make a drawing that shows how a walk through your community might be similar to or different from a walk through Jeff's community.

Raising Fruits

FOCUS *The Central Valley in California produces more fruits and vegetables than any other part of the nation.*

Different Kinds of Farms

Years ago, most farms were small and family owned. Most family farmers grew a variety of crops and raised some livestock too, both for their own use and for sale.

Today many farms are owned by large companies. Most of the products are sold. The **profit**, or money gained, goes to the company. A big company farm can afford to buy the machinery and other supplies that are needed to make large profits.

Many company farms today are specialized farms, growing only one or two crops. Or a specialized farm might raise only one kind of livestock, such as chickens, and the grains that they eat.

Some family farms have become more like company farms. They are specialized farms that have grown large enough to afford the machines that successful farms need today.

⭐ **profit** The money gained in a business after expenses have been subtracted

◀ A carrot harvester is a machine that picks carrots, removes their leaves, and loads them into a truck.

and Vegetables

Farming the Central Valley

Find the Central Valley in California on the map. A valley is a lowland between hills or mountains. The Central Valley is the largest farming area west of the Rocky Mountains. The valley has rich soil and a climate with hot, dry summers and a long growing season. It has two major rivers, the Sacramento and the San Joaquin (san waw KEEN).

Even with these rivers, the valley needs more water. In the 1930s, dams and canals were built to **irrigate** the land, or supply the area with more water. Irrigation makes it possible for farmers in California to produce half of the nation's fruits and vegetables.

⭐ **irrigate** To supply water through ditches, canals, and pipes

Central Valley, California

- ▨ Central Valley
- ▢ Deserts
- 🗻 Mountains

OREGON

NEVADA

COAST RANGES

SIERRA NEVADA

CENTRAL VALLEY

★ Sacramento

San Francisco

• Fresno

CALIFORNIA

• Bakersfield

PACIFIC OCEAN

MOJAVE DESERT

ARIZONA

Los Angeles

San Diego

SONORAN DESERT

```
0        100      200 miles
0   100    200 kilometers
```

Harvesting the Crops

Almost every kind of crop is grown in the Central Valley. Many farms in the valley are large and specialized. Machines are used to prepare the soil, irrigate the fields, and harvest the crops.

But many fruits and vegetables need to be picked by hand as soon as they ripen. Most of this work is done by migrant workers, or people who travel from place to place to harvest crops.

Some Central Valley farmers raise livestock, such as hogs and horses. Central Valley farmers also raise millions of cattle. Some cattle are raised for their beef, and others provide milk. In fact, California is the largest milk-producing state in our country.

Fruits and Vegetables of the Central Valley

Fruits

grapes
strawberries
oranges
melons
peaches
plums
apricots

Vegetables

tomatoes
lettuce
broccoli
cauliflower
carrots
potatoes

Nuts

almonds
walnuts

SHOW WHAT YOU KNOW!

REFOCUS

1. Why is the Central Valley a good place for growing fruits and vegetables?

2. What is irrigation?

THINK ABOUT IT

Why might a farmer decide to grow more than one kind of crop?

COMMUNITY CHECK

Make a list of fruits and vegetables that are raised in your community.

How It Works

⭐ KEY WORDS

dairy cow
pasture
bar graph

Dairy Farming

FOCUS *Many people work to bring dairy products from the farm to your table.*

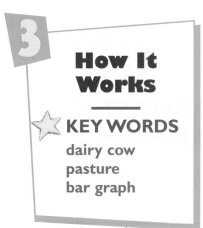

Dairy Farming

In the United States there are about 10 million **dairy cows** that supply dairy farmers with milk. Dairy farms are found in every state in our country. Although some dairy farms are small, other farms are huge, with up to 1,000 cows.

On some dairy farms, cows go outside to graze in **pastures**, or grassy fields. In cold weather the cows stay in the barn. On other dairy farms cows stay inside almost all the time and are fed hay and other foods.

A dairy cow eats about 50 pounds of food and drinks about 15 gallons of water each day. Most dairy cows produce about 1,800 gallons of milk in a single year.

Dairy Products

Dairy products are foods that are made from milk. They include butter, cheese, and yogurt. Find another dairy product shown on this page.

⭐ **dairy cow** A cow that produces milk
  pasture A grassland where animals eat

71

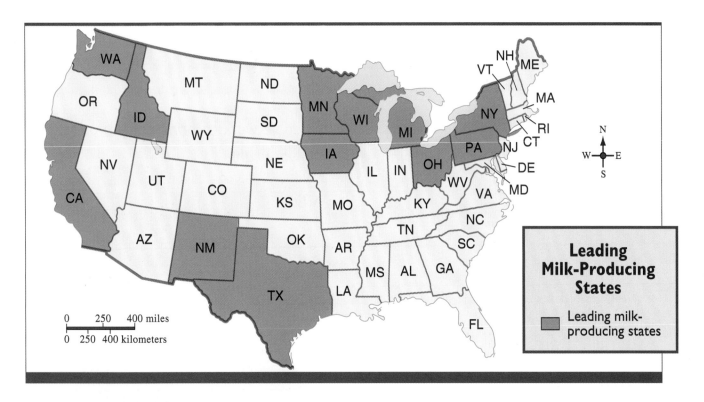

Dairy products are part of a healthful diet. You can read labels on containers to learn what we gain from eating these foods.

The map above shows the states that produce the most milk. The **bar graph** below shows how much milk is produced by each state. Use the map and the graph. Find out which state is the largest producer of milk, where the state is located, and how much milk is produced in that state. Then read the flowchart on the next page to see how milk gets to you.

⭐ **bar graph** A graph that uses bars to show information

FROM COW TO YOU!

1 Milking the Cows

Cows need to be milked twice a day. Milking machines are attached to the cows. In each machine the milk runs through a pipe to a tank that keeps the milk cold so that it won't spoil.

Farm to Dairy 2

The milk is checked to make sure it is of high quality. Then the milk is loaded onto a refrigerated truck that takes it to a dairy, or a place where the milk is prepared to be sold.

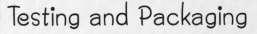

3 Testing and Packaging

At the dairy the milk is tested and heated to kill germs, and then it is put into containers. Some of the milk is made into other dairy products, like cream and butter.

Dairy to Store to You 4

The milk products are taken from the dairy and delivered to stores. Now your family can buy all the milk products it wants.

Family Farm

Thomas Locker

Read about what happened one day to Sarah and Mike, who live on their family's farm.

None of my friends sit with their sisters on the school bus, and neither do I. But the day we heard that our school was going to be closed, I did.

"Sarah, you said they'd never close down our school!"

"Leave me alone, Mike," she said, and she stared out the window.

"Why couldn't they close the school in Warren instead, and make those kids ride to our school? I don't want to sit on a bus for three hours every day! How are we supposed to have enough time to do our chores?"

"How should I know, Mike?" Sarah answered. "I guess we'll just have to get up earlier."

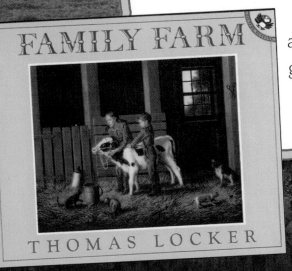

FAMILY FARM

THOMAS LOCKER

As soon as we got home, Sarah went looking for Mom. She was out in the garden, gathering the best pumpkins for tomorrow's trip to the market. Sarah told her the terrible news.

Dad and Grandpa had driven to town to deliver the last load of our corn crop, so I just started in on my own chores.

Before supper, Sarah and I went out to the barn to work with our calf, Derinda. We groomed her and tried to lead her around on the halter rope. Then we tried to get her to drink milk from the pail.

"Come on, Derinda," Sarah said, "you're too old to be drinking from that big baby bottle."

"She'll never win a ribbon at the fair if she doesn't start growing soon," I said.

Then we heard the brakes on our grain truck squeal as Dad and Grandpa pulled up.

"Suppertime!" Mom called.

Do you want to read more? Check out this book from your school or public library.

SHOW WHAT YOU KNOW!

REFOCUS

1. What jobs are needed to get milk from the cow to the store?

2. Why is milk heated at the dairy?

THINK ABOUT IT

What kinds of chores might Mike and Sarah have to do on their family's farm?

WORK TOGETHER

Work with a partner to make a picture book that shows how milk gets from the farm to the store.

Life on a

FOCUS *Sheep ranchers and their families raise animals for wool and for food.*

Ranching in the United States

Some large farms are called **ranches**. Livestock such as cattle, sheep, or horses are raised on ranches.

Cattle and sheep graze in the pastures and other fields of the ranch. Both sheep and cattle need lots of space to roam because they eat so much food each day.

Most ranches in the United States are in the West, which has the large areas of open land that ranching requires. Ranches can also be found in the Midwest—in Kansas and Nebraska—and in the Southwest, especially in Texas.

---

 ranch A large farm where cattle, sheep, or horses are raised

Sheep Ranch

Ranching in Texas

Texas raises more beef cattle and sheep than any other state. Much of Texas is covered by grassy plains, perfect for grazing. The southern part of the plains is called the Edwards Plateau. Look for it on the map. A **plateau** is a large raised area of flat land. The Edwards Plateau is sparsely covered with shrubs and grass. Almost 2 million sheep a year are raised here. These sheep produce more than 17 million pounds of wool each year.

⭐ **plateau** A raised level piece of land that covers a large area

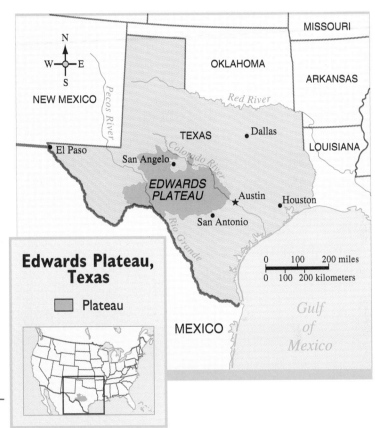

Edwards Plateau, Texas

▨ Plateau

Jobs on a Sheep Ranch

There are many jobs to be done on a sheep ranch. For one, the ranchers must make sure that the sheep are getting a good diet, which could include giving them extra food like hay, as shown in the photo. In addition, sheep ranchers must protect the sheep from natural enemies such as coyotes or wolves.

Some of the jobs on a sheep ranch are different from those on other ranches. Shearing, or clipping wool from a sheep, requires special skills. A sheep's coat grows all winter. In the spring it's time to shear the sheep. The wool is then packed and sent to a factory.

Herding the Sheep

Sheep ranchers often use sheep dogs to help them. A sheep dog works very hard to protect the sheep. These dogs also help herd the sheep when they need to be moved. Sheep dogs can separate a sick sheep from the flock, or group of sheep, as well. Ranchers give directions to their sheep dogs by using special hand signals and different whistling sounds.

FROM SHEEP TO SWEATER

Look at the flowchart to see how wool is turned into clothing. An expert can shear more than 200 sheep a day!

1 Getting wool from a sheep starts with shearing, or cutting the wool off the sheep. It's like getting a haircut.

2 The wool is sent to a factory to be weighed, sorted, and washed. Then the wool is dyed and untangled. Finally it is ready to be spun.

3 Spinning twists the wool into yarn. The yarn is then ready to be knit.

4 Knitting is done by hand, or by large machines in a factory. Many different types of clothing are made from wool.

SHOW WHAT YOU KNOW!

REFOCUS

1. What are some animals that may be raised on ranches?

2. What work does a sheep dog do?

THINK ABOUT IT

Why is spring a good time to shear sheep?

WRITE ABOUT IT

Research and write about an animal that works for people.

Global Connection

⭐ **KEY WORDS**

coast
trawl
seine

Fishing

FOCUS *People around the world fish the oceans for food.*

Fishing in the Ocean

For thousands of years, people have been catching fish for food. Millions of people around the world make their living by fishing or by working in fish-processing plants.

Do you eat lots of fish? Fish provide food for many of the world's people. In countries such as Japan and Norway, fish are a main source of food.

Lots of fish are caught in lakes and rivers. But the most fish are caught in the world's oceans—especially along the **coasts**, or edges of the continents. Look at the map to see where some fish are caught.

Different Types of Fishing

Cod, shrimp, and red snapper live on or near the ocean floor. To catch

⭐ **coast** Land along the sea or ocean

World Fishing Areas

▭	Major fisheries
🐟	Pollock
🐟	Cod
🐟	Sardine
🐟	Mackerel
🦐	Shrimp
🦞	Lobster
🐟	Anchovy
🐟	Salmon
🐟	Tuna
🐟	Herring

NORTH AMERICA

EUROPE

ASIA

ATLANTIC OCEAN

AFRICA

PACIFIC OCEAN

SOUTH AMERICA

PACIFIC OCEAN

INDIAN OCEAN

ATLANTIC OCEAN

AUSTRALIA

ANTARCTICA

Around the World

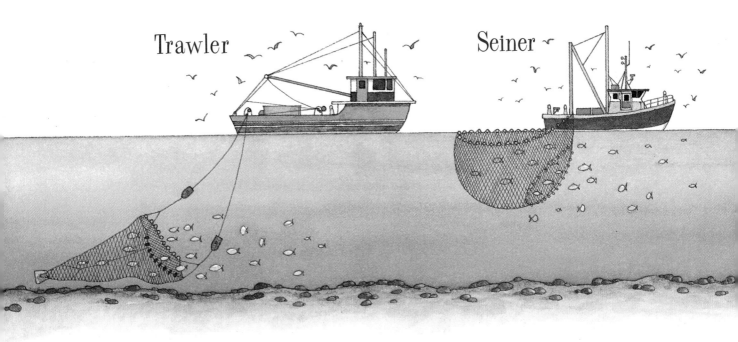

Trawler

Seiner

these fish, **trawls**, or nets shaped like funnels with one end closed, are cast out by boats called trawlers. The boats drag the trawls along the ocean floor. Fish and water flow into each net as it moves. Then water flows out and the fish are caught in the closed bottom of the net.

Other fish swim near the ocean's surface. To catch these fish, nets called **seines** (saynz) are cast out by boats called seiners. When a school, or a large group of fish, is spotted, the boat circles the fish and lays out the seine. When the school is surrounded, the net is pulled closed.

trawl A fishing net that is dragged along the ocean floor

seine A net that is used to catch fish near the surface of the water

SHOW WHAT YOU KNOW!

REFOCUS

1. In what part of the ocean are most fish caught?

2. What kind of boat is a trawler?

THINK ABOUT IT

Why might fish be such an important source of food for people in Japan?

COMMUNITY CHECK

Where do people in your community get fish to eat? In a paragraph, describe one place.

SUMMING UP

1 DO YOU REMEMBER...
COMPREHENSION

1. How have American farms changed over the years?

2. Where is the largest farming area west of the Rocky Mountains?

3. What are four kinds of dairy products?

4. Why are most ranches in the United States located in the West?

5. What two countries have fish as their main source of food?

3 WHAT DO YOU THINK?
CRITICAL THINKING

1. Why are towns important to people in rural areas?

2 Why might some fruits and vegetables need to be picked as soon as they are ripe?

3. Why does milk travel to the dairy in a refrigerated truck?

4. Why might a rancher want to remove a sick sheep from the rest of the herd?

5. Some countries are trying to limit ocean fishing. What might happen if too many fish are caught?

2 SKILL POWER
READING A FLOWCHART

In this chapter, flowcharts showed you how milk gets to stores and how wool is made into clothes. Look through encyclopedias, magazines, and other books for flowcharts. Share what you find with your classmates.

4 SAY IT, WRITE IT, USE IT
VOCABULARY

Write a paragraph that tells about the rural community in this chapter that you found most interesting. Use at least four key words.

bar graph	plateau
coast	profit
dairy cow	ranch
hatchery	rural area
irrigate	seine
pasture	technology
pie graph	trawl

5 GEOGRAPHY AND YOU
MAP STUDY

Look at the maps in this chapter to answer the questions below.

1. What states are leading fruit growers?

2. What states are leading cotton growers?

3. What mountains are east of the Central Valley?

4. What two rivers run through the Edwards Plateau?

6 TAKE ACTION
CITIZENSHIP

Many rivers in the United States are so polluted that fish cannot live in them or are not safe to eat. With a group of classmates, do some research and find out how rivers become polluted. Talk about ways that rivers could be made cleaner. Make a poster that shows your group's ideas.

7 GET CREATIVE
SCIENCE CONNECTION

The food groups below are the main foods that people should eat to stay healthy.

- bread, cereal, rice, pasta
- fruits
- vegetables
- meat
- milk

Make a chart that includes pictures of foods from each group. Write the names of some locations in the United States to show where these foods come from.

LOOKING AHEAD

Discover in the next chapter why so many people live, work, and play in cities.

Chapter 4

URBAN

How are New York, Los Angeles, Chicago, and Houston alike? If you think that they are all large cities, you're right! Cities and the people who live in them are what this chapter is about.

Where did these model dinosaurs come from? You can find out on page 91.

CONTENTS

COMMUNITIES

These books are about cities. Read one that interests you and fill out a book-review form.

READ AND RESEARCH

Urban Roosts by **Barbara Bash** (Little, Brown & Co., 1990)
Why do you think a city bird would choose to build its nest at the top of a traffic light? After reading this book you will want to visit the city to look for birds in some unusual places. *(nonfiction)*

My New York by **Kathy Jakobsen**
(Little, Brown & Co., 1993)
Becky's letter to her friend Martin describes all the places she is going to show him when he moves to New York City. You will find her paintings and her map fun to look at. *(fiction)*

The Last Dragon by **Susan Miho Nunes, illustrated by Chris K. Soentpiet** (Houghton Mifflin Co., 1995)
Peter Chang's summer turns out to be better than he expected. Find out how people in Chinatown use their talents to help him repair an old ten-man dragon. *(fiction)*

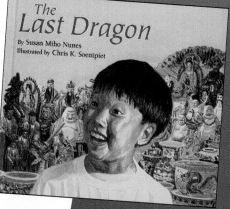

SKILL POWER

USING A

Knowing how to use a special-purpose map helps you learn interesting facts about places.

UNDERSTAND IT

Some maps are drawn for a special purpose, such as showing amounts of rainfall, historic places, or where corn is grown. A special-purpose map that shows how to get around in a community is called a transportation map. It might show subway or bus routes or where to walk. The routes on a transportation map are often color-coded or marked with arrows.

EXPLORE IT

The map on this page shows two bus routes you could take to do some sightseeing in Martin City. Use the map key and symbols to help you answer these questions.

• Which bus route would you take to see the space museum?

• On what bus route is the zoo located?

• Is City Hall on the same bus route as Jefferson Park?

• What place would you choose to visit on the yellow bus route?

MARTIN CITY BUS ROUTES

☐ Blue Bus Route
☐ Yellow Bus Route

Jefferson Park

ZOO Martin City Zoo

Union Train Station

Space Museum

City Hall

Pretzel Factory

SPECIAL-PURPOSE MAP

Z O O

Zoo Paths

Path 1	Path 2
- - - -	→ → →
elephants	birds
lions	seals
gift shop	fish
	snack bar

TRY IT

Work with several classmates to make a transportation map. Use an idea shown below or one of your own.

• School bus routes in a real or made-up place

• Walking paths through a zoo

Show two routes and include a map key with symbols for various sights found on each route. Use different colors to help tell the routes apart.

As a class you could create a display that shows the special-purpose maps that each group has made.

SKILL POWER SEARCH Look at the transportation maps in this chapter. Notice that each one shows a different way to get around in a city.

DAY AND

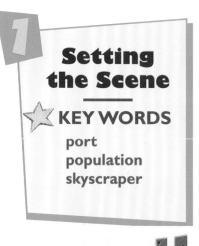

Setting the Scene

⭐ KEY WORDS

port
population
skyscraper

FOCUS *Large cities like New York City attract people because they offer jobs, housing, and services such as transportation and health care.*

The Growth of Cities

Long ago most people in this country lived in rural areas. Today most Americans live in urban areas, which include cities and places nearby. Cities grow for many reasons. Some cities started as trading centers, where people bought and sold goods. As trade grew, new jobs attracted more people to the cities.

Many cities are located near rivers, lakes, and oceans. These nearby waterways provide good **ports**, where ships can load or unload goods. Look at the map. How many of the nation's largest cities are located near water?

⭐ **port** A place where ships load and unload products

10 LARGEST CITIES IN THE U.S.

CITY	Millions of People
New York	(about 7.5)
Los Angeles	(about 3.5)
Chicago	(about 2.7)
Houston	(about 1.7)
Philadelphia	(about 1.5)
San Diego	(about 1.2)
Detroit	(about 1)
Dallas	(about 1)
Phoenix	(about 1)
San Antonio	(about 1)

Scale: 0 2 4 6 8
Millions of People

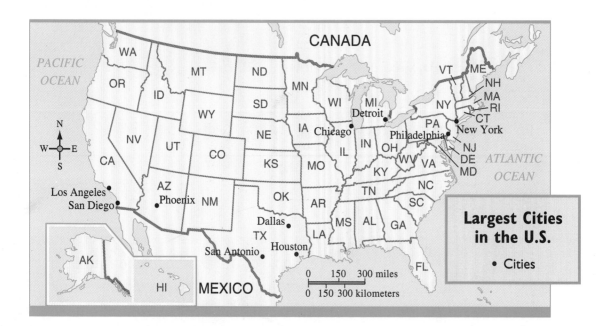

Largest Cities in the U.S.
• Cities

PACIFIC OCEAN

ATLANTIC OCEAN

CANADA

MEXICO

0 150 300 miles
0 150 300 kilometers

NIGHT IN THE CITY

What Is a City?

Cities are communities that have large **populations**, or numbers of people. Thousands and sometimes millions of people live in a city. Many cities are crowded places, where buildings are close together and open land is scarce. Some large cities have **skyscrapers**, very tall buildings that are built upward because there is so little open land to build on. Look at the graph on the left. Which cities have more than 2 million people?

⭐ **population** The number of people in a certain place
skyscraper A very tall building

Meeting People's Needs

New York City has a population of over 7 million people. Millions more live near New York and travel to work and school there. The city also attracts people because it meets their needs for housing, health care, and transportation. It is difficult to meet the needs of such a large population. Among the millions of residents of New York City are some people whose needs are not met. These people may have trouble finding a job or a home.

▼ People ice-skating in Central Park in New York City

Morning in the City

What would you see each day and night if you lived in New York City? In the morning, you would see stores opening, adults rushing to work, and children heading for school. People in a city always seem to be in a hurry.

New York has more than 300 neighborhoods. If you lived in Chinatown or Little Italy, you might hear Chinese or Italian spoken on the streets and in the shops. Around many parts of New York City, you would see and hear people from all over the world.

Afternoon in the City

It's noon, and cars and buses fill the streets. The sounds of sirens and car horns fill the air. People crowd the sidewalks.

Traffic jams are a problem. So many people are trying to get into, out of, or around the city at the same time. Fortunately, many people take buses and trains instead of driving their cars.

During the afternoon, many people are working. But some visitors and city residents are enjoying museums, theaters, parks, restaurants, and special places such as the Empire State Building.

▼ Schoolchildren from the city or nearby areas often visit the American Museum of Natural History in New York City.

Night in the City

Bright lights, traffic, and crowds of people make some parts of New York seem as busy at night as they are during the day. Many people attend sporting events, concerts, and plays at night.

Like people in other large cities, New Yorkers enjoy eating out at night. They have thousands of restaurants from which to choose. Many restaurants serve food from other countries, such as Mexico, India, and Thailand.

Night Workers

New York City is sometimes described as a city that "never sleeps." All night, people work to keep some stores, restaurants, offices, and other workplaces open. Night workers include train and bus drivers, toll collectors at bridges and tunnels, hotel clerks, radio-station announcers, newspaper printers, and street cleaners.

People also work throughout the night to bring food to New York. Fresh meat, fish, fruit, and vegetables are delivered in trucks, trains, ships, and planes. Workers at large food markets are busy at night receiving and unloading fresh foods.

▲ Workers at the Fulton Fish Market hurry to get fish ready to be sold in the morning.

Fresh, ripe tomatoes are unloaded for the day's customers.

Another Day Begins

The sun is almost up. The night workers are on their way home, and the day workers are starting another busy day. Some coffee shops, bakeries, and newspaper stands are getting ready to open for the new day's business.

Many city people are out early walking their dogs or jogging in the park. Others are sitting down to a breakfast of cereal from Michigan, bananas from Brazil, and orange juice from Florida. Soon many people will hurry off to work or school, as another busy day begins in New York City.

SHOW WHAT YOU KNOW!

REFOCUS

1. What are some jobs that need to be done in a city?

2. What are some activities that take place at night in a large city?

THINK ABOUT IT

What sights and sounds might you see and hear in a large city?

COMMUNITY CHECK

Make a booklet about jobs in your community. Talk to people you know about their work. You might use your local newspaper to identify jobs.

THE CHANGING

FOCUS *Different groups of people and events help cities like Los Angeles grow and change.*

Many Kinds of Change

Cities are always changing. Buildings grow old and need to be fixed up or torn down. Those that are torn down are often replaced with new buildings. New groups of people move in, and earlier groups move out.

Los Angeles, California, is a city with a history of rapid change. You can find Los Angeles on the map on page 88.

Early Settlers

In the 1500s, Native Americans called Gabrielinos (gay bree uh LEE-nohs) lived in the area of Los Angeles. Then in 1769, explorers from Spain arrived. Spanish priests built **missions**, or places of religious life, to convince Native Americans to join their religion. Soon others settled here, too. By 1800, about 300 people lived in the town of Los Angeles.

⭐ **mission** A small church and settlement where people were taught Christianity

CITY

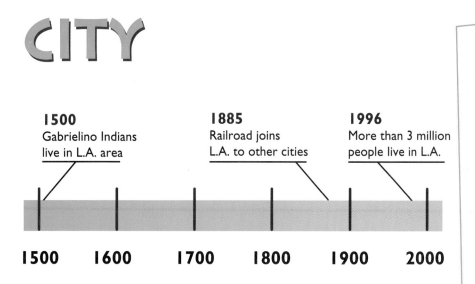

1500
Gabrielino Indians
live in L.A. area

1885
Railroad joins
L.A. to other cities

1996
More than 3 million
people live in L.A.

1500   1600   1700   1800   1900   2000

The Railroad Arrives

By 1885, two railroads connected Los Angeles to other parts of the United States. Many newcomers traveled to the city by train. Many farmers came and stayed. They planted groves of orange trees and used the trains to ship their crops across the country.

In the 1890s, oil was discovered in California. More people rushed to Los Angeles, hoping to strike it rich. By 1900 there were 100,000 people living there. Then a huge **harbor** where ships could dock was built. Los Angeles became a center for trade as well as farming.

A New Business Develops

About eighty years ago, a section of Los Angeles called Hollywood became the center of the growing movie business. The city's warm, dry climate made it possible to make movies outdoors all year long.

Los Angeles, also called L.A., is now the second largest city in the United States. It is home to more than 3 million people.

⭐ **harbor** A sheltered coastal place where ships can dock

SHOW WHAT YOU KNOW!

REFOCUS

1. Why did the Spaniards build missions when they settled in the Los Angeles area?

2. Why did Hollywood become the center of the movie business?

THINK ABOUT IT

How does transportation help cities change and grow?

COMMUNITY CHECK

Write about one important business in your city or a nearby city.

Map Adventure

⭐ KEY WORDS

taxi
public
 transportation
subway

How can we get to the park? We could take the bus, a taxi—or walk!

GETTING

FOCUS *Many people in cities like Chicago use public transportation to get around their cities.*

Travel in the City

People who live in and near cities need to get to many places. Large cities have more kinds of transportation than other communities. Many people walk. Others drive their cars or ride their bikes. Some people take **taxis**, cars that charge a fee to carry passengers. Many people in cities depend on **public transportation**, or transportation that is often run by the local government for everyone's use.

⭐ **taxi** An automobile that carries passengers for money
public transportation Transportation, often run by the local government, that anyone can pay to use

AROUND IN THE CITY

Buses and trains are types of public transportation. A **subway**, a train that runs underground, is another type. Does your community have any public transportation?

Some cities, such as Chicago, have electric railways that run above ground. Other cities have trolley buses, which are run by electricity that comes from overhead wires. One kind of public transportation system often has connections to another to help people get around the city.

Getting Around Chicago

People in Chicago can ride buses or take elevated trains around the Loop, an interesting downtown area shown on the map. Find the elevated train route on the map. How many stops does the train make on Wabash Avenue?

The map also shows a nearby area, Grant Park, that is filled with exciting places to visit. A special bus route starts at Union Station and explores this area. Find Union Station on the map. Then turn the page to travel the bus route.

⭐ **subway** A train that runs underground

LAKE
MICHIGAN

REFOCUS

1. What is public transportation?
2. What are three kinds of public transportation?

MAP IT

Chicago holds many treasures, such as famous paintings and dinosaur skeletons. A great way to enjoy these treasures is to sketch or write about them in a journal. The map shows the route of a Chicago bus that stops at buildings where treasures can be found.

1. Name a tall building where you could see the entire city.

2. Name a place where you could see moon rocks.

3. Start at Union Station and trace the bus route with your finger. What is the first stop you want to make?

4. How many stops does the bus make between Union Station and the Shedd Aquarium?

5. You want to stop for lunch at the food cart before you visit the Sears Tower. Where should you get off the bus?

EXPLORE IT

Plan the route of a walking tour that stops at buildings you would like to visit. Name the streets on your route.

Spotlight

★ KEY WORDS

volunteer
culture

CITY PRIDE

FOCUS *City residents, like those in Houston, take pride in many things about their city.*

Taking Pride in Cities

Many people who live in or near a city feel very proud of the city. Some residents are proud that their city is a center of government, like Washington, D.C. Others may be proud of a monument in their city, such as the Gateway Arch of St. Louis. A spectacular setting is another cause for pride. People in Denver love to show visitors the scenery of the nearby Rocky Mountains.

As the chart shows, people are often proud that their city was the first to have a special kind of building. There are many other reasons that people take pride in the cities they live in. Read on to find out why the people of Texas's largest city—Houston—are proud of their hometown.

Famous Firsts IN BUILDINGS

1884 The first skyscraper was built in Chicago, IL.

1893 The first children's room in a public library was in Minneapolis, MN.

1899 The first children's museum opened in Brooklyn, NY.

1956 The first circular office was built in Los Angeles, CA.

1965 The first domed sports arena was built in Houston, TX.

Pride in Houston

Houston residents are proud of many things about their city. These things include special events, such as the Houston Livestock Show and Rodeo. It is the biggest rodeo in the nation. There are parades, contests to test riding and roping skills, and contests to see who has raised the best horses and cattle. Schoolchildren like Sarah King enter pictures in the Rodeo's art contest. With the help of many **volunteers**, the Rodeo raises millions of dollars to support education throughout the state.

People in Houston are also proud that their community is home to people from many countries. Each year a different country is recognized and honored by the Houston International Festival. The Festival helps people learn about the **culture**, or way of life, of that country. People can see the dances, hear the music, and taste the food of the country.

Sarah King

Travis Elementary School

⭐ **volunteer** A person who chooses to do work and is not paid for it
culture A way of life

This child, at the Houston International Festival, is dressed in dancing clothes that show her Spanish background. ▶

Pride in City Services

Like all major cities, Houston must provide its people with a variety of services such as police and fire protection. Health care is another important service that must be provided in cities. The people of Houston are especially proud to have the world-famous Texas Medical Center in their city.

Did You Know?

- Building started on the Medical Center over 50 years ago and continues today.

- The Medical Center has 13 hospitals, 2 medical schools, and 4 schools of nursing.

- More than 100,000 people come to the Medical Center every day.

- The first successful heart transplant in the U.S. was performed here in 1968.

Young cancer patients at the M.D. Anderson Cancer Center design cards that are sold in stores throughout Houston. The money is used to help care for the children at the center.

A nurse watches a computer screen that provides information about a patient's breathing and heartbeat during an operation.

About 50,000 people work at the Medical Center. Patients and their families, visitors, doctors, volunteers, and students are some of the people who are seen at the Medical Center every day.

SHOW WHAT YOU KNOW!

REFOCUS

1. What are some things a city could have that a resident might feel proud of?

2. Why are the people who live in Houston proud of their city?

THINK ABOUT IT

Why do you suppose the Texas Medical Center is called "a city within a city"?

COMMUNITY CHECK

Interview one person at home or at school. Ask what things in your community make that person feel most proud.

MEXICO'S

Global Connection

⭐ **KEY WORDS**

tourism
artifact

FOCUS *Mexico City has a special heritage, but in many ways it is like other large cities.*

Cities Around the World

You have just learned about some of the largest cities in the United States. Other large cities around the world are similar in many ways to these American cities. Look at the map on the next page and discover where some of the world's largest cities are located. According to some experts, the largest city in population in the world is located just south of our country. Can you find it on the map? It's Mexico City, the capital of Mexico.

CAPITAL CITY

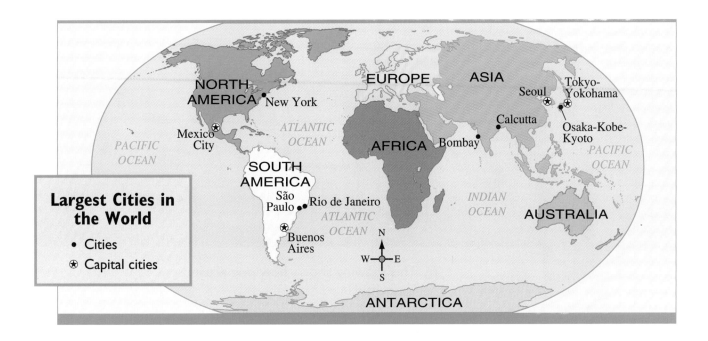

Largest Cities in the World
- Cities
- ⊛ Capital cities

NORTH AMERICA • New York
Mexico City ⊛
PACIFIC OCEAN
ATLANTIC OCEAN
SOUTH AMERICA
São Paulo
Rio de Janeiro • •
Buenos Aires ⊛
ATLANTIC OCEAN
EUROPE
AFRICA
Bombay •
ASIA
Seoul ⊛
Calcutta •
Tokyo-Yokohama ⊛
Osaka-Kobe-Kyoto
PACIFIC OCEAN
INDIAN OCEAN
AUSTRALIA
ANTARCTICA
N W—◯—E S

Mexico City

Mexico City, home to more than 20 million people, is located on high, flat land between two mountain ranges. It has skyscrapers and office buildings just like many other large cities. And like so many of the world's major cities, Mexico City is a center of trade and industry. About one third of the goods produced in Mexico are made in Mexico City. These goods include clothing and processed foods. Mexico City also has one of the world's best subway systems and many bus routes.

Life in the City

Today, one in every five Mexicans lives in Mexico City. Every week thousands of new people come from rural areas to the city in search of good jobs. This rapid growth in population creates serious challenges. Not everyone is able to find a job, and many people do not have good housing and basic services, such as running water and electricity.

Many people in Mexico City do have jobs, however. They work in factories, government offices, banks, companies that specialize in **tourism**, and other places.

⭐ **tourism** The business of serving people who travel

105

▲ This drawing shows how one artist pictured the city of Tenochtitlán.

▲ The original of this Aztec statue was found in Mexico City.

History of a City

Mexico City started its urban life more than 600 years ago when a people called the Aztecs (AZ teks) were searching for a new home. They chose to build their city, called Tenochtitlán (tay nawch tee-TLAHN), on an island in the middle of a lake. It was a well-planned city. The Aztec people built pyramids to honor their gods. They also built fine roads, bridges, and canals.

From this capital the Aztecs conquered new lands and peoples. For almost 200 years, until the Spaniards arrived, the Aztec culture ruled much of the region. Then the Spaniards destroyed Tenochtitlán and built Mexico City on top of it.

Pride in a City

Like citizens in all cities, the residents of Mexico City take pride in their city and all that it has to offer. They are proud of its great university and its beautiful old Spanish-style buildings that sit next to modern skyscrapers.

The people of Mexico City treasure the cultures of their past and present. When subways were being dug, workers uncovered an Aztec pyramid and various **artifacts**, or human-made objects from the past. It was decided to build the subway station around the pyramid. Now citizens point proudly to this ancient building, a part of the past that has been preserved within their modern city.

⭐ **artifact** An object, often old, made by humans

▲ A dancer performs a traditional Aztec dance at a festival in Mexico City.

SHOW WHAT YOU KNOW!

REFOCUS

1. How is Mexico City like other large cities?

2. Why is Mexico City growing so fast?

THINK ABOUT IT

Why might tourism be good or bad for a city?

WORK TOGETHER

With a partner, do research to learn more about one of the ten largest cities in the world. Prepare an illustrated talk to share what you learn.

SUMMING UP

1 DO YOU REMEMBER...
COMPREHENSION

1. In which of our states are the four largest cities?

2. How do cities change?

3. What are some ways that people travel around a city?

4. What are some reasons that people might be proud of the city in which they live?

5. Who were the Aztecs? What did they build?

2 SKILL POWER
USING A SPECIAL-PURPOSE MAP

Work with a group of classmates to find transportation maps for an area near you. You might check at home for maps of bus or train routes. Maybe your public library has tour maps. Compare the maps that you find. Decide which maps are easiest to read.

3 WHAT DO YOU THINK?
CRITICAL THINKING

1. How would you explain the saying "A city never sleeps"?

2. Would Los Angeles have become a great city without the movie and TV business?

3. Why does a city have more kinds of transportation than any other community?

4. Why is the work of volunteers important?

5. Which city on the map on page 105 do you think would be the most interesting to visit? Why?

4 SAY IT, WRITE IT, USE IT
VOCABULARY

Use five of the words below to write about an urban community. It could be the city you live in or one that you've visited.

artifact	public transportation
culture	skyscraper
harbor	subway
mission	taxi
population	tourism
port	volunteer

CHAPTER 4

5 GEOGRAPHY AND YOU
MAP STUDY

Use the map to answer these questions.

1. How many train stops are there on Lake Street?

2. Where does the train cross over the Chicago River?

3. Is there a train stop on Van Buren Street?

Chicago Loop Area
- Elevated train route
- T Train stops
- Union Station

Lake St.
Wells Street
Canal Street
Wacker Drive
Madison St.
State Street
Adams St.
Monroe Street
Jackson Drive
Van Buren St.
Grant Park
Eisenhower Expwy
Chicago River
Wells Street
State Street
Wabash Ave.
Michigan Ave.
Balbo St.
Columbus Drive
Lake Shore Drive
Lake Michigan
Roosevelt Rd
14th St.
N W E S

6 GET CREATIVE
MATH CONNECTION

Use an almanac to find out how many people live in each city listed below.

Philadelphia	New York
Los Angeles	Chicago
Phoenix	San Antonio

Use the math symbols shown to compare the populations.

> means "is greater than"

< means "is less than"

Philadelphia's population < New York's population

7 TAKE ACTION
CITIZENSHIP

It's hard to keep city streets clean. Work with a partner to think of ways to cut down on litter and encourage people to recycle. Share your ideas with the class.

LOOKING AHEAD

Read about suburbs in the next chapter and discover why more people live there than in any other kind of community.

Chapter 5

SUBURBAN

More people in the United States live in suburbs than anywhere else. Read the chapter to find out about these communities.

This boy is hanging a bird feeder. Find another bird feeder on page 128.

CONTENTS

COMMUNITIES

These books are about life in suburbs. Read one that interests you and fill out a book-review form.

READ AND RESEARCH

Aldo Applesauce by Johanna Hurwitz

(Penguin USA, 1989)
The first day at a new school can be scary, especially when things start going wrong. Read about how Aldo deals with school when he moves from a city to a suburb. *(fiction)*

The Adventures of Sugar and Junior by Angela Shelf Medearis, illustrated by Nancy Poydar

(Holiday House, 1995)
When Sugar moves in next door to Junior, they have fun playing and baking together. Find out how Sugar got her unusual name and who the screamer is at the spooky movie. *(fiction)*

Backyard Bear by Jim Murphy, illustrated by Jeffrey Greene (Scholastic, 1993)

Would you believe a bear in the suburbs? Read about the night a young bear smelled food and decided to find it. He came down from his mountain home and went right into a family's backyard. *(fiction)*

Knowing how to find the main idea and the details of a paragraph can help you remember and understand what you read.

UNDERSTAND IT

Do you ever read a paragraph and have trouble understanding it? What can you do?

• Start by finding the main idea, or most important part, of the paragraph. Main ideas are often found at the beginning or the end of a paragraph.

• Next look for details in the paragraph. The details give more information about the main idea. The main idea and the details work together to help you understand what you read.

EXPLORE IT

Read the paragraph below. Look for the main idea and the supporting details.

Feathers come in a rainbow of colors. They can be the gray of a sparrow. A crow is dressed in black feathers. A cardinal wears a bright red coat. Feathers of sky blue cover a jaybird.

Look at the main-idea bug below. The main idea of the paragraph is written on the bug's body. The details are written on the legs because they support the body. Which details are missing?

MAIN - IDEA BUG

Feathers come in many colors.

gray sparrow

black crow

THE MAIN IDEA

TRY IT

Find or write a paragraph that has a main idea and supporting details. Your paragraph might tell about a sport, an animal, or anything that interests you.

Now draw your own main-idea bug. Write the main idea of your paragraph on the body. Add as many legs as you need for details. Use your main-idea bug to tell your classmates about your paragraph.

Squirrels race up and down trees. On the ground, chipmunks dash around. Rabbits hop by, too. Birds are chirping happily. The park is home to many active and lively animals.

Active, lively animals live in the park.

Squirrels Chipmunks Rabbits Birds

SKILL POWER SEARCH As you read this chapter, practice finding the main ideas and supporting details of some of the paragraphs. Make main-idea bugs to help you.

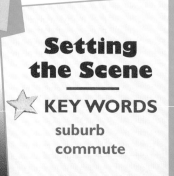

Setting the Scene

⭐ **KEY WORDS**

suburb
commute

ALL ABOUT

FOCUS *More people in the United States live in suburbs than in any other type of community.*

What Are Suburbs?

Many communities are located near large cities. These communities are called suburbs. There are different kinds of suburbs. They can be small, medium-sized, or large. Some suburbs have huge single-family homes with large lawns. Other suburbs have different kinds of homes, including apartment buildings and two-family houses. There are suburbs that have few businesses and suburbs that have large industries. Think about your own community. Do you think it is a suburb? Why or why not?

⭐ **suburb** A community located near a city

SUBURBS

Where Are Suburbs?

Every large city in the United States has suburbs. Many of these suburbs are growing faster every year. Often a city's suburbs grow more rapidly than the city itself.

The photo on this page shows some of the city and suburbs of Providence, Rhode Island. Find the tall buildings in the photo. These buildings are part of the city. Then look for the lower buildings that spread outward. These are part of the suburbs.

There are also suburbs in other parts of the world. In fact, the largest suburbs in the world are not in the United States. In another lesson in this chapter, you'll find out where they are.

The Suburbs Grow and Change

Not long ago most people lived in urban or rural areas. Some city people dreamed of owning homes in smaller communities in the suburbs. But these people couldn't leave their jobs in the city. Then came the trolley, train, and car. Once travel was made easier, more people moved away from the cities, and the suburbs began to grow.

In the 1940s most people who lived in the suburbs shopped and worked in the nearby cities. Many of these early suburbs were made up mostly of homes. Soon, though, stores and shopping centers sprang up in the suburbs. Then some businesses began moving out of the city, and even more people began moving to the suburbs. Compare the pie graphs. Where did most people live in the 1940s? Where do most people live today?

▼ This neighborhood is in a suburb of New York City.

Areas Where People Live in the U.S.

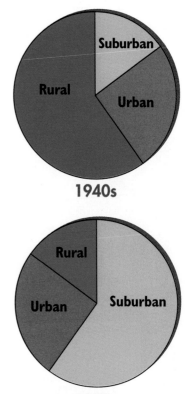

Rural
Suburban
Urban

1940s

Rural
Urban
Suburban

1990s

Getting Around

In the earliest suburbs many people relied on public transportation, such as trains, to get to their jobs in the city. Many people in the suburbs still **commute**, or travel to and from work, each day. The chart at the right shows a few of the ways that people in the United States commute.

In addition to commuting to work, people in the suburbs also have to travel to school, to stores, and to different activities. Cars and other forms of transportation have made life in the suburbs possible.

⭐ **commute** To travel to and from work

How People Commute

Method	Number of People
By car	100 million
On foot	4 million
By bus	3 million
By train	2 million

▲ How do most people commute to work?

The Suburbs Expand

You have learned that cities get bigger by growing upward with tall buildings. Instead of growing upward, suburbs usually get bigger by spreading out. For this reason, most people in the suburbs use cars to get around. Many people in the suburbs spend a lot of time driving from place to place.

The map below shows the suburbs of Milwaukee and Chicago. Notice how the suburbs have spread out and expanded around each city. Which city has the bigger suburban area?

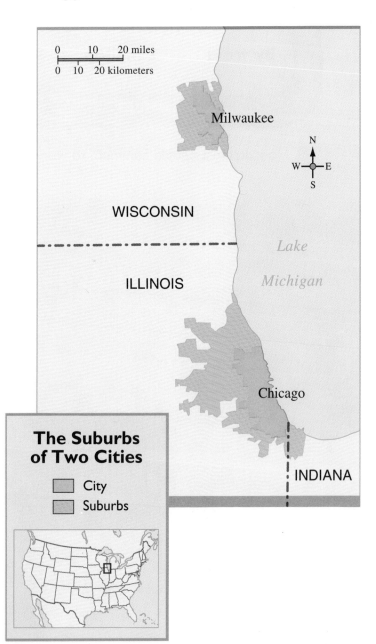

The Suburbs of Two Cities

☐ City
☐ Suburbs

Traveling Back and Forth

In addition to commuting to the city for work, many people who live in the suburbs often go to the city for other reasons. They might go for a special event such as a concert or a museum exhibit. And people from the city often go to the suburbs to shop and attend sporting events. Since large areas of land can be found in suburbs, malls and arenas have been built there.

Shopping in the Suburbs

Many people like to shop in a mall, or an indoor shopping center. Some people even use the mall as a meeting place to see their friends and neighbors. The photo above shows people in a mall in California.

One reason that malls are popular is that they have lots of different kinds of stores in one place. This way, people can do all their shopping at one site instead of having to drive to many places. Malls are easily reached by people with cars and they usually provide plenty of parking.

Suburban communities also have smaller stores located in the center of town. However, these shops sometimes lose money because many people choose to shop in malls.

SHOW WHAT YOU KNOW!

REFOCUS

1. What is a suburb?

2. Why are malls often built in the suburbs?

THINK ABOUT IT

Why, do you think, do so many people choose to live in the suburbs?

WRITE ABOUT IT

Write a paragraph about life in the suburbs. Make sure to have a main idea in your paragraph.

WHEELS AND

FOCUS *Over time, there have been many changes and improvements made to cars and roads.*

Learning to Love Cars

In the past, traveling was difficult. Horse-drawn buggies bumped along slowly on dirt roads. When the car was invented, it made many people nervous. Some towns passed laws that set a speed limit of 4 miles per hour. There were also no highways or street signs, so people often got lost.

Henry Ford believed people would eventually get used to cars. In 1903 he started the Ford Motor Company, which made cars such as the Model T, shown below. In his factory, people

worked on **assembly lines**. Each worker on the line worked on one small step of the process. This way, cars were built quickly and cheaply.

Ford was right—people soon learned to love cars. To make traveling by car easier, people paved roads and numbered highways. Many roads were built to connect cities to the new suburbs. Wide multilane highway systems, like the one shown above, were also built.

⭐ **assembly line** A row of people working in a line to put together a product

ROADS

Safety First

Since so many people rely on their cars to get to work or school, car safety is very important. Most new cars now come with air bags, which may protect people from injury during accidents. The man in the photo is testing air bags before they are put into new cars. Traffic lights, speed limits, and wider lanes have helped make roads safer.

Looking to the Future

One problem that has resulted from all these cars on the road is air pollution. The exhaust from burning gasoline has made the air dirty. There are many ways to lessen air pollution. Some people travel with other people in carpools. Others ride bicycles or take public transportation.

People are even building new kinds of cars such as the solar-powered car at right. This car runs on energy from the sun and doesn't cause any air pollution.

⭐ **pollution** The unclean state of air, land, or water

BUILDING A

FOCUS *In the mid-1940s, new ways of building houses helped suburban communities grow.*

The Levitt Plan

Abraham Levitt and his sons knew how to build houses. In 1946 they put this knowledge to work on land outside New York City. But they didn't just put up a few houses—they planned and built an entire suburban community. The map below shows part of the Levitts' plan. This Long Island suburb soon became known as Levittown.

Busy Builders

The Levitts' goal was to build houses as quickly and cheaply as possible. To do this, they used modern tools and new building methods. Each worker did the same job on every house. In this way the Levitts' builders were like Ford's assembly-line workers. The photos on the next page show a few Levitt workers in action in 1952.

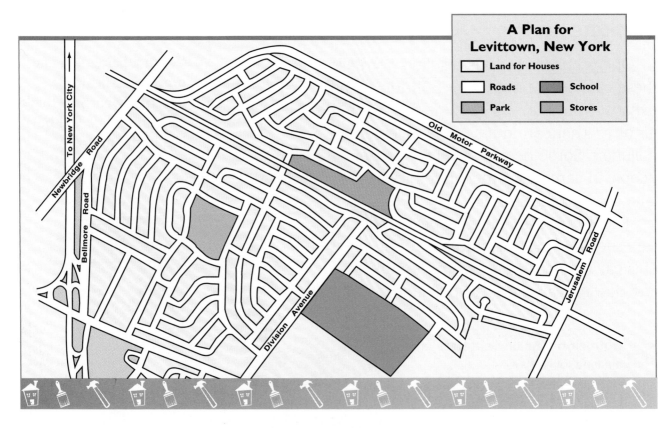

A Plan for Levittown, New York

☐ Land for Houses
☐ Roads   ■ School
▨ Park   ▨ Stores

SUBURB

Building a Levittown House

Levittown houses didn't have basements. Instead, they were built on concrete slabs, saving time and money. This Levitt worker is using a new power tool that smooths out wet cement. ▶

◀ These Levitt workers put up the framework for walls. The boards had already been measured, cut, and nailed together by other workers.

These workers are bolting and nailing the roof into place. After they finish this house, they will move on to the next house. The Levitt crews worked so fast that they could finish 30 houses a day! ▶

Families Need Homes

The Levittown, New York, suburb was a great success. It offered nice houses at a price that people could afford. Sometimes a stove or a refrigerator came with the house, too. Some people complained that the houses were too much alike, but most people didn't mind. When the Levitts first sold their houses, people stood in line for days to buy them. In March 1949 the Levitts sold 1,400 houses in one day!

A Planned Community

Since the first Levittown was such a success, the Levitts decided to build two more. All three Levittowns were **planned communities**.

Before building began, the Levitts planned every part of their towns. Most streets were narrow and curved so that heavy traffic wouldn't pass through the neighborhoods. Each street was given a pleasant name, such as Daisy Lane or Hilltop Road.

⭐ **planned community** A community in which the location of buildings and streets is decided on before building begins

▼ For many people, owning a Levittown home was a dream come true.

The Levitts planned other things, too. Trees were planted in each yard. Plans showed where to locate churches, gas stations, schools, stores, and parks. Tennis courts and swimming pools were also built.

After Levittown

The map shows the first Levittown in New York. Soon other builders began using the Levitts' ideas to build their own suburbs in other places around the country. They also began to use power tools, and many formed crews that worked like assembly lines. Suburbs outside other cities began to grow. Many of these suburbs looked like Levittown.

The Levitts and the builders who followed them made suburban life appealing and affordable to millions of people. These new ideas and new building methods helped America's suburbs grow.

Levittown, New York

- New York City
- New York State
- Levittown

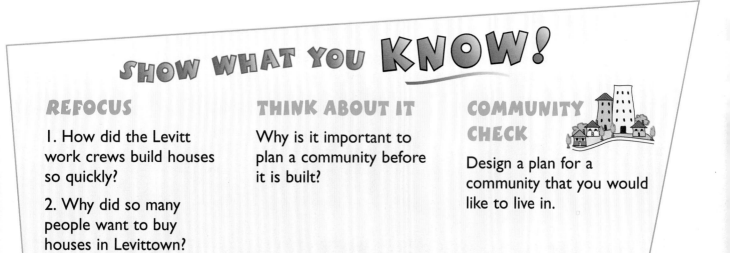

SHOW WHAT YOU KNOW!

REFOCUS

1. How did the Levitt work crews build houses so quickly?

2. Why did so many people want to buy houses in Levittown?

THINK ABOUT IT

Why is it important to plan a community before it is built?

COMMUNITY CHECK

Design a plan for a community that you would like to live in.

125

SHARING

Citizenship

⭐ **KEY WORD**

habitat

FOCUS *People in suburbs often share their community with animals. Sometimes this can lead to problems. Join the debate and decide what to do.*

Animal Neighbors

People and animals often share the same space in the suburbs. Skunks, raccoons, foxes, and even bears may live there. Many animals wander into people's yards, looking for food. Lawns, gardens, fruit trees, and garbage cans offer animals plenty of tasty treats! The photos on these pages show some animal neighbors you might find in the suburbs.

Squirrel

Coyote

THE SUBURBS

Common Problems

There can be problems when people and animals share the same community. Raccoons can create a mess by knocking over garbage cans. Groundhogs can eat quite a lot from people's gardens. A howling coyote can keep people up at night. Squirrels and birds can build nests that clog chimneys and rain gutters. Deer often eat plants from people's yards. In just one night, deer can destroy plants that took months to grow.

Deer

Groundhog

Raccoon

As Suburbs Grow

Many people live in the suburbs, and more suburbs are being built all the time. Homes, small stores, and schools all need to be built when the suburbs grow. Roads must be paved so that people can travel from one place to another.

All the building in the suburbs can disrupt the natural **habitat**, or home, of the animals. When this happens, animals may be left with no place to live and nothing to eat. Some people try to do things to keep the animals around, such as putting up bird feeders or feeding the squirrels.

New Ways to Share

In certain places, people are planning new kinds of communities to help preserve, or save, wildlife. Some of these communities have small houses clustered together in groups. The roads are made of dirt. There are many areas set aside for ponds and gardens. This way there is more room for the animals.

Some people hope that such communities will help people and animals share the suburbs. However, other people don't think these communities are a good idea. New ways of building can be expensive. Some people cannot afford to live in these new communities. Since more space is set aside for animals, these communities also have less room available for people.

⭐ **habitat** The place where an animal or a plant usually lives

Animals need a safe place to live. It's not fair that people take all the land to build new suburbs. What will happen to the animals?

People are more important than animals. Families need new homes and schools.

Each community should share the land with the animals. People can build in some areas and leave other areas open.

REFOCUS

1. What are some animals you might find in the suburbs?

2. What problems come up when people and animals must share the suburbs?

THINK ABOUT IT

What might happen if an animal's natural habitat is destroyed?

COMMUNITY CHECK

Animals are everywhere! Make a poster that tells about the animals that live in your community.

You Decide

Work with a small group and discuss how animals and people share the suburbs. What do you think?

Should people stop building in the suburbs to protect the natural habitat of animals? Why or why not? What suggestions do you and your classmates have for ways in which people and animals can share the suburbs?

SUBURBS OF

FOCUS *The suburbs of Sydney, Australia, are similar to suburbs in the United States.*

Where in the World?

Australia is known as the Land Down Under because it lies in the Southern Hemisphere. Australia is the only place in the world that is both a country *and* a continent.

Australia's largest city is Sydney. As the map shows, Sydney has a huge harbor. Hundreds of boats come and go from here every day. The city center has theaters, shops, and offices. Most people don't live in the center of the city, however. They live in suburbs outside it.

Sydney's Suburbs

Sydney's suburbs form the largest suburban area in the world. The suburbs near Sydney's center contain many apartment buildings. Farther out, most families own their own houses. Like American suburbs, these areas are filled with homes, schools, shopping centers, and roads. Almost every house has a garden, a garage, and space for a backyard barbecue.

AUSTRALIA

N
W E
S

PACIFIC OCEAN

Sydney

0   5 miles
0   5 kilometers

Suburbs of Sydney

☐ City center
☐ Suburbs

SYDNEY

Because of the warm, sunny weather, barbecues and picnics are an important part of life in Sydney's suburbs. And since Sydney's suburbs are close to big national parks, many people also enjoy hiking through the nearby wilderness. Hikers can sometimes spot a wallaby, which is a small animal like a kangaroo.

Getting Around

The suburbs in Sydney are spread out just like the suburbs found in the United States. So cars are just as popular in Australia as they are in our country. Many people also commute to work in Sydney by crossing the harbor in a large boat called a **ferry**.

The harbor cuts through the center of Sydney.

ferry A boat used for taking people or cars across a body of water

SHOW WHAT YOU KNOW!

REFOCUS

1. How are the suburbs of Sydney like American suburbs?

2. How do some people travel around Sydney?

THINK ABOUT IT

Why, do you think, have the suburbs of Sydney grown so big?

WORK TOGETHER

Work with a partner and make a list of things that you might like to do together if you lived in a suburb of Sydney.

SUMMING UP

1 DO YOU REMEMBER...
COMPREHENSION

1. Why do so many people live in suburbs today?

2. How did Henry Ford build cars quickly and cheaply?

3. Describe how Levittown, New York, was built.

4. How can building new suburbs cause problems for animals?

5. Where is the largest suburban area in the world?

3 WHAT DO YOU THINK?
CRITICAL THINKING

1. Why weren't there a lot of suburbs many years ago?

2. Why is an assembly line a fast way to build something?

3. What do you like about the Levitts' planned communities?

4. What can people do to help share the suburbs with animals?

5. How are the suburbs of Sydney, Australia, different from suburbs in the United States?

2 SKILL POWER
FINDING THE MAIN IDEA

With a partner, find a paragraph from this chapter that has a main idea and supporting details. Draw a main-idea bug and write the main idea in its body and the details in its legs.

4 SAY IT, WRITE IT, USE IT
VOCABULARY

Use four or more of the words below in a paragraph describing a suburban community you would like to build.

assembly line	pollution
commute	suburb
ferry	
habitat	
planned community	

⑤ TAKE ACTION
CITIZENSHIP

Wherever you live, you share your community with animals. With your classmates, talk about ways to help both pets and wild animals become "good citizens" in your neighborhood. Cleaning up after pets is one way. Picking up litter that might attract wild animals is another way. What other ideas do you have?

⑥ GEOGRAPHY AND YOU
MAP STUDY

Use the maps in this chapter to answer the following questions.

1. What body of water is north of Levittown, New York?

2. Which city has suburbs in two different states?

3. What do New York City and Sydney have in common?

⑦ GET CREATIVE
ART CONNECTION

As suburbs grow, it is important for communities to learn about the habitat of local animals. Work with several classmates to design posters that teach people about the needs of wildlife.

LOOKING AHEAD

Read the next chapter to discover how a community can move from one place to another.

Chapter 6

MOVABLE

Did you know that some communities move? When some people travel, they take their community with them. Read the chapter and find out how.

▼ What is this girl holding? What was it used for? Find out on page 143.

CONTENTS

COMMUNITIES

These books tell about communities that move. Read one that interests you and fill out a book-review form.

READ AND RESEARCH

Camping in the Temple of the Sun by **Deborah Gould, illustrated by Diane Paterson** (Simon & Schuster Books for Young Readers, 1992) Jeannie's family goes on its first weekend camping trip. Do you think that a pouring rain will spoil their fun? *(fiction)*

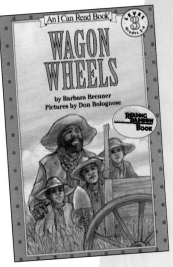

Wagon Wheels by **Barbara Brenner, pictures by Don Bolognese** (HarperCollins Publishers, 1978) While their father searches for better land, the Muldie brothers take care of themselves on the Kansas prairie. When their father sends for them, they must travel 150 miles, having many adventures along the way. *(historical fiction)*

Caitlin's Big Idea by **Gloria Skurzynski, illustrated by Cathy Diefendorf** (Troll Associates, 1995) Caitlin lives with her mom in a mobile home at the Three Peaks Trailer Court. Find out how she uses her mom's ski-cap business for her third-grade science project about the world. *(fiction)*

Knowing how to recognize cause and effect can help you understand what happened and why it happened.

UNDERSTAND IT

Things don't just happen. Something makes them happen. What happens is an **effect**. What makes it happen is its **cause**. Read the sentences that go with the pictures. *The ice cream melted* is an effect. The cause is *it was hot*. What is the cause and effect in the other picture?

It was hot, so the ice cream melted.

Because it was windy, my hair was a mess.

EXPLORE IT

When you read, watch for the words *because, so,* and *since.* They are often used to tell about cause and effect. Look at the sentences below. Does each question mark stand for a cause or for an effect?

Since I practiced karate every day, →	I earned a green belt.
(CAUSE)	(EFFECT)
We went home →	*since* the store was closed.
(EFFECT)	(CAUSE)
It is a weekend, →	*so* my friend can sleep over.
(?)	(?)
The game was called off →	*because* the field was wet.
(?)	(?)

CAUSE AND EFFECT

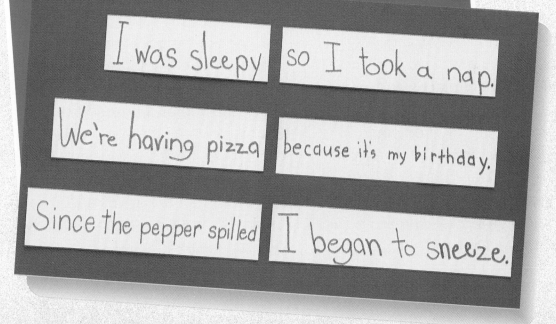

TRY IT

Play a cause-and-effect game with a group of your classmates. Take turns writing either a cause or an effect where everyone can see it. Then ask a volunteer to supply the missing part of your sentence. Can your sentence be completed in more than one way?

To get some ideas, look at the examples on this page.

I was sleepy   so I took a nap.

We're having pizza   because it's my birthday.

Since the pepper spilled   I began to sneeze.

SKILL POWER SEARCH *As you read this chapter, ask yourself these questions: What happened? Why did it happen? These questions will help you recognize effects and their causes.*

1

Setting the Scene

⭐ **KEY WORDS**

tipi
reservation
tradition

FOCUS *Americans have always been a people on the move. Long ago some Native Americans followed the buffalo, taking their movable homes with them.*

Let's Get Moving!

How would you feel if you were packing up and moving today? Most Americans do move several times in their lives. Americans have always enjoyed seeing new places and having new adventures. But it's hard to leave friends. If only you could take your friends with you when you go. Believe it or not, there are people who do just that. In movable communities, groups of people move from place to place together.

People on the Move

The idea of moving as a group is not new. In the 1800s the Crow Indians knew about movable communities. They lived in what is now Montana and Wyoming, where they followed and hunted buffalo. Each season as the buffalo moved, the Crows moved with them. Some Crow communities were large and included many relatives and friends. Other communities included only a few families.

THE BUFFALO

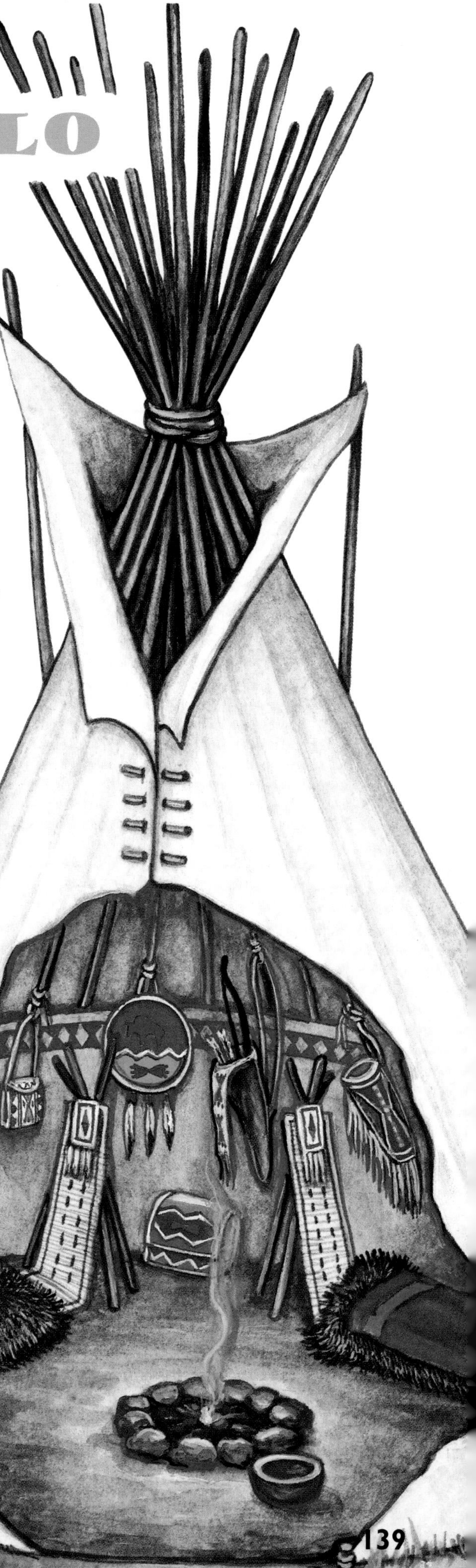

Homes for Moving

Because the Crows moved so often, they needed houses they could take with them. They used a kind of tent called a **tipi** (TEE pee). Tipis were made from wooden poles covered with buffalo skins.

Tipis were good homes for the Crows. A tipi kept out rain, snow, wind, and sun. Smoke from a cooking fire could escape through a hole at the top of the tipi. Best of all, tipis were easy to put up and take down. Two people could put one up in a few minutes. The poles and covering for a tipi could easily be carried from place to place.

Everything inside a tipi was movable, too. Crow women made beds from piles of animal skins. Backrests were made from wooden poles. When it was time to move, belongings could easily be taken along.

⭐ **tipi** A tent made of animal skins or other material and shaped like a cone

139

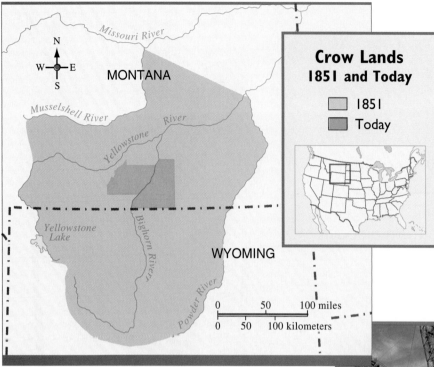

Crow Lands
1851 and Today

☐ 1851
☐ Today

Crow Communities Today

Today the Crows no longer follow the buffalo or live in tipis. Most Crows today live on a reservation. A **reservation** is land set aside for Native Americans. The map above shows the land the Crows traveled over in 1851 compared with the land of their reservation today. On their reservation the Crow people work at many jobs, such as teaching and farming. The man in the photo works for a company that mines coal on tribal land. Many other Crow people work outside the reservation.

Life has changed for Crow Indians. Still, many value their **traditions**, or old ways of doing things. Some Crow traditions come alive at the Crow Fair held every August on the reservation. The photo shows dancers at the Crow Fair. Crow families and friends dance, ride horses, and put up tipis, just as their ancestors did long ago.

⭐ **reservation** Land set aside for Native Americans
tradition A set of very old beliefs and ways of doing things

Creating Movable Communities

The Crows are not the only people with a tradition of moving from place to place. Other Americans have also valued the freedom to go where they wanted. For some, traveling in groups has worked best. That's the way settlers moved west in the 1800s. And it's the way some people still travel today. Let's take a closer look at some of these movable communities.

Each Crow shield had special meaning for the person who used it in battle. This shield includes storm clouds, lightning bolts, and eagle feathers.

SHOW WHAT YOU KNOW!

REFOCUS

1. Why did Crow Indians follow the buffalo?

2. How is your home like a tipi and different from a tipi?

THINK ABOUT IT

What caused the buffalo to move each season and what effect did this move have on the Crows?

WORK TOGETHER

One partner writes a sentence about Crow life. The other partner tells whether the sentence is about Crow life today or long ago.

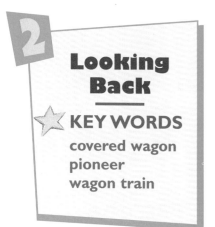
LIFE ON

FOCUS *Pioneers searching for opportunity and adventure traveled west in wagon train communities.*

Searching for a Better Life

In the 1840s many Americans were looking for opportunities and adventure. Some of them didn't own much land or have much money, but they all wanted a better life. How could they get it?

The land out west seemed inviting. People had heard that there was plenty of good land for farming. Soon thousands of people from the East began a journey west. In 1848, gold was discovered in California. That led even more people to travel westward. Families put everything they owned into **covered wagons** like the one shown here. Then they headed west.

A Long Journey

These people were **pioneers**. They were traveling to places they had never been before. Most hoped to reach California or the Oregon Territory. Pioneers had to cover miles of mountains, deserts, and prairies. Traveling alone could be dangerous, so many decided to travel in

▼ Wagon covers were made of strong cloth that protected travelers and supplies from rain and dust.

⭐ **covered wagon** A large wagon with an arched canvas cover

pioneer A person who goes before, opening the way for others to follow

THE TRAIL

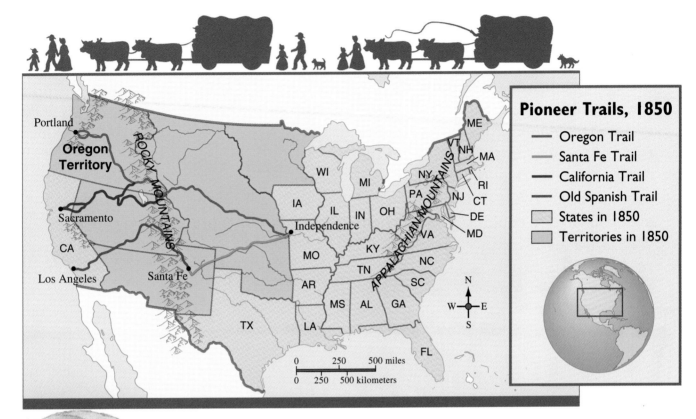

Pioneer Trails, 1850

- —— Oregon Trail
- —— Santa Fe Trail
- —— California Trail
- —— Old Spanish Trail
- ☐ States in 1850
- ☐ Territories in 1850

groups. Several trails, as you can see on the map, began in Independence, Missouri. A town such as this was called a jumping-off place because pioneers felt as if they were "jumping off" into the unknown.

Getting Ready to Go

Families spent many days in jumping-off places, gathering supplies for their trip. Each family packed its wagon with food, clothing, tools, and spare wagon parts. Meanwhile, the pioneers ran into others who were also preparing to "jump off." It made sense for these families to travel together since they could help each other along the way.

▼ A lantern holding a candle provided light for pioneers.

143

Forming Wagon Trains

Pioneer families formed **wagon trains**. These were groups of wagons that traveled together. A wagon train might have as many as 100 wagons. Before heading west the members of a wagon train would get together. They would choose leaders for the group. The leaders rode horses at the front of the wagon train. They set the daily schedule. They picked safe spots to cross rivers. They did everything they could to protect their wagon train.

⭐ **wagon train** A group or line of wagons traveling together

The Life of a Pioneer

For wagon train families, each day was long and hard. People had to be up before dawn. Soon after, they were on the trail. Wagons were packed so full that there was little space left for people. Besides, the inside of a wagon was often very hot, and the ride was bumpy. Most people ended up walking beside their wagons. Some days the sun beat down for hours. Other days, rain soaked everything. Many people became ill, and some died.

Wagon Train Communities

But life in a wagon train could be enjoyable. Children played tag with each other. Women shared recipes and medical advice. Men helped repair each other's wagons. At night the wagons formed a circle in which people could relax and talk with each other. Often someone played a fiddle. On special days, like the Fourth of July, people danced and sang songs.

Things didn't always go smoothly in wagon trains. Sometimes people didn't get along. For the most part, wagon train communities were peaceful. The pioneers needed each other in many ways. During their long months on the trail, these people learned to live together as friends and neighbors.

Travel the Oregon Trail Today

The small photo shows tourists who are reliving pioneer days by traveling the Oregon Trail in a wagon train. Wagon train rides are available at different locations along the trail. On these rides, people can learn about life on a wagon train as they eat dinner around a campfire.

SHOW WHAT YOU KNOW!

REFOCUS

1. Why did pioneers travel west?

2. What was life like for the members of a wagon train community?

THINK ABOUT IT

What problems might there be among the people traveling in a wagon train?

COMMUNITY CHECK

Make a chart. Compare the ways that people in your community help each other to the ways that people in a wagon train helped each other.

3

Spotlight
—
⭐ **KEY WORD**
mobile home

FOCUS *Today in the United States, many people live in mobile home communities.*

What Is a Mobile Home?

A **mobile home** is a special kind of home that has become very popular in the United States. Mobile homes developed from travel trailers, which were popular in the 1920s.

Today a mobile home, like almost any house, might have flowers by the front steps or a fence around the yard. However, unlike most other houses, a mobile home is built in a factory. A mobile home is different from most other homes in another way, too. It's movable. It has wheels, so it can be towed and moved from one location to another.

About 12 million Americans live in mobile homes. Some people take their mobile homes with them when they move. However, most people keep their homes in the same place, often in a mobile home park. This special community has roads, water pipes, and electric lines available to the people who live there.

⭐ **mobile home** A large movable home that is parked for a long time in one location

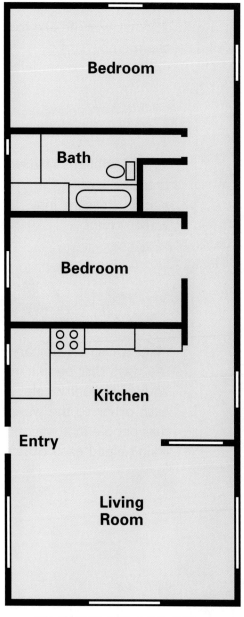

FLOOR PLAN OF
A MOBILE HOME

HOMES TODAY

Mobile Home Communities

More and more people in the United States, especially senior citizens and young families, are choosing to live in mobile home communities.

Mobile homes are well designed. Everything is handy and easy to keep clean and repair. Mobile homes often come complete with furniture and appliances such as stoves or refrigerators. They're often reasonably priced, too.

Today, many people enjoy living in mobile home communities. In some park communities, the neighbors may know each other. In many ways these communities are like those in suburbs, cities, or rural areas. They have streets, yards, and rules for being good neighbors. Each year, more and more Americans decide that a mobile home community is the best community for them.

SHOW WHAT YOU KNOW!

REFOCUS

1. How are mobile homes different from other types of homes?

2. Why do people choose to live in a mobile home?

THINK ABOUT IT

What services, in addition to roads and electricity, would be needed in a mobile home community?

WRITE ABOUT IT

Draw a picture to show how you would plan the inside of a mobile home. Write a paragraph describing your picture.

Map Adventure

★ **KEY WORDS**

caravan
rally
national park

A ROAD

FOCUS *In the United States today, some people travel in movable homes for pleasure.*

Taking a Ride in Your Home

The United States is a huge country. There are many places to go and much to see. One way to travel to these places is in an RV, or recreational vehicle. An RV is a home that can be driven. There are several styles of RVs. Some have their own engines. Others are built to be towed by cars or trucks.

Most people don't live in RVs all the time. They use them for vacations or for other long trips. There is space inside an RV for cooking and sleeping. There is usually a bathroom. Sometimes there is even a TV.

Taking a vacation in an RV can be lots of fun. No matter where you go, you are always right at home. You can even bring along your favorite games and toys. There are no restaurant and hotel bills to pay. You can eat and sleep right in your RV.

TRIP

Traveling Together

Some RV owners belong to special clubs. These clubs plan trips to interesting places. That way, members can vacation together. If you belong to an RV club, you have more than a movable home. You have a movable community.

Club members often form a caravan, or a string of vehicles on the road, and drive to their vacation spot together. They park their RVs next to each other. Then they relax and enjoy a vacation among friends.

⭐ **caravan** A group of people traveling together

Being With Friends

There are several RV clubs across the nation. The clubs arrange trips that include rallies, or meetings of members from different places. Here people may dance, put on pet shows, and share meals. Rallies such as the one in the photo are called Silver Cities. Can you see why?

The next two pages invite you to take a road trip of your own in an RV. You can travel on highways and visit national parks, areas of land protected by the United States government for the public to visit.

⭐ **rally** A large meeting held for a particular purpose
national park Land cared for and protected by the U.S. government

149

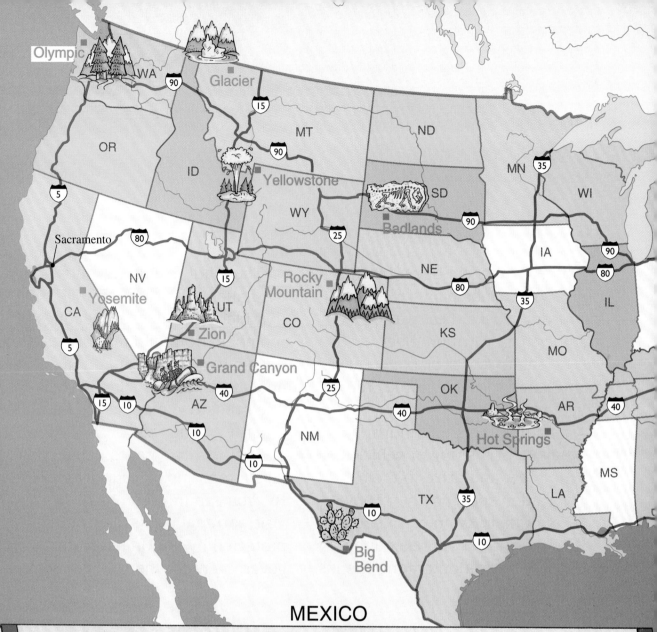

Olympic

WA

Glacier

90

15

OR

MT

ND

MN

35

WI

ID

Yellowstone

SD

Badlands

90

IA

90

Sacramento

80

WY

25

NE

80

35

80

NV

Rocky Mountain

IL

Yosemite

UT

CO

KS

MO

CA

Zion

5

Grand Canyon

OK

AR

40

15

10

40

AZ

10

NM

10

Hot Springs

MS

10

TX

35

LA

Big Bend

10

MEXICO

A NATIONAL PARKS ROAD TRIP

 Great Smoky Mountains— huge forests and many streams

Grand Canyon—deep river canyon

Yosemite—nation's highest waterfall

Yellowstone—first national park, opened in 1872

Olympic—rain forests and rare elk

Rocky Mountain—high, rugged mountain peaks

Acadia—mountainous sea coast

Zion—colorful canyons and rocks

Glacier—50 mountain glaciers and 250 lakes

Shenandoah—mountains and wilderness trails

Big Bend—desert land along Rio Grande

Badlands—rugged land and fossils of mammals

Everglades—swampland with alligators

Hot Springs—hot mineral springs

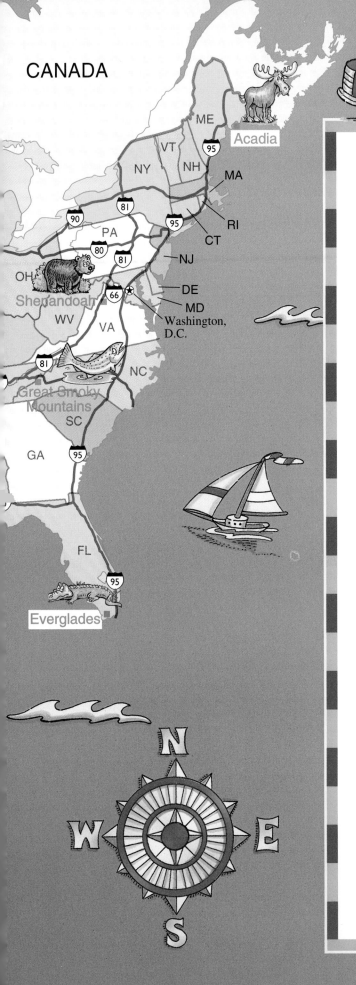

CANADA

Acadia

ME
VT
NY   NH
90   81   MA
PA   95
80   RI
81   CT
NJ
OH   DE
66   MD
Shenandoah   Washington, D.C.
WV   VA
81
Great Smoky
Mountains   NC
SC
GA   95
FL
95

Everglades

N
W   E
S

REFOCUS

1. How is an RV different from other homes?

2. How do the members of an RV club form communities?

MAP IT

The map shows some main highways you could use to drive to many national parks. Start your road trip from Sacramento, California.

1. What national park will you be near if you drive as far north on Highway 5 as you can? What can you see there?

2. From Highway 5, you drive east on Highway 90 and then south on Highway 25. What national park is close to this route? What can you do there?

3. From Rocky Mountain National Park, what highways could you take to reach Great Smoky Mountains National Park?

4. What is the national park that is the farthest northeast?

EXPLORE IT

Plan your own tour of our national parks. Start anywhere you'd like. What parks will you visit and what highways will you use?

Global Connection

⭐ KEY WORDS

herder
reindeer

HERDING IN

FOCUS *In some parts of the world today, there are groups of people who live a traditional lifestyle of moving from place to place.*

Who Are the Saami?

The Saami (SAHR mee) are a people who have lived for thousands of years in northern Europe. The Saami hunt, fish, and farm for a living. The map shows areas where the Saami live. The best-known Saami are traditional herders. They take care of reindeer, large deer found in northern areas. Many Saami herders live in the far northern areas, where they move about. In the spring they move into the mountains. In the fall they move back to lower ground.

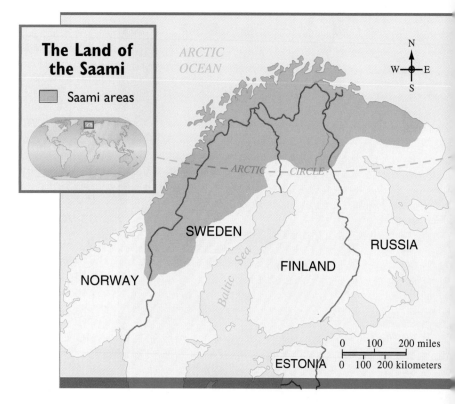

The Land of the Saami

Saami areas

ARCTIC OCEAN

ARCTIC CIRCLE

SWEDEN

NORWAY

Baltic Sea

FINLAND

RUSSIA

ESTONIA

0   100   200 miles
0   100   200 kilometers

The reindeer-herding Saami live in a land where the climate is cold and the ground is covered with snow most of the time. They make skis to travel over the snow. They wear heavy clothing that keeps them warm and dry. Most important of all, they raise reindeer.

⭐ **herder** A person who takes care of a herd, or group, of moving animals
reindeer Large deer found in northern regions

THE FAR NORTH

Reindeer and the Saami

The Saami use reindeer in many ways. They eat the meat and use the skin to make clothing. They carve tools from the bones. The Saami need reindeer to stay healthy and strong. That's why the Saami move so often. In summer, reindeer need the grasses that grow in the mountain pastures. But in winter, reindeer can't find food in the mountains, so they need to be brought down to lower ground.

Each Saami family has its own herd of reindeer. But it takes cooperation to care for these herds. Men work together to round up the animals and move them to new grazing land. The men help each other make marks in the animals' ears so that each reindeer can be identified by its owner.

▲ A Saami man stuffs his shoes with hay to help keep his feet warm.

A Saami family sits around the fire inside its tent while dinner cooks.

Saami Homes

The Saami need several homes because they move so often. In winter the Saami stay down in a village. They live up in the mountains the rest of the time. They don't stay too long in any one mountain home. They need to keep moving so that the reindeer can find fresh food.

Some families stay in huts. As summer goes by, the families move from one hut to the next. Other families spend the summer in tents shaped like tipis. The Saami carry these tents with them as they travel with their reindeer.

A Special Way of Life

The traditional Saami way of life involves hard work, but the Saami people know a special kind of freedom. They feel at home in several different places. They are always close to nature. And they are part of a community that shares a way of life.

The closeness of the Saami communities can be seen each spring. That's when the Saami have a big party to celebrate the end of winter. Everyone wears colorful clothing. People play games and have contests. They even have a reindeer race.

Shoes for a Saami child's doll are often made of reindeer skin.

154

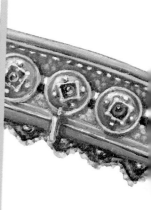
This man is throwing his lasso, or rope, to show his skill at catching reindeer.

Changes in Saami Life

Today, life is changing for most Saami people. Most of them travel by snowmobile instead of skis. Some children live at school instead of moving around with their parents. Some Saami have given up raising reindeer and now work in factories, teach in schools, or do other jobs. Still, many Saami value their traditions. They take pride in wearing Saami clothing. They want their children to learn the Saami language. They don't want their Saami traditions to disappear.

REFOCUS

1. Why do the Saami move from place to place?

2. What do the Saami use reindeer for?

THINK ABOUT IT

What might be some reasons that the Saami celebrate the end of winter?

WRITE ABOUT IT

Make a poster that shows what traditional Saami life is like. Include pictures and descriptive writing on your poster.

SUMMING UP

1 DO YOU REMEMBER...
COMPREHENSION

1. What is a movable community?

2. Describe the job of a wagon train leader.

3. How is a mobile home like and different from other homes?

4. What are recreational vehicles used for?

5. How do the Saami take care of reindeer?

2 SKILL POWER
UNDERSTANDING CAUSE AND EFFECT

Work with a partner to write three sentences that tell about causes and effects you learned about in this chapter. Take turns writing the cause and effect for the sentences.

3 WHAT DO YOU THINK?
CRITICAL THINKING

1. Why do you think the Crows value their traditions?

2. What was the most difficult problem that the pioneers faced? Explain your opinion.

3. Why were mobile homes not invented before the 1920s?

4. How is an RV caravan like and different from a wagon train?

5. Do you think that the Saami traditions will disappear? Why or why not?

4 SAY IT, WRITE IT, USE IT
VOCABULARY

Suppose you lived in one of the movable communities described in this chapter. Write a journal entry that describes your community. Try to use four or more of the vocabulary words below.

caravan	rally
covered wagon	reindeer
herder	reservation
mobile home	tipi
national park	tradition
pioneer	wagon train

5 GEOGRAPHY AND YOU
MAP STUDY

Use the map to answer the questions below.

1. In what state is the Crow reservation found?

2. What river runs through the reservation?

3. What state borders the Crow reservation?

4. How does the size of the Crows' land today compare with their land in 1851?

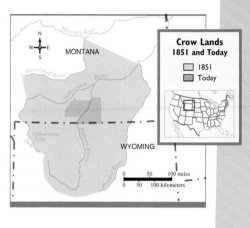

Crow Lands
1851 and Today
☐ 1851
☐ Today

MONTANA

WYOMING

Missouri River

Musselshell River

Yellowstone River

Bighorn River

Powder River

Yellowstone Lake

0   50   100 miles
0   50   100 kilometers

6 TAKE ACTION
CITIZENSHIP

Are there students in your school or neighborhood who have moved a lot? Think of ways to help these students feel at home in your community. You might tell them about special places in your community or draw them a map that shows how to get to the library. What else could you do?

7 GET CREATIVE
MUSIC CONNECTION

Pioneers sang songs from home or made up new ones. Here are some lines from "Sweet Betsy from Pike."

Oh, don't you remember sweet Betsy from Pike?

She crossed the wide prairies with her husband, Ike,

With two yoke of oxen, an old yellow dog,

A tall Shanghai rooster and one spotted hog.

Find other songs about traveling and share them with the class.

LOOKING AHEAD

In the next chapter you'll learn more about **Native Americans** and our country's heritage.

American Indians by forest and sea
   lived close to nature in harmony.
Then the Pilgrims set sail on a very rough sea
   to find a new home where they could live free.
More people journeyed to settle the land—
   this was how cities and towns first began.
As pioneers settled this vast frontier,
   more people arrived from both far and near.
America grew and soon came to be
   a land and its people with rich history.

THE NATIVE

Who were the very first Americans? Learn about Native Americans, their traditional ways of life, and their lives today.

▼ What plant is this girl holding? Look for it three times in this chapter.

CONTENTS

AMERICANS

These books are about Native Americans, today and long ago.
Read one that interests you and fill out a book-review form.

READ AND RESEARCH

Cherokee Summer by Diane Hoyt-Goldsmith,
photographs by Lawrence Migdale (Holiday House, 1993)
Bridget is a Cherokee girl living in Tahlequah, Oklahoma.
Find out how the traditions of her people are kept alive.
Bridget's school uses computers to help children learn the
Cherokee language. *(nonfiction)*

*Eagle Drum: On the Powwow Trail with a
Young Grass Dancer* by Robert Crum
(Simon & Schuster Books for Young Readers, 1994)
Meet Louise Pierre who lives on a reservation in
Montana. Wearing an outfit of his own design, he
performs a grass dance at a powwow. *(nonfiction)*

*Thirteen Moons on Turtle's Back: A Native
American Year of Moons* by Joseph Bruchac and
Jonathan London, illustrated by Thomas Locker
(Philomel Books, 1992)
Many Native Americans based their calendar on the
stages of the moon. Here's a collection of poems, each
telling a story about the seasons. *(poetry)*

Knowing how to read a line graph can help you understand changes that take place over time.

UNDERSTAND IT

A line graph shows changes that take place over a period of time. The time might be measured in days, weeks, months, or years. You can look to see if there have been any changes by seeing if the line of the graph goes up or down.

EXPLORE IT

The school cafeteria needs to know how much ice cream is needed for lunches. Look at the line graph that was made to show on which days students buy the most ice cream.

On which school day did students buy the most ice cream?

On which school day did students buy the least ice cream?

Was more ice cream bought at the beginning or the end of the week?

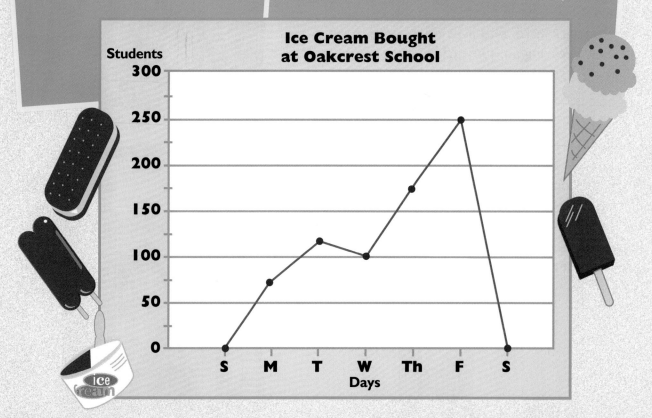

Ice Cream Bought at Oakcrest School

A LINE GRAPH

TRY IT

How do you and your classmates spend your time during a week? Find out by choosing one of the following to make a line graph of your week's activities.

- The number of hours you spend playing with friends in a week

- The number of hours you spend watching TV in a week

- The number of hours you spend doing homework in a week

When you are finished, compare your graph with those of your classmates. Discuss the way the class spends its time.

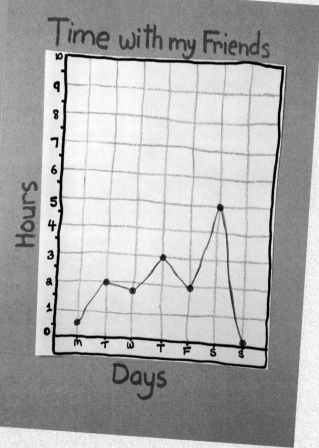

SKILL POWER SEARCH *Look ahead for a line graph in this chapter. Use the graph to practice your new skill.*

Setting the Scene

⭐ **KEY WORDS**

adapt
ancestor
legend

THE FIRST

FOCUS *North America has been home to Native Americans for thousands of years. They developed ways of life suited to the areas in which they lived.*

Many Nations

The Navajo artist in the photo makes clay masks that are similar to the leather masks used in traditional Southwestern American Indian ceremonies. Like many American Indians today, he is trying to keep some of the old ways and pass them on to the next generation.

American Indians were the first people to live in North America. They lived here for thousands of years before European explorers arrived. The people spoke different languages, and each nation had its own traditions and way of living. An American Indian nation is a community of people with lands, a way of life, and a language in common. Once there were several hundred nations of American Indians.

AMERICANS

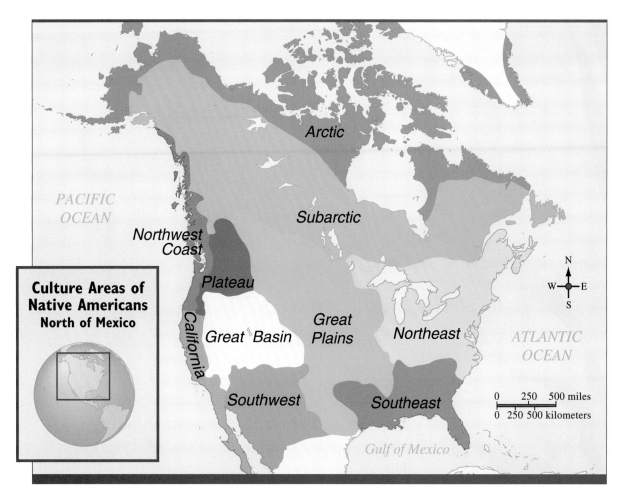

Culture Areas of Native Americans North of Mexico

Arctic

Subarctic

PACIFIC OCEAN

Northwest Coast

Plateau

California

Great Basin

Great Plains

Northeast

ATLANTIC OCEAN

Southwest

Southeast

Gulf of Mexico

N
W — E
S

0   250   500 miles
0   250 500 kilometers

Ways of Living

North America is a land of varied geography with different plants, animals, and natural resources. American Indians adapted, or changed, their ways of life to suit the areas in which they lived. Different nations of American Indians, or Native Americans, in the same area often had similar ways of living. An area where people live and share a way of life, or a culture, is called a culture area. The map shows the different culture areas where nations of Native Americans lived.

The artist shown on page 164 is a member of the Navajo nation. His ancestors lived in the hot, dry desert of the Southwest culture area. Find that area on the map. Today, many Navajo people still live in this area.

American Indians today—like those of the past—have different ways of living but still share some basic ideas about the world.

⭐ **adapt** To change in order to fit new conditions

⭐ **ancestor** A person from whom one is descended

Respect for the Earth

Respect for the earth has been an important tradition in Native American cultures. The earth was honored for its beauty and for everything it provided, including food and shelter. Native Americans felt close to nature and believed that all living things should be respected. They were careful not to waste things in nature. The Native Americans in the picture above are guarding their cornfields from crows.

Native Americans organized their lives around the changing seasons. Since the seasons came and went in a cycle, they viewed time in a cycle. Spring was the time to plant, summer was the time to hunt, fall was the time to harvest and celebrate, and winter was the time to stay inside and tell traditional stories. Many Native Americans still follow these beliefs.

A bowl used to hold corn and seeds, from the Southwest culture area

Art for Every Day

American Indians thought that the earth was filled with beautiful things, and so they tried to create beautiful things, too. They decorated everyday objects, such as baskets, bowls, and blankets, to increase their beauty and to emphasize their importance as useful objects. What designs do you see on the handle of this wooden spoon from the Northwest Coast culture area? Many American Indians today continue the artistic traditions of their ancestors. Look for more examples in the pages that follow.

The Spoken Word

Most Native American nations had no written languages. All Native American cultures valued the ability to speak well before an audience. Speechmaking and storytelling were important skills. News and ideas were shared in speeches. Knowledge and beliefs were passed from generation to generation by telling **legends**, stories about the past. Many stories had lessons that helped people solve problems and get along with each other. Young people learned the history and traditions of their people by listening to stories.

legend A story that is handed down among a people through the years

A wooden bowl shaped like a sea otter, from the Northwest Coast culture area ▶

SHOW WHAT YOU KNOW!

REFOCUS

1. Who were the first Americans?

2. What culture areas did they live in?

THINK ABOUT IT

Explain how the place where people live can affect how they live.

WRITE ABOUT IT

Write a short summary that describes some basic ideas about the world that many Native Americans still share.

NORTHWEST

FOCUS *The Native Americans of the Northwest Coast lived in a region that offered many natural resources from the ocean, rivers, and forests.*

People of the Northwest Coast

Native Americans of the Northwest Coast lived along the Pacific Ocean from southern Alaska to northern California. The culture area map shows where they lived. This area is warm and mild in the summer and cool and rainy in the winter.

The waters were filled with fish, and the forests grew large because of the mild, rainy climate. Bears, deer, and mountain goats lived in the wooded mountain areas. The forests also provided plants and fruit to eat.

Northwest Coast Culture Area

The Native Americans who lived here were able to collect most of the year's supply of food between May and September. During the other months of the year, which were very rainy, they had time to develop a culture rich in storytelling and ceremonies. The line graph on the next page shows the **precipitation** for one area of the Northwest Coast. Precipitation includes all the forms of water that fall to the earth. Which months have the most precipitation? A rain hat like the one on the graph was made from roots and protected people from rain.

⭐ **precipitation** Rain, snow, or any other moisture that falls from the sky

▼ This is a copy of a wooden bowl that was used to serve food to important people.

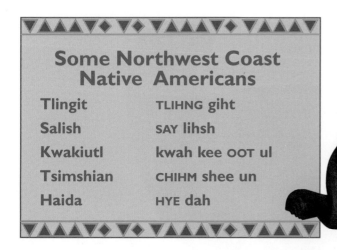

Some Northwest Coast Native Americans

Tlingit	TLIHNG giht
Salish	SAY lihsh
Kwakiutl	kwah kee OOT ul
Tsimshian	CHIHM shee un
Haida	HYE dah

COAST PEOPLE

Villages of Wood

Nearly every village of the Northwest Coast people faced the water. The houses were large and made of wood. Even taller than the houses were the **totem poles**, the carved posts that the people made. Many everyday objects were carved from wood, too, including dishes and spoons. What do you see that is made of wood in the Northwest Coast village in the painting above?

Canoes, the major form of transportation, were made from the wood of red cedar trees. Skilled carvers built the canoes to hold as few as one or two people or as many as 60 people. The Tlingit people and the Salish people were noted for their fine canoes.

⭐ **totem pole** A post carved with animals and other natural objects that tells a story or a legend

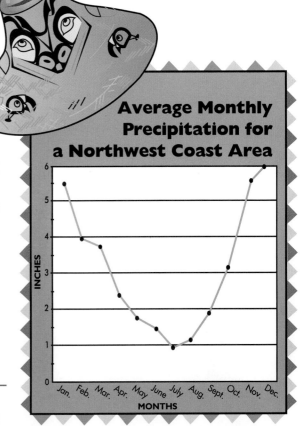

Average Monthly Precipitation for a Northwest Coast Area

INCHES

MONTHS

Jan. Feb. Mar. Apr. May June July Aug. Sept. Oct. Nov. Dec.

Fishing for Food

The Native Americans of the Northwest Coast didn't grow any food, since the land and water supplied what they needed. Fishing was their most important way of getting food. Fish were caught with a net, a hook, or a **harpoon**, a type of spear. The main catch was salmon. In many Northwest Coast languages, the word for *fish* and *salmon* is the same. A ceremony of thanksgiving was held every spring after the first salmon was caught. Everyone was given a taste of this first fish. All the villagers worked to dry the salmon over slow fires. Dried fish provided food for the winter months.

⭐ **harpoon** A spear with a sharp barbed point at one end and a cord attached to the other end

This song honors the river and Chief Kalakuyuwish, who made the first totem pole for his people. ▶

SONG OF THE TOTEM POLE

NOW DOTH IT RISE, OUR RIVER;
OUR RIVER IS WAKIASH, GOOD IS HE.

NOW DOTH IT CREAK, THIS TOTEM POLE;
CLOUDS REST ON ITS TOP.
KALAKUYUWISH, GREAT AS THE SKY-POLE IS HE!

Carving History

Carved and painted totem poles, such as this one, were part of the Northwest Coast culture. They were carved from cedar trees and had animal-like figures on them. Many totem poles told the story of a family's history. Sometimes a totem pole was put up by a new chief to honor the old chief.

When a totem pole was finished, a potlatch, or feast, might be held to celebrate the event. Sometimes one family would have a potlatch to honor another family. Everyone received gifts and spent days feasting and telling stories.

Northwest Coast People Today

Many Northwest Coast Native Americans today work to keep their traditional arts alive. Some Kwakiutls continue to carve totem poles. Some Tlingits still weave their blankets of goat hair and cedar bark. Every two years the Tlingits, Tsimshians, and Haidas unite for a four-day celebration of their heritage.

SHOW WHAT YOU KNOW!

REFOCUS

1. What natural resources were available in the Northwest Coast region?

2. What food was most important to the people who lived there?

THINK ABOUT IT

Why was rain important to the Northwest Coast region?

COMMUNITY CHECK

If you were to carve a totem pole to represent your classroom, what things might you show?

Spotlight

★ **KEY WORDS**

mesa
hogan
clan

SOUTHWEST

FOCUS *The Southwest was home to many Native American groups, including the Navajo.*

The Southwest

The land of the Southwest culture area is not only beautiful, but it also includes many different environments. It has desert areas and flat-topped **mesas**, or hills with very steep sides. There are mountain grasslands, pine forests, and snow-covered mountains as well.

Southwest Culture Area

The Southwest culture area was home to many Native American groups. The Jicarilla people (heek uh REE yuh) hunted and gardened in the hills. The Hopi (HOH pee) and Zuni (ZOO nee) people lived in villages and farmed the mesas. The Navajos (NAV uh hohz) were desert hunters and farmers who later learned to herd sheep.

★ **mesa** A flat-topped hill with steep sides

PEOPLE

Navajo Communities

The Navajos didn't live in towns but in small family groups. The Navajo word for *family* also meant "generosity" and "cooperation." Each family lived in a **hogan**, a round house made of logs covered with mud. When a Navajo woman married, her husband moved in with her and her mother. Families were organized around women because ancestors were traced through women. People who had common ancestors formed **clans**, large groups of relatives who worked together. Clan members helped each other to grow corn and herd sheep.

This Navajo pottery jar was used to hold seeds.

hogan A house made of logs covered with mud
clan A group of people who claim to be related to a common ancestor

The door of a hogan always faces east, the direction of the rising sun.

Daily Life

In Navajo settlements the oldest woman was the head of the family. She was respected because of her wisdom and experience. She made sure that all work was completed.

Women took care of the children, worked in the fields, and herded sheep. Many Navajo women were expert weavers, providing blankets and rugs not only for their own families but also to sell to outsiders. The men built the hogans and cleared the land for farming. They hunted for deer, rabbits, and mountain sheep. The main crop grown by the Navajos was corn.

Navajo Beliefs

The Navajos believed that by respecting all living things, a person would lead a healthy, peaceful life. The Navajos say such a person "walks in beauty." The Navajo Blessingway ceremony was a special ceremony used to increase happiness, goodness, and beauty. It was performed for many different reasons, such as protecting sheep herds or blessing a new marriage.

Navajo tradition holds that all people should be treated as equals, with equal rights. Thus, an important decision would not be made unless all members in a settlement agreed.

▼ Corn, beans, and squash are important in Navajo cooking.

The Navajo chant, or song, that follows shows how much the Navajos respected—and continue to treasure—the earth and all living things.

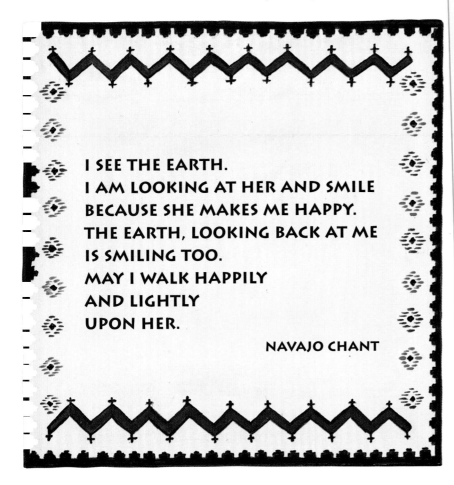

I SEE THE EARTH.
I AM LOOKING AT HER AND SMILE
BECAUSE SHE MAKES ME HAPPY.
THE EARTH, LOOKING BACK AT ME
IS SMILING TOO.
MAY I WALK HAPPILY
AND LIGHTLY
UPON HER.

NAVAJO CHANT

Navajos Today

Many members of the Navajo nation live on the Navajo Reservation, the largest reservation in the United States. Covering more than 15 million acres, this reservation is located in the area where New Mexico, Arizona, Utah, and Colorado meet. This region is often called "Four Corners."

Many Navajos still follow the ways of their ancestors by tending flocks of sheep, though many hold other kinds of jobs, such as teacher or health care worker. The Navajos have created community schools so that their children can be taught the Navajo language, and they have also opened a community college.

REFOCUS

1. How are Navajo communities organized?

2. What are some Navajo beliefs?

THINK ABOUT IT

What are some advantages to having members of a clan help each other?

WORK TOGETHER

Work with a partner to create a song or a poem about something that you both respect.

GROWING UP

FOCUS *As a Native American child growing up on the plains, you would be part of a farming family and live in an earth lodge.*

People of the Plains

The Great Plains area stretches from the Mississippi River west to the Rocky Mountains, and from southern Canada to central Texas. The Great Plains culture area was home to two major groups of Native Americans.

Native Americans such as the Piegans (PEE gunz) and Crows lived in the drier western part of the plains and

Great Plains Culture Area

hunted and gathered food. You read in Chapter 6 about the Crow people, who hunted buffalo and lived in tipis.

Rainfall was more frequent in the eastern part of the plains. The Native Americans who lived there were farmers who also did some buffalo hunting. The Mandans (MAN danz) and Omahas (OH muh hawz) were two nations that occupied this area.

In this painting of a Mandan village, people relax on the roofs of their earth lodges.

ON THE PLAINS

A Child of the Omaha Nation

Suppose you were a child growing up on the plains and your family was part of the Omaha nation. What would your life be like? Your family members are farmers, and you live with them in an earth lodge in a village. Your earth lodge home is partially below ground so that it stays cool in the summer and warm in the winter. Sometimes your family leaves home in search of buffalo, and then you camp in a tipi.

Family Life

Your parents raise you and your brothers and sisters in a way similar to that of most other Native Americans. They don't believe in harsh punishment for children. Your grandparents and other family members teach you how to behave by telling stories. Children are so loved that when a child is born, he or she is given a special name. A child's first hunting trip is a special event for the whole nation.

▼ Plains people often gave a newborn baby a good-luck charm shaped like a turtle.

Some earth lodges, such as the one shown here, were very simple. Others were more complicated and housed many people.

Special Times

When you were a baby, a naming ceremony was held for you. Prayers were said, and you were given a name and a special pair of **moccasins**, which are soft leather shoes. As a baby your mother carried you about in a **cradleboard**, which protected you.

When you began to walk, another ceremony called "turning the child" took place. If you were a boy, you may have gotten a haircut that showed the clan you belonged to.

▲ A Plains cradleboard

▼ A child of the plains stands in front of her miniature tipi.

Play and Games

You and the other children in your village play games. You especially like to play games with balls. Sometimes you play house in a small tipi or make believe you are going on a buffalo hunt. You use clay to make dishes and dolls and many other toys. In summer you and your friends love to go swimming.

Learning Manners

As you grow up, you are taught to follow the rules of your family and to respect older people. You and your brothers and sisters are also expected to get along with each other. If you're a girl, you learn how to sit and move quietly. If you're a boy, you learn how to sit on your heels and get up quickly.

⭐ **moccasin** A shoe made of soft leather
cradleboard A carrier for babies, made from leather, wood, and other materials

Keeping Traditional Ways

On winter nights you sit around the fire and listen to older people tell stories. One night, you learn the story of a brave man who makes himself invisible and plays tricks on Thunder until Thunder becomes nice. Thunder used to always harm people but now helps people by bringing summer rains. In this way you and the other children learn about the history and traditions of your nation.

The Omahas Today

There are about 6,000 members of the Omaha nation today. About 2,000 live on the Omaha Reservation in Nebraska. The people there work in agriculture, small businesses, and reservation offices. In school, students can learn the Omaha language along with their other subjects. Dancing and the giving of gifts are important modern ceremonies, and the old Omaha warrior songs are sung by many nations at gatherings today.

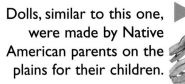
Dolls, similar to this one, were made by Native American parents on the plains for their children.

SHOW WHAT YOU KNOW!

REFOCUS

1. What were two ways of life of the Native Americans who lived on the Great Plains?

2. How did Omaha children learn the history of their nation?

THINK ABOUT IT

How did some games that children played help them know what to do when they grew up?

COMMUNITY CHECK

What rules did Omaha children have to obey that are similar to and different from the rules in your life?

KEEPING

FOCUS *Many Native Americans across the United States value their traditions and work hard to keep them alive for their children.*

Native American Traditions

Many Native Americans today, whether they live in cities or on reservations, still value the traditions that have been part of their heritage for hundreds of years. They are working in many ways to save these traditions and pass them on to their children.

Learning an Art

The Navajo people of the Southwest have a tradition of weaving. This tradition continues as you can see in the photo. A Navajo mother is teaching her daughter how to weave a blanket with Navajo designs.

The Northwest Coast people were expert canoe builders. In recent years the art of canoe building has been renewed among Northwest Coast nations. Canoe carving and paddling is taught at some Northwest Coast American Indian schools.

TRADITIONS ALIVE

Sharing the Dance

Most Native American nations share a tradition of dancing. One way that this tradition continues today is at a powwow, a celebration of Native American culture. Powwows, such as the one in the photo below, are held all across the United States.

Most dancing at powwows is done in a circle. A group of men sit in the center of the circle around a drum similar to one shown below. As the men sing and beat the drum, the dancers circle around them. The beat of the drum drives the singing and dancing that can last far into the night.

Members of many nations attend each powwow. Non-Native Americans also attend to enjoy and learn about this traditional culture. There are more than 1,000 powwows held in the United States each year.

powwow A celebration of Native American culture that includes dances, songs, and traditional dress

Learning the Language

Native Americans have traditionally passed their culture on through stories and songs. Today more of their languages are being written down. So, many Native American children (who already speak English) are today learning their traditional language in both written and spoken forms.

Respecting the Land

Native Americans still feel a special closeness to the land. For centuries these people organized their lives around the cycles of nature. Many Native Americans still teach their children to respect the land. The photo shows a Hopi father explaining the growing cycle of corn to his children.

Sharing Cultures

American Indians are proud to share their traditions with others. For a long time the National Museum of the American Indian was housed in an old building in New York City. Then in 1994, the Heye Center opened in New York City. It is part of the National Museum of the American Indian.

The first three exhibits shown at the Heye Center included nearly 500 objects from the museum's collection. American Indians wrote descriptions for the objects. The museum has a program called Talking Circles, in which visitors can ask American Indian artists and elders, or respected older people, questions about Native American life.

Another building of the National Museum of the American Indian is planned. It will be built on the last available site, or land, on the National Mall, in Washington, D.C.

elder An older person who is respected in a community
site A piece of land to be used for a special purpose

SHOW WHAT YOU KNOW!

REFOCUS

1. What traditions are important to Native Americans?

2. Why is the newly opened museum in New York City important?

THINK ABOUT IT

What questions about Native American life would you ask if you visited the Heye Center?

COMMUNITY CHECK

What events does your community hold that help keep traditions alive?

SUMMING UP

1 DO YOU REMEMBER...
COMPREHENSION

1. What ideas about the world do Native Americans share?

2. What kinds of things did the Northwest Coast people make out of wood?

3. How are Navajo communities organized?

4. In what ways did most Native American parents raise their children?

5. In what ways are Native Americans today saving and sharing their traditions?

3 WHAT DO YOU THINK?
CRITICAL THINKING

1. What are some reasons that could explain why American Indians organized their lives around the seasons?

2. Why were canoes the main source of transportation for the Northwest Coast people?

3. Explain some of the beliefs of the Navajo people.

4. How did the amount of rainfall in the Great Plains affect how Native Americans lived?

5. Is it important that traditions be passed on? Why or why not?

2 SKILL POWER
USING A LINE GRAPH

The line graph on page 169 shows the precipitation in one area of North America. Look in an almanac to find the precipitation in another area of North America. Make a line graph that shows the precipitation in that area.

4 SAY IT, WRITE IT, USE IT
VOCABULARY

Write five questions about the first Americans. Use at least one word below in each question. Trade questions with a friend and answer each other's questions.

adapt	legend
ancestor	mesa
clan	moccasin
cradleboard	powwow
elder	precipitation
harpoon	site
hogan	totem pole

184

5 GEOGRAPHY AND YOU
MAP STUDY

Use the map on page 165 to answer the following questions.

1. How many Native American culture areas were there?

2. Was there any area in North America where Native Americans did not live?

3. What culture area is south of the Northwest Coast culture area?

6 TAKE ACTION
CITIZENSHIP

Today, Native American children speak English. Many are also learning the language of their ancestors. Share any words that you know from other languages. Maybe you know some words from the language of your ancestors, neighbors, or friends. Add your words and their meanings to a class chart for everyone to share.

7 GET CREATIVE
SCIENCE

Find out about some foods that Native Americans ate. Make a poster with words and pictures that compares some Native American foods with some foods that you eat. Note similarities and differences.

LOOKING AHEAD

The next chapter continues the story of America by telling about the Pilgrims and their new community.

Chapter 8

What was it like to travel aboard the *Mayflower*? Find out on page 206.

What would it be like to start a new community in a faraway land? Read about the challenges the Pilgrims faced as they started their community in Plymouth.

CONTENTS

PILGRIMS

These books are about the Pilgrims and other related subjects.
Read one that interests you and fill out a book-review form.

READ AND RESEARCH

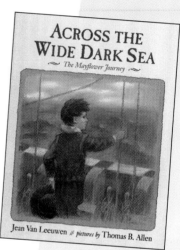

Across the Wide Dark Sea: The Mayflower Journey
by Jean Van Leeuwen, illustrated by Thomas B. Allen
(Penguin USA, 1995)
Listen as young Love Brewster describes the stormy voyage
on the *Mayflower*. Follow him through the first difficult year
at Plymouth. *(historical fiction)*
• *You can read a selection from this book on page 208.*

Clambake: A Wampanoag Tradition by Russell
M. Peters, photography by John Madama
(Lerner Publications Co., 1992)
Clambakes have been part of the Wampanoag
tradition since before the Pilgrims arrived. Read along
as Steven learns from his grandfather, Fast Turtle, how
to prepare for a clambake. *(nonfiction)*

Three Young Pilgrims by Cheryl Harness
(Simon & Schuster Books for Young Readers, 1992)
The rich paintings, labeled with interesting facts, tell
the story of three Pilgrim children. *(historical fiction)*

Reading a time line can help you understand the order in which different events happened.

UNDERSTAND IT

A time line shows when events happen and the order they occur in. Most time lines show events from the past. Each segment on a time line stands for the same amount of time. In the time line below, each segment stands for ten years. In other time lines, segments may stand for more or less time.

EXPLORE IT

The time line below shows some of the dates on which particular coins were first made in the United States. Read the time line from left to right. Did the buffalo nickel come before or after the Jefferson nickel? How can you tell?

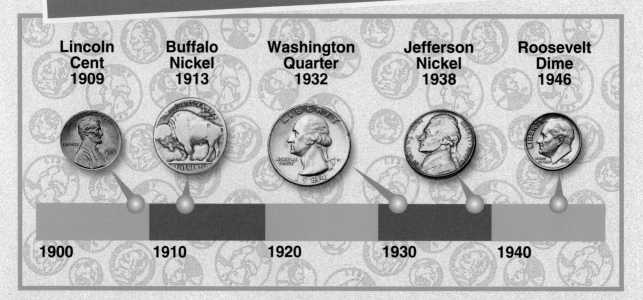

| Lincoln Cent 1909 | Buffalo Nickel 1913 | Washington Quarter 1932 | Jefferson Nickel 1938 | Roosevelt Dime 1946 |

1900   1910   1920   1930   1940

A TIME LINE

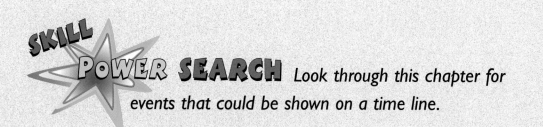

SKILL

POWER SEARCH *Look through this chapter for events that could be shown on a time line.*

Setting the Scene

⭐ KEY WORDS

Pilgrim
colony

A LIVING

FOCUS *In a living-history museum, people can visit and learn about communities from the past.*

Learning About the Past

There are many ways to learn about the past. You can read books or talk to people who have lived a long time. You can look at old photos. You can also visit a place called a living-history museum.

A living-history museum re-creates the past—right before your eyes. In a living-history museum, a town or village is made to look just as it did long ago. The people who work there often dress, talk, and act as the people did in the past.

The map below shows some living-history museums across the country. There are others, too. Can you find one near your community?

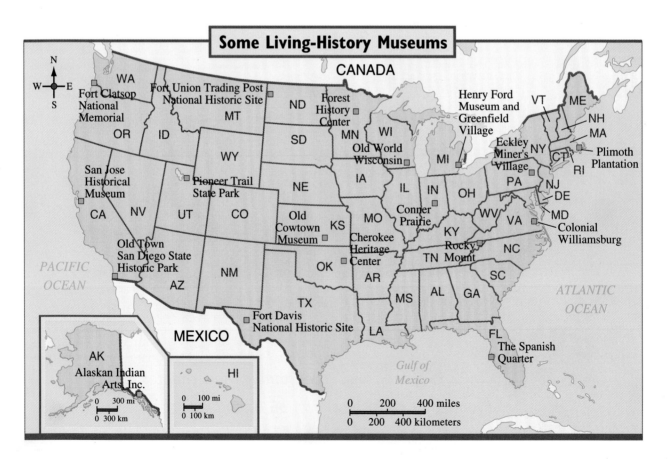

Some Living-History Museums

N W E S

CANADA

WA
Fort Clatsop National Memorial

Fort Union Trading Post National Historic Site

MT

ND

Forest History Center

OR ID

WY

SD

MN WI

Old World Wisconsin

MI

Henry Ford Museum and Greenfield Village

VT ME
NH
MA

Eckley Miner's Village

NY CT
RI

Plimoth Plantation

San Jose Historical Museum

Pioneer Trail State Park

NE

IA

IL IN OH

PA

NJ
DE

CA NV UT CO

Old Cowtown Museum

KS MO

Conner Prairie

WV VA

MD

Colonial Williamsburg

Old Town San Diego State Historic Park

NM AZ

OK

Cherokee Heritage Center

AR

KY

Rocky Mount

TN

NC

SC

PACIFIC OCEAN

TX

Fort Davis National Historic Site

MS AL GA

LA

ATLANTIC OCEAN

MEXICO

Gulf of Mexico

FL

The Spanish Quarter

AK
Alaskan Indian Arts, Inc.

0 300 mi
0 300 km

HI

0 100 mi
0 100 km

0   200   400 miles
0   200   400 kilometers

A Visit to Plimoth Plantation

On the next few pages you can visit Plimoth Plantation, a living-history museum where the life of the **Pilgrims** in 1627 has been re-created.

The photo on this page shows the main street of the Pilgrim **colony**. This dirt path slopes down the hill to the ocean. The street is lined with two rows of small houses. Each house is covered with uneven wooden planks. Some of the houses have straw roofs. Each house has a vegetable garden.

The people dressed as Pilgrims are museum guides, or interpreters. They study the history of Plymouth so that they can build houses, plant crops, and dress as the actual Pilgrims did almost 400 years ago.

⭐ **Pilgrim** One of the group of people who settled in Plymouth, Massachusetts, in 1620
colony A place that is settled by people from a faraway country and ruled by that country

Pilgrim women used a butter churn like this one to turn milk into butter.

Meeting the Pilgrims

If you visited Plimoth Plantation, you could watch the Pilgrims feed animals, chop wood, fix fences, and tend their gardens—just as the real Pilgrims did years ago. You would also see cattle, goats, sheep, and chickens. The photo above shows some children visiting with one of the Pilgrim guides at Plimoth.

The Pilgrims' houses are small and dark. The tiny windows don't let in much light. Inside one house a woman and her daughter are cooking dinner, the midday meal. The daughter stirs something in a big kettle. They are both wearing heavy clothing. Their long skirts and aprons reach the floor.

The floor of the house is made of dirt. The small room is the kitchen, living room, and bedroom all in one. There isn't much furniture. There are shelves with tools, pots, and bowls. There is a bed behind a curtain.

The father and son come home from their work in the fields. Then the whole family gets ready for dinner.

A Family Meal

The quiet house is now full of noise and activity. Everyone helps get things ready for the meal. The father and son take out a big board that is the family's table. They place it on two wooden barrels.

The daughter puts wooden bowls, knives, and spoons on the table. The family doesn't own forks. But that doesn't matter—around here, it's all right to dig in with your hands. Everyone has a big cloth napkin to wipe off sticky fingers.

Dinner is a lamb stew with vegetables. There aren't enough chairs for everyone, so the children may stand to eat.

▼ Although this family at Plimoth Plantation has only two children, many Pilgrim families had six or more.

REFOCUS

1. What is a living-history museum?

2. Describe what dinner might be like in a Pilgrim home.

THINK ABOUT IT

What do you think it would be like to work as a guide in a living-history museum?

COMMUNITY CHECK

With a small group, use a local telephone book to make a list of museums in your area.

FOCUS *The Pilgrims faced many challenges during the first year as they started their new community.*

Who Were the Pilgrims?

The Pilgrims lived in England during the early 1600s. Their religious beliefs were different from those of England's rulers, who wanted everyone to belong to the same church. The Pilgrims wanted freedom to worship God in their own way. So some of them decided to leave.

After trying another place in Europe, the Pilgrims decided on America as the place to start their new community. America was far from England and its harsh laws, and America had lots of land with many natural resources. By September of 1620, the Pilgrims were ready to begin their journey.

▼ This painting shows the Pilgrims as they might have looked as they prepared to leave England.

PLYMOUTH

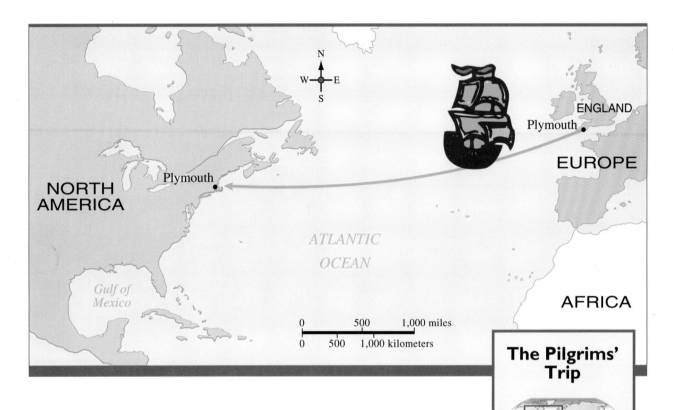

N
W—E
S

ENGLAND
Plymouth •

EUROPE

NORTH
AMERICA

Plymouth •

ATLANTIC
OCEAN

Gulf of
Mexico

AFRICA

0   500   1,000 miles
0   500   1,000 kilometers

The Pilgrims' Trip

A Trip Across the Ocean

The Pilgrims left England on the *Mayflower* in September 1620. There were 102 passengers on the ship—50 men, 20 women, and 32 children.

Forty-one passengers belonged to the church group called separatists. Most of the others were people who thought they could be happier in America. Although the separatists called these people "strangers," today we refer to all the *Mayflower* passengers as Pilgrims.

The trip across the ocean was long and stormy. After 66 days at sea, the Pilgrims finally saw land. But they were in the wrong place. They were supposed to be landing near what is now New York City. Instead, they had landed many miles to the north.

▲ During their first winter at Plymouth, the Pilgrims worked very hard to start their new community.

The First Winter

The Pilgrims were finally in America, but they had a lot of hard work ahead of them. The winter would bring cold weather, and they had no houses to shelter them. They were also running low on food.

They first needed to find a place to live. They found a cleared area near a brook, which looked good. The families started to build houses. Until the first house was built, everyone lived on the cold, wet ship. Many of the Pilgrims became sick. By the end of the winter, half of them had died.

By the spring of 1621, the Pilgrims had built a few houses and a small meetinghouse. They had started to make Plymouth their new home.

Springtime

In March 1621 the Pilgrim settlers met a Native American for the first time. His name was Samoset. Samoset had learned to speak English from some English fishers who had visited America earlier.

Samoset brought another man, Squanto, to meet the Pilgrims. Squanto was a member of the Wampanoag (wahm puh NOH ag) tribe. The Pilgrims didn't know it, but they had settled on Wampanoag land.

Samoset and Squanto introduced the Pilgrims to the leader of the Wampanoags. The Pilgrims and the Wampanoags signed a treaty, or agreement, to help protect each other.

Squanto stayed at Plymouth to help the Pilgrims. He showed them how to plant native corn and where to fish and hunt. Squanto taught the Pilgrims to gather wild plants that were good to eat. Without Squanto's help during the first year, the Pilgrims may have starved.

⭐ **settler** A person who makes a home in a new place

▼ Read the time line to find out what happened to the Pilgrims.

THE PILGRIMS' FIRST YEAR

NOVEMEBER 1620 TO OCTOBER 1621

Pilgrims see land

Nov. 1620

Dec.

Jan. 1621

Feb.

Mar.

Apr.

May

June

July

Aug.

Sept.

Oct.

Good harvest

Hard winter

Pilgrims meet the Wampanoags

First Thanksgiving

The Harvest Feast

After the Pilgrims had a good harvest in the fall of 1621, they had a celebration to thank God. This harvest feast has become known as the first Thanksgiving.

The Pilgrims invited the Wampanoags to join them. Though the Wampanoags usually had their own harvest celebration, this year they also celebrated with the Pilgrims. For three days the 52 Pilgrims and 90 Wampanoags ate, danced, and played games.

Four Pilgrim women and a few girls cooked the food. They probably baked corn bread and cooked carrots, turnips, onions, and beets. They most likely served fish, geese, ducks, and wild turkeys. The Wampanoags brought five deer for the feast.

Thanksgiving didn't become a national holiday until about 200 years later. We celebrate it today on the fourth Thursday in November.

▼ This painting shows what the first Thanksgiving might have looked like.

SHOW WHAT YOU KNOW!

REFOCUS

1. Why did the Pilgrims leave England?

2. Why was the first winter so difficult for the Pilgrims?

THINK ABOUT IT

What do you think might have happened if the Wampanoags hadn't helped the Pilgrims?

WRITE ABOUT IT

Write a paragraph telling why Thanksgiving is an important holiday.

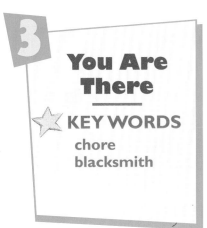

You Are There

⭐ **KEY WORDS**
chore
blacksmith

DAILY LIFE

FOCUS *A day in the life of a Pilgrim child was filled with chores, lessons, and games.*

Growing Up in Plymouth

The year is 1627, and you are a child in Plymouth. The drawing below shows what Plymouth looked like at this time. What is it like to live there?

You spend most of your time behind the walls of this small village. You have walked up and down the main street hundreds of times. The building at the left is the fort. The fort was used as a meetinghouse, a church, a courthouse, and a jail. Most of the other buildings are houses. You know each little house and every person who lives there. One of the houses is where you live.

Plymouth in 1627

Fort

A Day of Work

Girls do chores to help their mothers. If you are a girl, you tend the vegetable garden, milk the goats, and feed the chickens. You mend clothing and clean the house. You might pound spices while your mother churns butter.

Early to Rise

On most days you get up at sunrise. You dress quickly in the cold house. You wash your face and hands in a bowl of cold water. You might take a bath once a month in summer. In winter you hardly bathe at all.

After dressing you roll up your blankets and pillows and then you gather sticks for the breakfast fire.

Your breakfast is oatmeal or cornmeal mush. Your father says a prayer, and everyone eats. After breakfast you start your chores.

Boys mostly work with the men. If you're a boy, you sometimes work in the fields to help with the harvest. You might take care of a trap in the forest like the boy shown on the next page. You might also work with a carpenter, farmer, or blacksmith to learn a skill.

⭐ **chore** A task that has to be done on a regular basis

⭐ **blacksmith** A person who shapes iron to make things, such as horseshoes

200

Lessons and Games

There is no school in Plymouth. But if your father can read and write, he might teach you.

Religion is very important to your family. You pray several times each day. You spend all of Sunday at church. It's hard to sit for hours on the wooden benches, but in winter the cold keeps you awake.

Even though you work hard, you do have some free time to play with your friends. You might play marbles or blow bubbles. But most of your day is spent helping your parents.

SHOW WHAT YOU KNOW!

REFOCUS

1. What are some of the chores that Pilgrim children did every day?

2. What might a Pilgrim child have done for fun?

THINK ABOUT IT

How would your life be different if you were growing up in Plymouth in 1627?

WRITE ABOUT IT

Make a time line showing all of the activities a Pilgrim boy or girl might have done in one day.

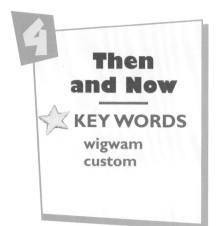

PEOPLE OF

FOCUS *The Wampanoags' way of life changed when the Europeans arrived in America.*

The Wampanoags

When the Pilgrims arrived at Plymouth, they found that there were already many people living in the area. The Native Americans called the Wampanoags had been living there for ten thousand years. The name *Wampanoag* means "people of the dawn."

The Wampanoags had many settlement areas, or villages, in what is now Massachusetts and Rhode Island. They met all their needs from the natural world around them. The Wampanoags had a great respect for nature. They were careful to protect the land and use it wisely.

▼ A woman tends her garden in the re-created Wampanoag village at Plimoth Plantation.

▼ Baskets like these were used for gathering food.

THE DAWN

Moving With the Seasons

The lives of the Wampanoags changed with the seasons. They planted their fields in spring. The warm weather of spring and summer was the best time to catch fish. Fall was harvest time. In fall and winter they hunted for deer and bear. They also trapped animals.

The Wampanoags did not live in the same place all year long. In spring and summer they lived in small settlements near their fields. These settlements were usually near rivers. In fall they moved to their winter settlements, which were closer to the hunting grounds.

▼ Two Wampanoags work together to build a wigwam at Plimoth Plantation.

Family Life

As in Pilgrim families, men and women in Wampanoag families had different jobs. Men hunted and trapped and made tools such as arrows and knives. They also made canoes.

Wampanoag women cooked and made clothes. They also tended the crops. They grew three main crops— beans, corn, and squash. The women also took care of the children.

Both men and women built Wampanoag homes, or **wigwams**. The wigwams were made by bending saplings, or young trees, into a dome shape and covering them with mats made of grasses or bark.

⭐ **wigwam** A traditional Native American home sometimes shaped like a dome

▲ The Wampanoags taught the Pilgrims how to enrich the soil with fish to help corn grow.

A Changing World

When people from Europe arrived in America, the Wampanoags' way of life was changed forever. One change was increased trade. In exchange for furs the Europeans traded farm tools, beads, and cloth with the Indians.

In addition to bringing goods, the explorers and traders from Europe also brought diseases. Many Native Americans died from these diseases. About half of the total population of Wampanoags—10,000 to 12,000 people—died. The cleared fields where the Pilgrims built Plymouth was a Wampanoag settlement that was left empty when many Wampanoags died.

Sharing the Land

In 1621 the Wampanoags signed a treaty with the Pilgrims. The peace lasted for many years. Some Wampanoags helped the Pilgrims survive by teaching them how to fish and farm successfully. But the peace did not last forever.

Each year more English settlers arrived. At first the Wampanoags were willing to share the land. But the English settlers didn't want to share— they wanted to push the Native Americans out of the way. In 1675 a war started. After more than a year of fighting, the Wampanoags lost the war and much of their land.

The Wampanoags Today

Today there are about 2,000 to 3,000 Wampanoags living in Massachusetts. The Wampanoags have special celebrations to show their respect for their ancestors and their culture. At these times they may wear special clothing, sing or dance, and eat traditional foods.

The appanaug (AP uh nawg), or clambake, is one important Wampanoag custom. The Wampanoags may decide to have an appanaug to honor someone or to celebrate the change in seasons. In the photo below, you can see Steven, a young Wampanoag boy, with his grandfather, helping to prepare for an appanaug.

⭐ **custom** A way of doing things

SHOW WHAT YOU KNOW!

REFOCUS

1. Why did the Wampanoags move when the seasons changed?

2. What were the three main crops the Wampanoags harvested?

THINK ABOUT IT

Why do the Wampanoags think it's important to remember their ancestors?

WORK TOGETHER

With a partner, make a list of the ways the Wampanoags and the Pilgrims were alike and different.

How It Works

KEY WORD
crew

A TRIP ON

FOCUS *The Pilgrims lived in crowded and uncomfortable conditions as they sailed on the* Mayflower *to their new home.*

Across the Sea

Have you ever taken a long trip in a car or bus? If the trip took several hours, you probably couldn't move around much. Remember how you couldn't wait to get out?

Now think about what it would have been like to be on the *Mayflower* for 66 days. There are more than 100 other people with you. It's dark, wet, cold, and smelly. People are shouting and babies are crying.

The diagram shows some of the ship's important areas. Read the captions to find out how the **crew** and passengers lived and worked.

▼ At Plimoth Plantation you can take a tour on *Mayflower II,* a reproduction of the original ship.

⭐ **crew** All the people who work on a ship

THE *MAYFLOWER*

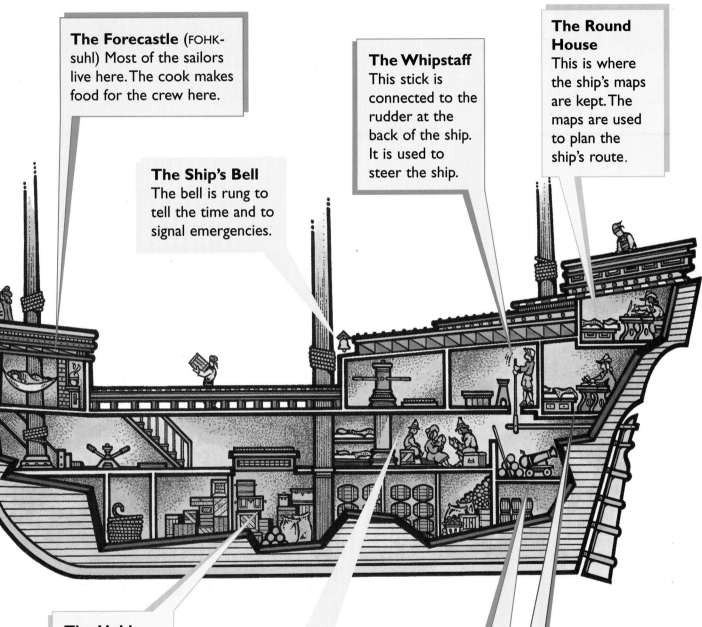

The Forecastle (FOHK-suhl) Most of the sailors live here. The cook makes food for the crew here.

The Ship's Bell The bell is rung to tell the time and to signal emergencies.

The Whipstaff This stick is connected to the rudder at the back of the ship. It is used to steer the ship.

The Round House This is where the ship's maps are kept. The maps are used to plan the ship's route.

The Hold Most of the supplies and food are stored here.

Between Decks Most of the passengers live here during the trip.

The Gun Room The ship's cannons are kept here. They are needed to protect the ship from pirate attack.

The Great Cabin This is where the ship's master, or captain, lives.

Across the Wide Dark Sea: The Mayflower Journey

by Jean Van Leeuwen, illustrated by Thomas B. Allen

Read about a young boy's life as he and his family cross the ocean on the Mayflower.

I stood close to my father as the anchor was pulled dripping from the sea. Above us, white sails rose against a bright blue sky. They fluttered, then filled with wind. Our ship began to move.

My father was waving to friends on shore. I looked back at their faces growing smaller and smaller, and ahead at the wide dark sea. And I clung to my father's hand.

We were off on a journey to an unknown land.

The ship was packed tight with people—near a hundred, my father said. We were crowded below deck in a space so low that my father could barely stand upright, and so cramped that we could scarcely stretch out to sleep.

ACROSS THE WIDE DARK SEA
~ The Mayflower Journey ~

Jean Van Leeuwen *pictures by* Thomas B. Allen

Packed in tight, too, was everything we would need in the new land: tools for building and planting, goods for trading, guns for hunting. Food, furniture, clothing, books. A few crates of chickens, two dogs, and a striped orange cat.

Our family was luckier than most. We had a corner out of the damp and cold. Some had to sleep in the ship's small work boat.

The first days were fair, with a stiff wind.

My mother and brother were seasick down below. But I stood on deck and watched the sailors hauling on ropes, climbing in the rigging, and perched at the very top of the mast, looking out to sea.

What a fine life it must be, I thought, to be a sailor.

One day clouds piled up in the sky. Birds with black wings circled the ship, and the choppy sea seemed angry.

"Storm's coming," I heard a sailor say.

We were all sent below as the sailors raced to furl the sails.

You can find out more about the Mayflower journey by checking the book out of your school or public library.

SHOW WHAT YOU KNOW!

REFOCUS

1. Where did most of the passengers live as they sailed to America?

2. What were the conditions like on the *Mayflower*?

THINK ABOUT IT

How do you think the Pilgrims felt when they first saw land?

WRITE ABOUT IT

Write a paragraph describing what might happen next in the story.

SUMMING UP

1 DO YOU REMEMBER...
COMPREHENSION

1. What is Plimoth Plantation?

2. What was the harvest feast of 1621?

3. What did Pilgrim children spend most of their time doing?

4. Describe the Wampanoags' homes.

5. How long were the Pilgrims on the *Mayflower*?

2 SKILL POWER
READING A TIME LINE

Make a time line that shows events from your life. First choose what time period you want to show. Do you want to show events from last week, last year, or your entire life? Draw the time line with segments of days, months, or years. Include four or more events on your time line.

3 WHAT DO YOU THINK?
CRITICAL THINKING

1. Do you think living-history museums are important? Why or why not?

2. How might things have been different if the Pilgrims and the Wampanoags had never met?

3. Why did Pilgrim boys and girls have different chores?

4. Why did the Wampanoags help the Pilgrims?

5. Why were people willing to live in the crowded and uncomfortable conditions on the *Mayflower*?

4 SAY IT, WRITE IT, USE IT
VOCABULARY

Write an advertisement for the Plimoth Plantation living-history museum. Use at least four of the words below.

blacksmith	custom
chore	Pilgrim
colony	settler
crew	wigwam

5 GEOGRAPHY AND YOU
MAP STUDY

Use the maps in this chapter to answer these questions.

1. Which ocean did the Pilgrims cross to get to America?

2. What is one living-history museum you can find in Indiana?

3. What living-history museum in Virginia shows life as it was during colonial times?

6 TAKE ACTION
CITIZENSHIP

The Wampanoags are proud of their culture. They know it is important to pass down their ancestors' customs and stories. Find out about your ancestors. If you wish, tell your classmates about your ancestors' culture. Listen to stories about your classmates' ancestors, too.

7 GET CREATIVE
LANGUAGE ARTS CONNECTION

Write a short story about something in this chapter. You might choose to write a story about a child growing up in Plymouth, or you could write about life in a Wampanoag village. Draw pictures to illustrate your story.

LOOKING AHEAD

In the next chapter, learn about the people who settled in areas all across our country.

Chapter 9

Learn about the people long ago who braved hardship and danger to settle in different areas of our country.

CONTENTS

▼ What is this boy looking at? Find out on page 224.

Pioneers

These books are about the pioneers who settled our country.
Read one that interests you and fill out a book-review form.

READ AND RESEARCH

Paul Bunyan and Babe the Blue Ox by Jan Gleiter
and Kathleen Thompson, illustrated by Yoshi Miyake
(Steck-Vaughn Co., 1993)
Meet big Paul Bunyan in these tall tales about his logging days
in the forests of America. Follow him and Babe, the giant blue
ox, in their adventures across the country. *(folk tales)*

• *You can read a selection from this book on page 232.*

*The Quilt-Block History of Pioneer Days:
With Projects Kids Can Make* by Mary Cobb,
illustrated by Jan Davey Ellis (Millbrook Press, 1995)
You can learn about the daily lives of the pioneers by
studying the quilt patterns in this book. Discover how
to decorate cards, bookmarks, boxes, and diaries by
using pioneer patterns. *(nonfiction)*

Grandma Essie's Covered Wagon by
David Williams, illustrated by Wiktor
Sadowski (Alfred A. Knopf, 1993)
Grandma Essie tells the story of her family's
travels in a covered wagon from Missouri to
Kansas. Life is hard, but Grandma Essie also
remembers the good times. *(historical fiction)*

SKILL POWER

USING A

Knowing how to use the scale on a map helps you understand how big a place is as well as the distances between places.

UNDERSTAND IT

A map shows you where places and things are located. You can find out how big a place is and the distances between places shown on a map by using the map scale.

Look at the scale on the map below. It stands for a certain number of miles.

EXPLORE IT

Place a ruler under the scale of the map. Do you see that one inch stands for 100 miles on the map?

Use a ruler to measure how many inches there are from Scotts Bluff to Center. Now you can figure out the number of miles between the two cities.

$$100 + 100 + 100 = 300 \text{ miles}$$

- How many inches are there between Valentine and Columbus?

- About how many miles apart are these two cities?

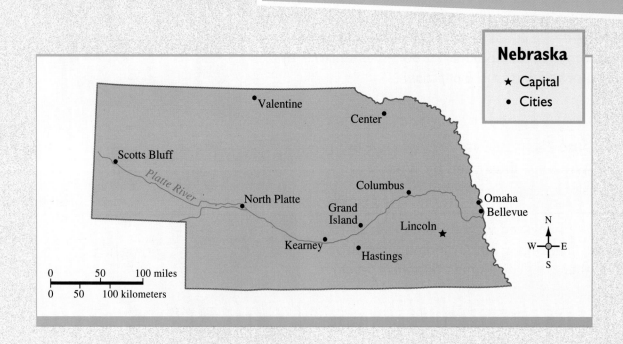

Nebraska
★ Capital
• Cities

Valentine
Center
Scotts Bluff
Platte River
Columbus
North Platte
Omaha
Bellevue
Grand Island
Lincoln
Kearney
Hastings

N
W ◆ E
S

0   50   100 miles
0   50   100 kilometers

MAP SCALE

TRY IT

You're beginning your visit at Happy Wildlife Park. You're at the Cheetah Grasslands exhibit. A minibus takes you from one exhibit to another. With a partner, use a ruler and the map scale to find and write down the distance between each exhibit. About how many miles will you ride the minibus if you visit every exhibit? Don't forget to include the miles you'll travel back.

0 ———————— 1 mile

Happy Wildlife Park
—— **Minibus route**
⬤ **Cheetah Grasslands**
◯ **Baboon Mountain**
⬤ **Sea Lion Island**
⬤ **Camel Desert**
◯ **Crocodile Creek**
◯ **Parrot Paradise**
◯ **Swan Lake**
⬤ **Zebra Zone**

SKILL
POWER SEARCH Use other map scales in this chapter to measure distances from one place to another.

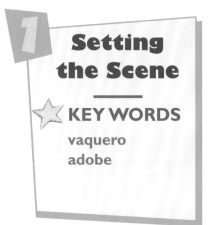

1 Setting the Scene

⭐ KEY WORDS

vaquero

adobe

Southwest

FOCUS *The Spaniards were the first Europeans to settle in North America.*

People and Place Names

How did places on the map below get their names? Many place names come from the language of the people who first lived in these places. American Indians were the first people to live in our country. Find Omaha and Miami, cities with American Indian names, on the map. The English, Dutch, and French were early settlers in our country. Find

Norfolk on the map—a city with an English name. Find Detroit, a city with a French name. Can you find a city with a Dutch name?

The Spaniards were the very first Europeans to settle in the United States. Many cities in the Southwest have Spanish names. Find one on the map. Let's start in the Southwest to learn about some of the people who settled our country.

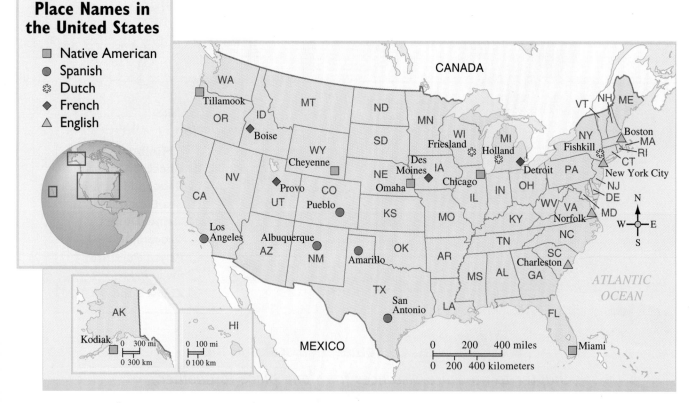

Place Names in the United States

- ■ Native American
- ● Spanish
- ❋ Dutch
- ◆ French
- △ English

216

Settlements

The Spanish Southwest

The Spaniards came to the Americas in search of gold and silver. Spanish soldiers conquered the Aztecs of Mexico in 1521. Spanish explorers pushed northward during the 1500s, claiming more and more land for Spain. Soon, Spain began to set up colonies in the present-day states of Florida, New Mexico, Texas, and California. Find these states on the map.

Today this mission is a part of the San Antonio Missions National Park in Texas. A painting from the ceiling is also shown.

Missions and Forts

Spanish settlers, priests, and soldiers from Mexico arrived in New Mexico in 1598. By 1690 there was a small mission in Texas. In 1769 the Spaniards had a mission in California. The priests started missions to teach their religion to Native Americans. The soldiers built presidios, or forts, to defend the missions.

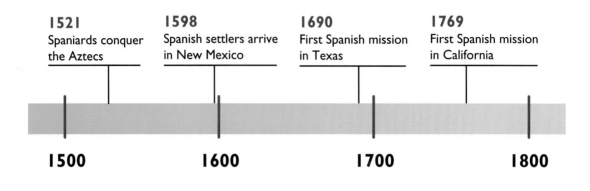

1521
Spaniards conquer
the Aztecs

1598
Spanish settlers arrive
in New Mexico

1690
First Spanish mission
in Texas

1769
First Spanish mission
in California

1500　　　　**1600**　　　　**1700**　　　　**1800**

The First Ranches

Some settlers in the Spanish Southwest lived in farming villages or in towns. Many people lived on ranches and raised cattle, horses, and sheep. The workers hired to care for these animals were called **vaqueros** (vah KER ohs). *Vaquero* comes from the Spanish word *vaca*, which means "cow." Many of the vaqueros' clothes and equipment were later used by cowboys of the American West.

Ranching was important to the Spanish Southwest. The livestock raised on ranches supplied the nearby missions, villages, and towns with food, leather, and tallow, animal fat used in making candles and soap.

⭐ **vaquero** A person hired to care for cattle

▲ This painting shows cowboys working on a ranch.

◀ A pair of goatskin leg coverings used by vaqueros

218

Spanish Culture

If you were to travel through the southwestern United States today, you would see many ways in which Spanish culture has become a part of the culture of the United States.

Many place names, including *Montana* and *Nevada,* come from the Spanish language. Some rivers in Texas, such as the *Rio Grande* and the *Brazos,* also have Spanish names.

American cowboys still practice the skills of roping and herding cattle learned from Mexican cowboys. Many cowboy terms, such as *ranch* and *lasso,* come from the Spanish language.

The Spanish style of building also found a home in the Southwest. Here many beautiful buildings have tan walls of **adobe**, a type of hardened clay.

The Indians in Mexico taught the Spaniards to use tomatoes, corn, and many types of beans. Together the Spaniards and the Indians of Mexico have given us tortillas, chili, and tacos.

⭐ **adobe** A clay brick that has dried in the sun

REFOCUS

1. Who were the first Europeans to settle in North America?

2. In what parts of the American Southwest did these Europeans settle?

THINK ABOUT IT

Give an example of a Spanish contribution to the culture of our country and explain its importance.

COMMUNITY CHECK

Look at a map of your community and make a list of place names. Do some research to find out what language some of the place names come from.

Spotlight

⭐ KEY WORDS

immigrant
tornado
sod
bee

Settling

FOCUS *The people who moved westward to the plains in search of land faced many challenges.*

Moving Westward

While settlers from Mexico moved to the American Southwest, people from Europe and Africa came to the East Coast in the early 1600s and settled there. During the 1700s, people began to search for new lands. Leading the way were explorers, hunters, and trappers. The explorers went to see what the land was like. Hunters and trappers traveled west to make a living. They earned money by selling animal furs to be made into clothes back East. People began to hear about the beauty and richness of western lands. And so they too began to travel west.

▲ Hunters used an animal's horn to carry gunpowder. A pigskin bag held bullets.

Cities in the United States, 1850

- ✪ National capital
- • Other cities
- — Present-day boundaries

the Plains

Who Were the Pioneers?

Many people who went west in the 1840s and 1850s lived on farms and in cities in the eastern United States. As the map shows, the western part of our country had few cities. Use the map scale to find out how many miles a person would travel to get from New York City to Salt Lake City.

People from Europe also landed in the East and traveled to the West. People who settle in a new country are called immigrants. Most settlers were white. There were some black settlers too, many who went west when they were given their freedom after the Civil War. Asian immigrants didn't travel across the country in the early 1800s. Instead, they went directly to California to be miners and railroad workers.

The West was already home to Native Americans, who had been living there for thousands of years. When Mexican, Spanish, white, black, and Asian peoples settled on lands in the West, Native Americans were often forced to leave.

Some settlers who made their home in Oklahoma

⭐ **immigrant** A person who settles in a new country

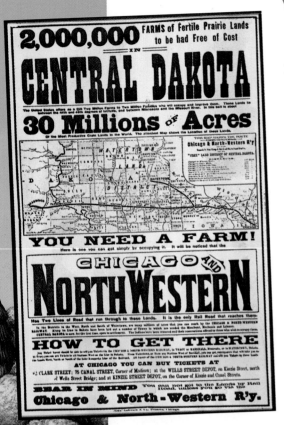

Why Go West?

Land was the biggest reason why so many people traveled west. The Homestead Act of 1862 provided for a settler to get 160 acres of land if he or she farmed the land for five years.

Railroads sold the land they owned along their routes to settlers. They printed posters like the one shown at left to encourage people to settle in the West.

Where They Went

In the early 1800s, pioneers settled in the forests and river valleys of Ohio, Illinois, and Minnesota. Soon people moved farther west. In the 1840s many settlers went to Oregon for its forests and rich soil. Families who settled in forested areas built log cabins.

Other settlers went to California, hoping to get rich after gold was found there. Most failed to find gold but stayed to work and farm.

Settlers traveled through the Great Plains on their way west. By the 1870s this was the only open land left, so people began to settle there. Once again, American Indians were forced off their lands.

What They Found

Families who settled on the Great Plains didn't have an easy life. This region was very hot in the summer and very cold in the winter. It was a place of blizzards and **tornadoes**, or dangerous windstorms. Find the Great Plains on the map below. Was it an area of forests or few trees? The region didn't receive much rain, and having enough water for crops was a problem.

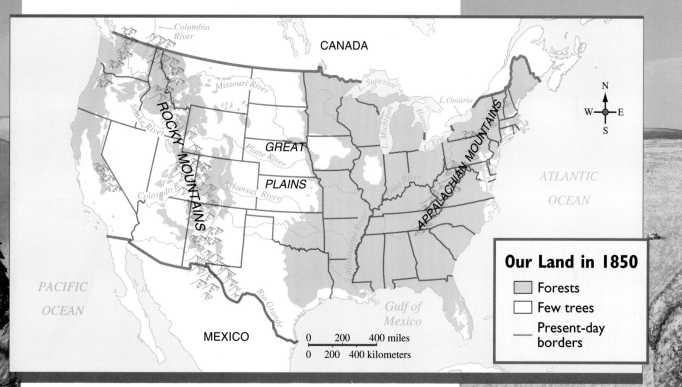

The settlers learned to live in this new land that had little wood for houses or fuel. They grew crops that needed less water and learned new ways to build homes. Some families found life too hard on the Great Plains and gave up and went back home. But many others stayed and survived.

⭐ **tornado** A dangerous windstorm that whirls very fast and can cause destruction

A stereoscope made photos seem very real. Photos of faraway places were popular with pioneer families.

Building a House

Families on the Great Plains used what they had to build a house—dirt and grass. Some settlers dug holes into the sides of hills and cut blocks of sod, or the top layer of earth, to make the fronts of their houses. Others built their whole houses with sod. These homes were called soddies. Wind and snow came in through openings in the sod walls, and the roof often leaked when it rained. The photo above shows a pioneer family in front of their soddie.

Family Life

Work was the center of family life. Men worked in the fields. Women cooked, made clothing, and raised vegetables. Women also worked in the fields with their husbands. Children took care of younger brothers and sisters and helped with the planting of crops.

In the evenings, families might take a break from chores. They would tell stories, read, play games, or look at photos through a recent invention called a stereoscope.

⭐ **sod** The top layer of earth containing grass with its roots

Community Life

As more settlers moved to the Great Plains, towns, such as Fremont, Nebraska, and Topeka, Kansas, grew. Families went to the general store to buy things that they couldn't grow or make, such as sugar or special tools. They also picked up their mail.

Sometimes there were dances in town. Country fairs, like the one in this painting, were popular. People liked to show off the animals they had raised. Many fairs had horse races, too.

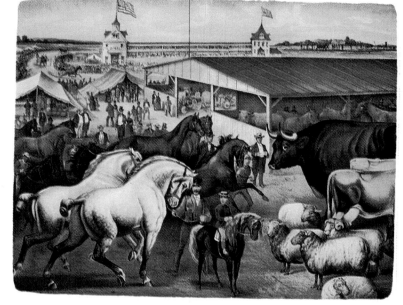

Pioneer families often got together to work in gatherings called **bees**. Families might have a house-building bee. Women got together at sewing bees to make quilts, or coverings for beds, such as the one shown here. Everyone would bring food to a bee, and people had fun sharing work and visiting.

⭐ **bee** A meeting of people to work on something together

SHOW WHAT YOU KNOW!

REFOCUS

1. Why did people choose to settle in the West?

2. What hardships did settlers face on the plains?

THINK ABOUT IT

Why were bees a good way for pioneers to get work done?

WORK TOGETHER

Work with a partner and build a model soddie. Write a few sentences that tell about living in such a house.

School Days

FOCUS *Pioneer children went to school to learn basic things to help them make a living.*

Work Comes First

The year is 1874 and your family has recently settled on the plains. You go to school when you don't have work to do at home. One of your chores is to gather cow or buffalo chips, or chunks of dried manure. The chips provide fuel for your family's stove and fireplace. Often you help plant crops in the spring and harvest crops in the fall. During those times, there is no school.

Building a Schoolhouse

Every community wants a school. When more people move to your area, they decide to start a school. They advertise for a teacher in eastern newspapers. You hope the new teacher will be nice.

Before finding a teacher, work starts on the school. Everyone helps to build a small school with one room for children in all grades. Men work on the building, and women cook food for the workers. When the day ends, everyone eats together and celebrates the work that has been completed.

◀ Children collecting cow chips

A Day at School

You get up early to do chores before school. After breakfast you walk to school. Each school day begins with the flag being raised outside. Then you start your work. Your classmates are of different ages and include students from first through eighth grades. Most of the day, you work at your seat.

When the teacher calls your name, you read a lesson or solve an arithmetic problem on the chalkboard. Pioneer schools don't have much money, so you and the other students share books. Usually you write with chalk on a thin stone known as a slate.

At the end of the day, everyone cleans the classroom. You don't have much homework because your teacher knows that you have chores to do at home.

▲ Teachers often used a bell to signal the start of the school day.

★ **slate** A thin piece of smooth rock that is used as a chalkboard

A farmer needs to use arithmetic to figure out how much seed to buy.

Cash registers similar to this one were used in general stores in the 1800s.

Learning Lessons

Your teacher is told by the adults in your community what they want their children to learn. So mostly you are taught subjects that can help you make a living. You learn skills that will help you grow crops or work in a store or at a small newspaper.

What subjects do you study? First you learn arithmetic. You learn to add, subtract, multiply, and divide. You practice reading every day in front of your teacher and sometimes in front of the whole class. You learn how to write by practicing each letter of the alphabet on your slate. You memorize the spelling of many words. As you get older, you study other subjects, such as American history or geography.

Learning From Stories

Your teachers and your parents believe that school should help to make you a good member of the community. So the stories in your schoolbooks don't just help you to read— they teach you other important lessons such as knowing the difference between right and wrong. Many stories are about the importance of working hard and being honest. Such books also teach you to be proud of your country.

Having Fun

Around noon you get to have lunch and recess. You carry your lunch to school in a bucket or box. You bring foods that don't spoil in the summer heat. Today for lunch you eat cheese, bread, and fruit, and you drink water from the well.

You eat your lunch as fast as you can so that you have more time to play. You might play tag and then hopscotch with your friends. Your school has a seesaw and other wooden things to play on in the yard, so sometimes you play on those, too.

SHOW WHAT YOU KNOW!

REFOCUS

1. What did pioneer children learn at school?

2. Why did pioneer children go to school for only part of the year?

THINK ABOUT IT

Why were children needed to help with chores at home on the plains?

COMMUNITY CHECK

Compare a day at your school with a day in a pioneer school. How are they alike and different?

Citizenship

KEY WORD
heritage

Stories of

FOCUS *Stories are a part of the history of the United States. They can help us learn about our country's people and our land.*

Stories About Our Past

Native Americans created stories to explain their beliefs about the world. People who came to America from other countries created stories about the land that they found here. Such stories can teach us about the past and the beliefs of our ancestors. These stories are an important part of our heritage—our past. As members of the United States community, we should know some of these stories. The photo shows a storyteller at a recent National Storytelling Festival in Jonesborough, Tennessee.

The Pioneer Spirit

The pioneers survived difficult times by creating tall tales, stories about people who did impossible things. From tall tales, we learn about the courage of the pioneers. Some tall tales start with a real person or event and add things that didn't actually happen. You'll read part of a tall tale on page 232.

A North Dakota Story

This story from North Dakota tells of a Native American who watched a pioneer plowing the prairie. The Native American picked up a piece of sod. He said, "Wrong-side up," and turned the sod over so that the grassy side was up. By this he meant that the prairie should not be plowed under. People thought this showed how little Native Americans knew about plowing. But years later when winds blew much of the soil away, people understood: The Native American knew that prairie grasses hold the soil in place.

A Michigan Tale

Michigan is a state with cold winters and strong winds. Here is one "windy" story from Michigan.

⭐ **heritage** Something that is handed down from one's ancestors or the past

America

A man sat on his doorstep, eating apple pie. Suddenly, the wind blew the man up into a tree. As the man sat in the tree, a board flew by. The man grabbed it and held it in front of his face to block the wind so that he could finish eating his pie. What does this story tell you about how the people of Michigan feel about their climate?

LITERATURE

Paul Bunyan and Babe the Blue Ox

by Jan Gleiter and Kathleen Thompson

Read part of a tall tale about Paul Bunyan, the mighty lumberjack, who cut down trees in the forests across America.

One of Paul's biggest jobs was in North Dakota. Back then, there wasn't an inch of land in North Dakota that wasn't covered with trees. And people wanted farms. So Paul said that he would clear the whole state. He made the biggest logging camp that the world has ever seen.

Every building in the camp was as big as a town. The dining room was so big that the loggers would get hungry just waiting in line for their food. So Paul built lunch counters every mile or so. That way, the loggers could have snacks while they were waiting for their meals.

Paul and Babe carried water to the camp from the Great Lakes. Paul put a big tank on Babe's back and filled it. As Babe walked to North Dakota, his hoofprints made holes in the ground. The water splashing from the tank filled the holes. That's why there are so many lakes in Minnesota. Once, Babe tripped. All of the water spilled from the tank and started the Mississippi River.

You can read more about the adventures of Paul Bunyan by checking this book out of your school or public library.

SHOW WHAT YOU KNOW!

REFOCUS

1. What can you learn from stories about America?

2. Why did American pioneers create tall tales?

THINK ABOUT IT

When people created the tale of Paul Bunyan, what were they trying to say about the work they did clearing the land?

COMMUNITY CHECK

Find out what stories your state has and make one of the stories into a picture book for young children.

A Railroad

FOCUS In 1869 the first railroad was built to connect people in the East to people in the West.

Railroad Needed

People wanted to get from the East to the West in less time than wagons took. There were trains in the East but few in the West. A transcontinental railroad, connecting one side of the continent to the other, was needed. In 1862 the U.S. government gave two companies the right to build the Pacific Railroad.

The Work Begins

The Union Pacific Railroad started in Omaha, Nebraska. Many of the workers who built it were Irish immigrants. The workers faced heavy snows and attacks from American Indians who saw the railroad as a threat to their way of life.

The Central Pacific Railroad started in Sacramento, California. Many of the workers who built it were Chinese immigrants. They did the dangerous work of blasting tunnels through mountains.

⭐ **transcontinental** That which goes from one side of a continent to the other

Across the Country

The Last Spike

Seven long years later the railroad was completed. The railroad owners and the workers gathered at Promontory, in Utah, on May 10, 1869. The last spike, a special one made of gold, was tapped into place. The trains from east and west moved across the final piece of track and touched each other. Americans everywhere celebrated this great achievement—the completion of a railroad that spanned the country. Now instead of taking months, it would take only a few days to travel from New York to San Francisco.

▼ This photo shows the railroad owners and workers celebrating the completion of the railroad.

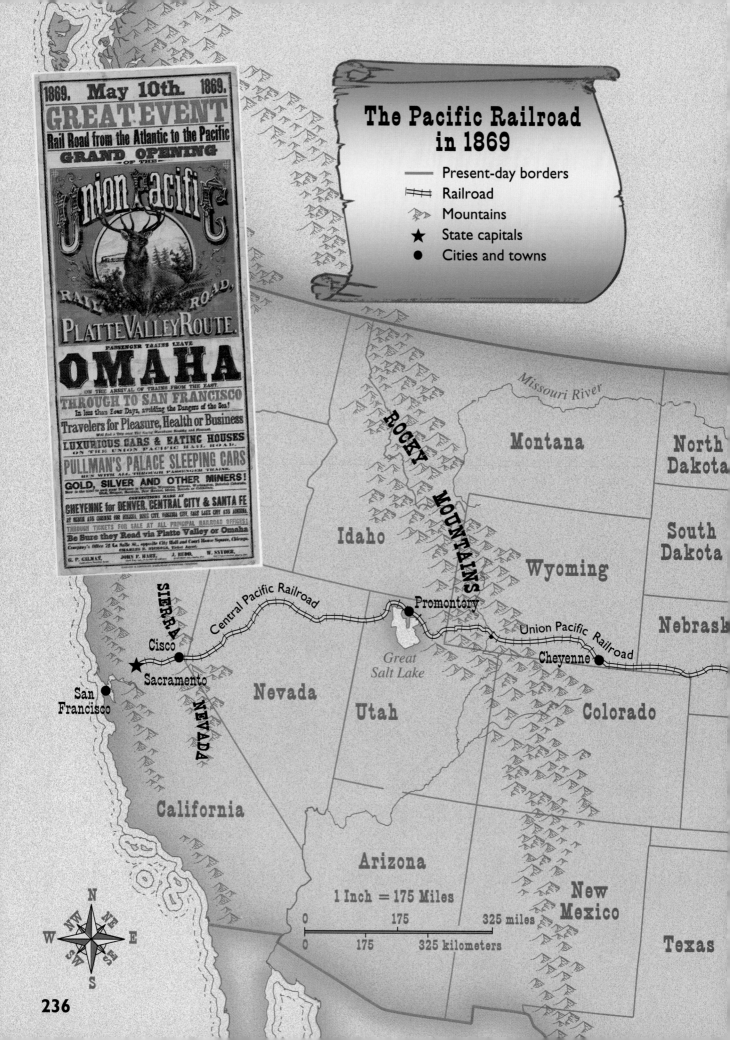

The Pacific Railroad in 1869

- —— Present-day borders
- Railroad
- Mountains
- ★ State capitals
- ● Cities and towns

1869. **May 10th.** 1869.
GREAT EVENT
Rail Road from the Atlantic to the Pacific
GRAND OPENING
OF THE
Union Pacific
RAIL ROAD,
PLATTE VALLEY ROUTE.
PASSENGER TRAINS LEAVE
OMAHA
ON THE ARRIVAL OF TRAINS FROM THE EAST.
THROUGH TO SAN FRANCISCO
In less than Four Days, avoiding the Dangers of the Sea!
Travelers for Pleasure, Health or Business
LUXURIOUS CARS & EATING HOUSES
ON THE UNION PACIFIC RAIL ROAD.
PULLMAN'S PALACE SLEEPING CARS
RUN WITH ALL THROUGH PASSENGER TRAINS.
GOLD, SILVER AND OTHER MINERS!
CHEYENNE for DENVER, CENTRAL CITY & SANTA FE
AT OGDEN AND CORINNE FOR HELENA, DEER CITY, VIRGINIA CITY, SALT LAKE CITY AND MONTANA
THROUGH TICKETS FOR SALE AT ALL PRINCIPAL RAILROAD OFFICES!
Be Sure they Read via Platte Valley or Omaha
Company's Office 72 La Salle St., opposite City Hall and Court House Square, Chicago.
CHARLES E. NICHOLS, Ticket Agent.
G. P. GILMAN,   JOHN P. HART,   J. BUDD,   W. SNYDER.

Missouri River

Montana

North Dakota

ROCKY

Idaho

Wyoming

South Dakota

MOUNTAINS

Central Pacific Railroad

Promontory

Union Pacific Railroad

Nebraska

SIERRA

Cisco

Great Salt Lake

Cheyenne

★ Sacramento

San Francisco

NEVADA

Nevada

Utah

Colorado

California

Arizona

1 Inch = 175 Miles

0   175   325 miles

0   175   325 kilometers

New Mexico

Texas

N
NW NE
W E
SW SE
S

236

REFOCUS

1. Why was a railroad across the United States needed?
2. What dangers did the workers of each railroad face?

MAP IT

Suppose you worked on the Central Pacific Railroad. Your friend worked on the Union Pacific.

1. You started work at Sacramento. In what direction did the Central Pacific Railroad begin to put down tracks? Your friend started work at Omaha. About how many miles did each of you travel to Promontory, Utah?

2. Many of your Chinese co-workers on the Central Pacific came to the United States through San Francisco. About how far did they travel to get to the start of the job, in Sacramento?

3. As your friend and the other workers on the Union Pacific approach Great Salt Lake, in what direction are they putting down tracks?

EXPLORE IT

Find a map that shows railroad routes today. How does it compare to the map on this page? Can you find the railroad today that follows part of the Central Pacific route?

Omaha

Kansas

Oklahoma

SUMMING UP

1 DO YOU REMEMBER...
COMPREHENSION

1. Why was ranching important to the pioneers of the Southwest?

2. What challenges did settlers of the plains face?

3. Describe a typical school day on the plains long ago.

4. What is a tall tale?

5. What two railroads built the transcontinental railroad, and from where did each one start?

2 SKILL POWER
USING A MAP SCALE

Look at the map on page 220. Use the map scale to figure out about how many miles it is from Richmond, Virginia, to San Diego, California.

3 WHAT DO YOU THINK?
CRITICAL THINKING

1. Why do so many cities in the southwestern part of the United States today have Spanish names?

2. Why did Asian settlers come to the West Coast instead of the East Coast?

3. How can school help to make you a good member of your community?

4. Which parts of the story that you read about Paul Bunyan are true, and which parts are not true?

5. Why was the last spike of the transcontinental railroad made of gold?

4 SAY IT, WRITE IT, USE IT
VOCABULARY

Write the words to a song about the pioneers. Try to include at least 4 words. Sing your song to a friend.

adobe
bee
heritage
immigrant
slate

sod
tornado
transcontinental
vaquero

CHAPTER 9

5 GEOGRAPHY AND YOU
MAP STUDY

Use the maps in this chapter to answer the following questions.

1. What city in Idaho has a French name?

2. Name some eastern cities in the United States in 1850.

3. What area of our country had the most forests in 1850?

6 TAKE ACTION
CITIZENSHIP

Pioneer parents wanted their children to be proud of the United States. There are many things in our country to be proud of. Talk to people at school and in your neighborhood to find out what makes them proud to be Americans. Make a list of their answers. Add your own ideas to the list. Display your list alongside others from the class.

7 GET CREATIVE
COMPUTER CONNECTION

What else would you like to know about the pioneers? Use the computer to write your questions. Your classmates can add questions, too. Everyone can do some research and enter answers to the questions. If you have a drawing program, add pictures to the answers. The class might make a book of questions and answers about the pioneers.

LOOKING AHEAD

Discover in the next chapter why communities need government.

People and Citizenship

America's the place to be
    for hope and opportunity.
We have so many families
    in this great big community.
Where citizens work side by side
    to show we care, to show our pride.
Our country is a land that's free—
    our country stands for liberty.
So raise our flag and celebrate
    and sing out why our country's great!

Chapter 10

Government

Why do we need government? Find out how people in local, state, and national governments work to help communities.

▼ Do you have class elections? Find out how we elect our leaders on page 248.

CONTENTS

Vote for Me!

at Work

These books are about communities and government. Read one that interests you and fill out a book-review form.

READ AND RESEARCH

Local Governments **by Barbara Silberdick Feinberg**

(Franklin Watts, 1993)
One thing you can learn from this book is how a town decides to use its tax money to take care of its schools, fire department, and library. *(nonfiction)*

Class President **by Johanna Hurwitz, illustrated by Sheila Hamanaka**

(Scholastic, 1991)
Julio's class is planning on electing a class president. Julio is sure that Cricket, the teacher's pet, will win. But you may be surprised at the results of the election. *(fiction)*

Firehouse **by Katherine K. Winkleman, illustrations by John S. Winkleman**

(Walker & Co., 1994)
Learn about the importance of firehouses to towns and cities all over our country. Find out why firehouses had a special kind of staircase in the past. *(nonfiction)*

SKILL POWER RECOGNIZING

Understanding the difference between fact and opinion can help you become a careful listener and reader.

UNDERSTAND IT

Have you ever heard the saying "Don't believe everything you hear"? It means that what you read or hear may be a person's opinion. An *opinion* tells what a person feels or believes. A *fact* is a statement that is true and can be proved.

EXPLORE IT

How can you tell what is a fact and what is an opinion? A fact can be checked to see if it is true. An opinion can't be checked.

FACT: George Washington was the first President of the United States. (You can check this information in a book.)

OPINION: George Washington was the best President. (There is no way to prove this statement to be true or false.)

Though opinions can't be proved, they are still important. We all like to know what others think. But sometimes people try to make us believe their opinions are facts. That's when it is especially important to know the difference between fact and opinion.

FACT AND OPINION

TRY IT

Choose something shown below. Write two sentences about it that are facts and two sentences that are opinions. Exchange your paper with a partner. Mark each other's sentences with an *F* for fact or an *O* for opinion. Discuss why each sentence is a fact or an opinion.

cat

broccoli

book

rain

TV show

airplane

My Cat

My cat is the best cat in the world. O

My cat is black and white. F

My cat weighs eight pounds. F

My cat leads an exciting life. O

SKILL POWER SEARCH

Write an opinion about something in this chapter. Show your opinion to a classmate. Do you both share that opinion?

1 **Setting the Scene**

⭐ **KEY WORDS**

county
vote
citizen
representative
tax

Learning

FOCUS *People in the local, state, and national government work to make laws and provide services.*

What Is Government?

What would happen if there were no government? Look around your community. What would be different? There would be no street lights, public schools, or police officers. Although you may not know it, government affects you in many ways.

Government is a group of people that works together to make laws and provide services. Some services provided by our government leaders are fire and police departments, public libraries, and schools. The map on the next page shows how one place can be part of each of the different levels of government.

About Government

Levels of Government

The first level of government is community government. Next there is **county** government. Then there is state government, which is centered in the state capital. For example, the map shows that Austin is the capital of Texas. Our national government is the highest level of government. It is centered in Washington, D.C. You'll learn more about Washington, our national capital, in the next chapter.

⭐ **county** A part of a state

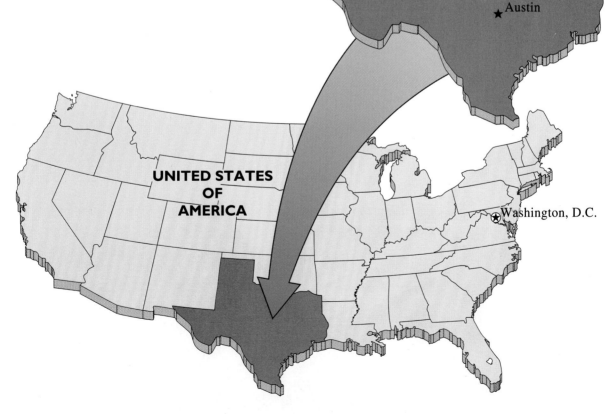

City of El Paso

El Paso County

State of Texas
★ Austin

UNITED STATES OF AMERICA

⭐ Washington, D.C.

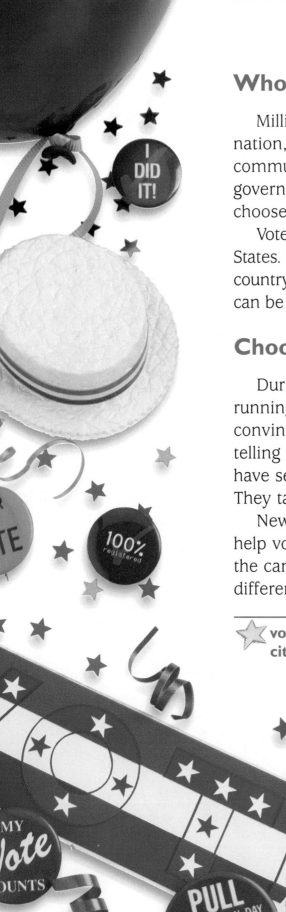

Who Runs Government?

Millions of people live in the United States. Our nation, our states, our counties, and most of our communities have too many people for everyone to be government leaders. So people **vote** in elections to choose their government leaders.

Voters must be **citizens**, or members of the United States. The right to vote is a special freedom in our country. It is one of the most important ways that people can be active in government.

Choosing Our Leaders

During an election the candidates—the people running for office—usually have several months to convince others to vote for them. They put up posters telling people why they should be elected. You may have seen people on TV who are running for office. They talk about what they'll do if they are elected.

Newspapers, radio, and television news stations also help voters get to know the candidates. Reporters ask the candidates questions about how they will solve different problems.

---

vote To express one's choice in an election
citizen A person who is a member of a nation

Voters listen to the people who are running for office because they want to know what the candidates think. They want to choose leaders whom they can trust. Voters must listen carefully to tell the difference between facts and opinions.

Election Day

When election day comes, the voters make their decisions. They think about all the things they have heard from the candidates. They hope that each candidate they vote for will be a good leader. Usually when people vote they go into a voting booth to make their choice.

▼ In the United States, when people vote, no one is allowed to see their choices.

Elected officials have an important job to do. As government leaders, they are **representatives** of the people who elected them. Elected officials work to make their communities better places for people to live and work.

☆ **representative** A person who acts or speaks for others

Who Pays for Services?

Running a government takes money. Firefighters, police officers, teachers, and other government workers must be paid. Parks have to be kept clean. Government buildings, such as schools, libraries, and post offices, need heat and electricity. School buses and garbage trucks sometimes need repairs.

Where does the money come from to pay for these services? The government gets some of this money by collecting **taxes** from people who earn money and own property.

⭐ **tax** Money collected by a government

Kinds of Taxes

Taxes are collected in many different ways. Income tax, sales tax, and property tax are three examples of taxes.

Most of the workers in our nation pay an *income tax* on the money they earn. Many state governments also have an income tax. Sometimes when people buy things in a store, they pay for the items, plus a little extra money. The extra money is the *sales tax*. Almost everyone who owns land, a house, a store, or some other business pays a *property tax*.

▼ A sales tax is one way government collects money. This picture shows some of things tax money may be used for.

Government

Meeting Needs

A large portion of tax money goes to pay government workers. Another portion buys supplies and equipment that the workers use.

Government leaders also use the tax money to help people. They may help in many different ways. For example, there may be people who need help finding jobs or finding places to live. A traffic light may be needed to make a road safer. A community may want to start a summer recreation program for children.

Each program or need will cost a certain amount of money. The government leaders decide how to spend the money they have to help the most people.

SHOW WHAT YOU KNOW!

REFOCUS

1. What are four levels of government?

2. How are government leaders chosen?

THINK ABOUT IT

What might happen to a community if the people in it did not pay their taxes?

COMMUNITY CHECK

Make a list of places in which you see government at work in your community.

Libraries

Parks

Road work

Safety

Schools

A Community

FOCUS *Community leaders must work hard to make their city or town a better place.*

My Mom, the Mayor

My friends have told me that some of the swings in the park playground are broken. I said I would tell my mom about the park. She's the **mayor**.

As the mayor, my mom is the leader of our community government. I'm very proud of my mom. She cares about our community and works hard to make it a great place to live. There's a picture of my family below.

My mom works with the town **council**, which is a group of men and women elected by the people of our town. The council and my mom work together to govern, or rule, our town.

⭐ **mayor** The leader of a town or city

⭐ **council** A group of people that works for the community government

Leader

Becoming Mayor

My mom had always worked hard for our community, so some of the leaders of our town thought she would make a good mayor. They asked her to run for office.

The whole family helped her run for election. We put up posters, mailed letters, and passed out buttons. When my mom gave her first speech as mayor, I stood right next to her. As everyone cheered, she thanked all the people who had voted for her. She said her work had just begun.

Now that she's the mayor, my mom works in an office in the town hall. She talks to people on the phone or meets with them in person. They work together to solve problems in our community.

▼ Here's my mom getting her picture taken. She was giving an award to the firehouse.

Making Decisions

Right now my mom is studying a request from a company that wants to build a new shopping plaza. Some people in town want the plaza. They say the stores will mean more jobs for the people who live here. Other people don't want the plaza. They say there are enough stores in our town and they think new stores might take away business from the ones that are already here. Some people also think the new stores might cause traffic.

My Mom, the Mayor

Local Firehouse Receives Award

Mom came to School on Career Day to talk about what it's like to be the mayor.

I save all the newspaper articles about my mom.

My mom will meet with the town council to talk about this problem. They will hold a town meeting to hear what other people have to say. Sometimes these town meetings can be very loud and very long. Afterward Mom and the town council must decide what to do about the plaza.

Helping the Community

My mom has been the mayor for almost two years. During this time, she has worked hard to help our community in many ways. In another two years her term of office will be finished. Then she will decide if she wants to run for mayor again. If she does run again, I'll be there to help mail letters and pass out more buttons.

◀ I made this scrapbook for my mom.

Campaign buttons ↩

REFOCUS

1. What are two parts of most community governments?

2. What are some of the jobs of a mayor?

THINK ABOUT IT

What kind of person makes a good mayor?

COMMUNITY CHECK

Write about how you would solve the problems in your town if you were the mayor or other leader.

255

3

Citizenship

⭐ KEY WORDS

budget
debate

Join the

FOCUS *Sometimes, communities must make difficult decisions. Join the debate in one community and decide what you would do.*

A Town Meeting

A town meeting is about to start. The meeting room is crowded. There are many children here with their parents. Tonight the council and the mayor are going to talk about the town's **budget**. A budget is a plan for how the town government will spend its money.

One concern is about summer activities for children. The town can't afford to have the same programs as last year. The townspeople are here to say what they think the town government should do. Before you join the meeting, you should know what programs the town has to choose from.

Learning to Swim

Last year the town government had a program at the community pool to teach children how to swim. A lot of children signed up for the program. Now these children know how to swim safely. There is a private pool in town, but many families do not have the money to join.

⭐ **budget** A plan for using money

256

Town Council

Playing Baseball

Another popular summer program is the baseball clinic. The town pays coaches to teach children how to play baseball. Children who already know how to play can get tips on how to play better. The coaches work with players on batting, throwing, catching, and being part of a team.

Arts and Crafts

Another summer program is an arts and crafts class. Children meet in a park twice a week to make different art projects. The money to pay the teachers for this program comes from the town's recreation budget. Although not as many children take part in this program as in the swimming lessons or the baseball clinic, it is still a popular program.

Making Choices

Now that you know the choices, you can join the town meeting. Many people stand up to **debate** the different choices. When people debate they discuss their ideas for or against something.

Many people give reasons to support the programs. Some of the children who have been in a program also talk about why they want to keep that program.

One person suggests keeping the swimming lessons and cutting out the other two programs since the swimming lessons are the most popular program. But others disagree.

Instead of cutting one or two programs, some people come up with other ideas. One idea is to cut a little money from each program. But others say this will hurt each program and every participant, or person who takes part in the program.

The table below lists some of the ideas people suggested. Do you agree with any of these suggestions? What other ideas could you add to the list?

⭐ **debate** To discuss different sides of a question

CURRENT SUMMER PROGRAMS

Swimming Lessons, Baseball Clinic, Arts and Crafts

IDEA 1

Cut the program that has had the fewest participants. Keep the other two programs.

IDEA 2

Have one program each summer. Have the swimming lessons this summer, the baseball clinic next summer, and the arts and crafts class the third summer.

IDEA 3

Keep all three programs. Find ways to save money. For example, shorten the pool hours or find arts and crafts teachers that will volunteer.

REFOCUS

1. What happens in a town meeting?

2. What does it mean to debate something?

THINK ABOUT IT

Why do community governments have town meetings?

WRITE ABOUT IT

Write a paragraph describing what you would do if you were on this town council.

You Decide

With your class, have your own town meeting. First elect people to play the parts of the council members. The mayor might be played by your teacher. The rest of the class should be divided into three groups. Each group will support a different idea. These ideas can be from the table at the left, or you can make up your own.

Each group will decide what it will say to get the council to support and vote for its ideas. Each group should elect one person to speak during the debate.

After each group speaks to the council, the council members talk about what they have heard. They decide which idea is best. Then they vote. This vote will decide what the summer programs will be.

Map Adventure

⭐ **KEY WORDS**

governor
legislature

Visiting a

FOCUS *A visit to a state capital can teach you about state history and government.*

State Government

As you know, each of the 50 states has its own government. The leader of a state government is the **governor**. Other government leaders are part of a state **legislature**. The state legislature makes laws for the state. The state leaders also plan the budget and decide what services the government will offer people in the state. The people who live in a state elect the governor and the representatives to the state legislature. The governor and legislature govern from the state's capital city. What is the capital of your state?

▼ This statue stands atop the State Capitol in Madison, Wisconsin.

⭐ **governor** The leader of a state government
legislature A group of people that makes laws

▼ The University of Wisconsin Hospital is located in Madison, the state capital.

State Capital

A Capital City

When people visit their state capital, they may visit museums or other government buildings. Many of these buildings are public property—they belong to all the citizens of the state.

One building you can visit in a state capital is the capitol. This building is where the state legislature meets. The State Capitol in Madison, Wisconsin, is shown at right.

Universities and other schools are also often located in state capitals. Find the University of Wisconsin on the map of Madison on the next page. Then take a walking tour to explore the rest of this capital city.

◀ People picnic around the State Capitol during a summer concert.

Madison, Wisconsin

State Capitol

State Historical
Society Museum

Henry Vilas
Park Zoo

Lake
Mendota

N
W   E
S

Tenney
Park

Sherman Avenue

East Gorham Street
East Johnson Street
Butler Street
Paterson Street
Williamson Avenue

East Washington Street

Williamson Street

Langdon Street

State Street

Henry Street

West Wilson Street

John Nolen Drive

University of Wisconsin

Observatory Drive

University Avenue

University Avenue

West Johnson Street

West Dayton Street

Broom Street

Basset Street

Bedford Street

Willow Drive

Lake Mendota Dr.

Highland Avenue

University Avenue

Franklin Avenue

Regent Street

Breese Terrace

Allen Street

Speedway Road

Virginia Terrace

Regent Street

Monroe Street

South Randall Avenue

Mills Street

Park Street

West Washington Ave.

Brittingham
Park

Lake
Monona

Henry Vilas
Park

Drake Street

Monona
Bay

Wingra
Park

Monroe Street

Lake Wingra

North Wingra Drive

Fish Hatchery Road

South Park Street

West Olin Avenue

Franklin
Field

Quann
Park

Olin &
Turville
Park

John Nolen Drive

Dane
County
Exposition
Center

University of Wisconsin Arboretum

South Park Street

West Badger Road

Highway 12/18

Rimrock Road

John Nolen Drive

0   .25   .5 mile
0   .25   .5 kilometer

Highway 12/18

A view of the Wisconsin State Capitol from Lake Mendota

REFOCUS

1. What are two parts of a state government?

2. What are some of the things you might do if you visited a state capital?

MAP IT

Take a walking tour around Madison, Wisconsin, to discover some things you can do in this capital city.

1. From the University of Wisconsin, what direction would you walk along State Street to get to the State Capitol?

2. On the observation deck of the State Capitol, you have a view of the city and three lakes. What are the names of these lakes?

3. Across the street from the State Capitol is the State Historical Society Museum. After visiting the museum, you want to see the animals and take a camel ride at Henry Vilas Park Zoo. From the museum, what streets could you take to reach the zoo?

EXPLORE IT

Every state has a capital. Find the important and interesting buildings that are located in your state capital and design your own walking tour.

SUMMING UP

1 DO YOU REMEMBER . . .
COMPREHENSION

1. What kinds of services does government provide?

2. How are people taxed?

3. Who is the leader of a town or city government?

4. What is a budget?

5. Where does a state legislature meet?

3 WHAT DO YOU THINK?
CRITICAL THINKING

1. Why is it important for voters to learn about the candidates running for election?

2. Why do we need several levels of government?

3. Would you want to be a mayor or serve on a town council? Explain why or why not.

4. Why do towns and cities need budgets?

5. Why do states need capitals?

2 SKILL POWER
RECOGNIZING FACT AND OPINION

Work with a partner to see if you can recognize facts and opinions. Go through a newspaper to find two examples of facts and two examples of opinions. Hint: You are likely to find some opinions in advertisements.

4 SAY IT, WRITE IT, USE IT
VOCABULARY

You are a candidate running in an election. Write a short campaign speech using five of the words below.

budget	legislature
citizen	mayor
council	representative
county	tax
debate	vote
governor	

5 TAKE ACTION
CITIZENSHIP

Voters have an important job. They need to know as much as they can about candidates before they make a decision. Ask your parents and other adults how they find out about people running for office. Do they watch TV, read the newspaper, or talk to other people? Make a list of all the ways they get information before voting.

6 GEOGRAPHY AND YOU
MAP STUDY

Use the map on page 262 to answer the following questions.

1. What is the name of the park which surrounds Monona Bay?

2. If you walked south to the end of South Randall Avenue, where would you be?

3. From Tenney Park, what streets could you take to get to the University of Wisconsin?

7 GET CREATIVE
LANGUAGE ARTS CONNECTION

When people run for election, they often put up signs and posters. Make up a catchy slogan or phrase that would get people to vote for you. Here are two examples.

★★ I Like Mike ★★

Win with Wendy

LOOKING AHEAD

In the next chapter, learn about our national capital—Washington, D.C.

Chapter 11

Our National

Do you know where the capital of the United States is? Read this chapter to learn all about our national government and our capital city–Washington, D.C.

▼ How many times can you find the flag in this chapter?

CONTENTS

Capital

These books are about Washington, D.C., and our government.
Read one that interests you and fill out a book-review form.

READ AND RESEARCH

Look Out, Washington, D.C.! by Patricia Reilly Giff,
illustrated by Blanche Sims (Dell, 1995)
Ms. Rooney's class takes an exciting trip to our nation's
capital city. There is even a map to help you find the Polk
Street School Kids' favorite places. *(fiction)*
• *You can read a selection from this book on page 280.*

Dear Benjamin Banneker by Andrea Davis
Pinkney, illustrated by Brian Pinkney
(Harcourt Brace & Co., 1994)
Benjamin learned as much as he could about the night
sky when he was a boy. This knowledge later helped
him to lay out the boundaries for the city of
Washington, D.C. *(biography)*

The Story of the White House by Kate Waters
(Scholastic, 1991)
Reading this book is like going on a tour of the
White House. Along the way, you can learn
interesting facts about each of the Presidents
who lived and worked there. *(nonfiction)*

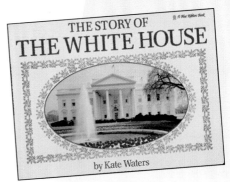

Knowing how to use a grid makes it easier to find places on a map.

UNDERSTAND IT

All you need to know to read a grid map are numbers and letters. A grid map is just a regular map. The only difference is that lines forming boxes have been drawn on the map. These lines help you find places easily.

EXPLORE IT

Here you are at a theme park. How do you get to the rides you want? Use the grid! For example, to find the Undersea Express, put one finger of your left hand on the letter C. Put a finger from your right hand on the number 3. Move your left finger across and your right finger down until they meet. Now you're in box C-3. Go ride the Undersea Express!

Index

Food Court	🍔	A-3	Log Ride	B-1
Mystery Castle	🏰	B-3	Runaway Coach	C-2
Space Walk	🚀	A-1	Undersea Express	C-3

A GRID MAP

TRY IT

Try your hand at map making. Working with a small group, turn this unfinished map of a park into a grid map. First, copy the map and the grid onto a piece of paper. Then write letters on the left side and numbers on the top.

Next, make an index of places for the park. Be creative. Add as many places to the map as you wish. Compare your grid map with those of other groups. Take turns locating places on your classmates' maps.

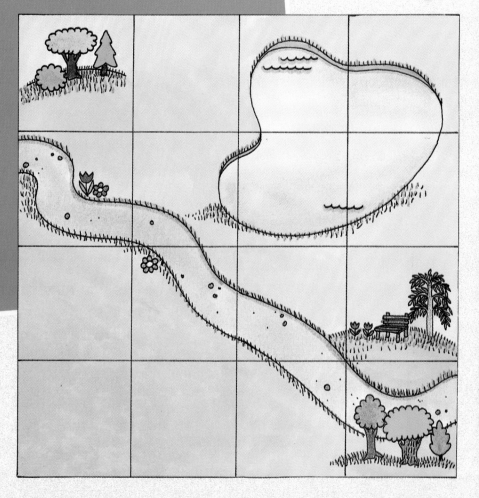

Use this unfinished map of a park to create your own grid map. ▶

SKILL

POWER SEARCH *Look ahead for a grid map of Washington, D.C. Use this map to practice your new skill.*

Setting the Scene

⭐ **KEY WORDS**

Constitution
President
Congress
Supreme Court

Our National

FOCUS Our national government is located in our nation's capital, Washington, D.C. The people in government make decisions that affect our lives.

Our National Capital

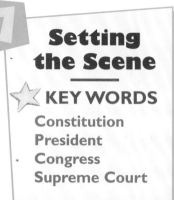

Washington, D.C. ✪

What Our Government Does

As you have learned, each state has a government—so does our country. The center of our country's government is in our nation's capital, Washington, D.C. Find Washington, D.C., on the map. Many of our government leaders live and work in Washington. They come from every state in the country to be a part of our national government.

Our national government has many different jobs. One important job is to create laws that make our country a better place to live. Our government also provides services for people. Building roads, printing money, providing health care to people in need, and helping schools are just some of these services.

Government

Choosing Our Leaders

In the last chapter you learned how we elect our leaders. The Constitution of the United States is a written plan for our government. It outlines the basic laws of our country and tells how our leaders should be chosen. Although the Constitution was written more than 200 years ago, in 1787, we still depend on it today.

Any citizen of the United States who is at least 18 years old and a registered voter can vote for the President and other leaders. A citizen is a person who is a member of a nation. Voters from every state choose people to go to Washington to represent them in our national government.

Constitution The set of laws by which the United States is governed
President The leader of the United States

The Three Branches of Government

The Congress writes and passes new national laws.

The President signs new laws and makes sure laws are enforced.

The Supreme Court decides if the laws agree with the Constitution.

The Three Branches

The chart above shows the three branches, or main sections, of our national government. There are three branches of government so that each one will balance and limit the others. This way, no one branch has too much power.

Each branch of our government has an important role in making the laws for our country. After Congress writes a new law, it is sent to the President for approval. The President can either sign the new law or veto it. The President will veto, or reject, a law if he disagrees with it. The Supreme Court decides whether the laws are fair.

The President

The President has many jobs. One is to send a plan to Congress for how the money collected from taxes should be spent. As head of our armed forces, the President chooses the leader for each branch of the military. The President also works with leaders from other countries.

With all these different jobs, it's not surprising that the President is often very busy. In any one day the President might give a speech, read reports and newspapers, meet with members of Congress, and visit with leaders from other countries. Many people believe our President is the most powerful leader in the world.

Congress The group of elected people who make our country's laws
Supreme Court A court of nine judges that decides if laws are fair

President Clinton's daughter ▶ has a pet cat named Socks.

Running the Country

The President, who has a lot to do to run the country, depends on many people to help out. One person who helps is the Vice President. The Vice President is elected with the President. If for some reason the President cannot govern, the Vice President takes over.

The President's wife is called the First Lady. She also helps the President and is in charge of social events in the White House. The role of the First Lady has been changing. Many First Ladies have taken on important projects.

Eleanor Roosevelt worked for world peace and human rights. Nancy Reagan asked all young people to "just say no!" to drugs. Barbara Bush focused on reading education. Hillary Rodham Clinton has worked on many problems, such as trying to provide health care for everyone.

▼ Barbara Bush worked hard to help children and adults learn to read.

▼ President Bill Clinton gives a radio speech from the Oval Office.

Congress

The members of Congress are elected by citizens and work in the Capitol building, shown below. The smaller photo shows some members of Congress with their families as Congress starts a new session.

Each state elects people to go to Congress to represent that state. A representative acts or speaks for the people of his or her state.

You have learned that Congress is the branch of our government that creates the nation's laws. Besides making laws, Congress has other jobs. Congress works with the President in many ways to help run the country.

The Supreme Court

The third branch of government is headed by the Supreme Court, which is made up of nine judges. These judges are not elected. The President chooses the judges, but Congress must approve the choices. A judge stays on the Supreme Court for life or until he or she decides to retire.

The Supreme Court is the highest court in the United States. It hears cases about local, state, and national laws. The judges use the Constitution as a guide. They sometimes decide that a law goes against what the Constitution says. Then the law has to be changed or erased.

Supreme Court Decisions

The decisions made by the Supreme Court can change people's lives. In the past the Supreme Court has decided which schools people can attend. The Court also has ruled on what people can say or write and how people charged with crimes should be treated. The courts try to make sure that people's rights are protected.

The judges hear cases in the Supreme Court Building.

SHOW WHAT YOU KNOW!

REFOCUS

1. What are some of the things the government does?

2. How are the President and Vice President chosen?

THINK ABOUT IT

Why is it important that there are three separate branches of government?

COMMUNITY CHECK

With a small group, find out about the people who represent your state in Congress. Share with your class what you find.

A Capital City

FOCUS *As our capital city, Washington, D.C., has a special history that all citizens share.*

Choosing the Location

When the United States first became a nation, members of the new government needed a place to meet. The leaders had already tried New York City and Philadelphia. But some people in the South thought it was unfair to have the nation's capital in the North. So it was decided that a new city would be built about halfway between the North and the South.

George Washington, our first President, chose the place for the new capital city in 1791. Washington decided to build the city along the Potomac River. Find the Potomac River on the map of Washington, D.C., below. The land that Washington marked off for the city belonged to two states, Maryland and Virginia. These states gave the land to the government to use for the new city.

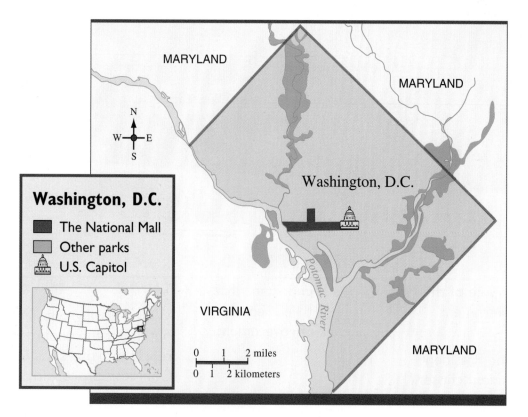

MARYLAND

MARYLAND

N
W E
S

Washington, D.C.

Washington, D.C.

■ The National Mall
■ Other parks
🏛 U.S. Capitol

VIRGINIA

Potomac River

MARYLAND

0 1 2 miles
0 1 2 kilometers

Planning the City

George Washington hired Pierre L'Enfant (pee AIR lahn FAHN) to plan the city. L'Enfant's plan placed the Capitol building in the center of the city. Wide streets spread out from the center like the spokes of a wheel. L'Enfant also included large parks and planned where to put the President's house. The painting on the right shows Washington on horseback, talking with L'Enfant about his plans for the new city.

A New City Is Built

Benjamin Banneker, shown at right, and Andrew Ellicott helped to carry out L'Enfant's plan. They **surveyed** the land to show where the buildings, the streets, and the parks would be placed.

The new capital city took many years to build. The government finally moved into its new home in 1800. The city was named Washington, D.C., in honor of George Washington. The letters *D.C.* stand for "**District** of Columbia." A district is a place set aside for a special purpose. The name *Columbia* honors Christopher Columbus.

⭐ **survey** To measure and mark the boundaries of a piece of land

district An area set aside for a special purpose

The Early City

In the beginning, Washington, D.C., was a very small city. Even though it was our new capital city, many people did not want to live there. Summers were often very hot and humid. People did not like the marshy land and the mosquitoes. In fact, Thomas Jefferson, our third President, called the new city a "swamp in the wilderness."

Slowly, people began to move to the new city, and Washington did begin to grow. People often moved to Washington in times of war and times when the country was in trouble.

The City Grows

But for many years the city remained small and unfinished. The roads were muddy and unpaved. Pigs and cows often roamed around freely.

In the late 1860s, people decided to improve the city. Congress set aside money to pave the streets, plant trees, and construct new buildings. People wanted a beautiful capital city they could be proud of. The photo on this page shows how Washington looked in 1880, when the Washington Monument was still under construction.

Washington Today

More than 4 million people live in the Washington, D.C., area today. The city has many of the advantages of and some of the same challenges as other cities. Because it is our nation's capital, the city will always be special. Many important events in our country's history have happened in Washington.

People from all over the world and the United States visit Washington, D.C., every year. They come to learn about our country's history and to visit the city's many famous sights.

One sight many visitors come to see is the Korean War Veterans Memorial. Later in the chapter you'll take a tour of some of the other famous places in our capital city.

The Korean War Veterans Memorial opened on July 27, 1995. ▶

LITERATURE

Look Out, Washington, D.C.!

by Patricia Reilly Giff, illustrated by Blanche Sims

Emily and her class are on a two-day class trip to Washington, D.C. Read about their adventure as they visit the National Air and Space Museum.

Ms. Rooney stood up. She held on to the rail. "We're coming to a special part of the trip now. The National Air and Space Museum."

Timothy opened his diary. "I wrote about it already," he said. "It's the museum about flying, and missiles, and . . ."

He raised his shoulders in the air. "It's all about the air around us . . . the space . . . out as far as—"

"—the planets and even farther than that," said Dawn in a rush. "Are we going to sit here forever?"

The bus doors opened.

Derrick turned to Emily. "This is where I'll get my best picture. It's the moon rock."

"What's a moon rock?" Emily asked.

Derrick pointed. "Look up. What do you see?"

"The sky," Emily said. "A tiny cloud—"

"The moon," said Derrick. "Look at it."

"I am," Emily said. She remembered her mother showing her the daytime moon when she was in kindergarten.

She remembered her mother holding her up, saying, "See, Emily, it doesn't go away."

"Emily?" Derrick asked. "Are you listening?"

She nodded. "It's big and round and—"

"Missing a rock," said Derrick. "A piece of rock from the moon is right inside the museum. We can even touch it."

"*The moon isn't round like a plate*," she remembered her mother telling her. "*It's round like an orange.*"

It had been hard to believe that in kindergarten.

And now, staring up at the moon, she could see dark spots.

"Mountains," said Derrick. "Deep holes . . ."

Dawn came up behind them.

"Look at the moon," Emily told her.

Dawn pushed her hair back. She was wearing tiny moon earrings. "Out of my way, guys. I'm on my way to see *Skylab*. I'll probably live in space someday."

Emily made a fish face as Dawn pushed past.

Then she looked up at the moon again. She walked backwards into the museum.

You can find out what happens next to Emily and her friends by checking the book out of your school or public library.

SHOW WHAT YOU KNOW!

REFOCUS

1. What did L'Enfant put in his plan for the new capital city?

2. Why did Washington, D.C., grow slowly at first?

THINK ABOUT IT

Why might people move to Washington during hard times?

WORK TOGETHER

With a small group, plan a class trip to Washington, D.C. Decide where to visit, what to bring, and how to get there.

A Home With

FOCUS *The White House is the home and office of the President and the President's family.*

The White House

The most famous home in the United States is found at 1600 Pennsylvania Avenue in Washington, D.C. This is the White House. Every President except George Washington has lived here.

The White House has 132 rooms in all. The President and the President's family live in the top two floors of the Main Building. Find the President's office in the diagram below. The East Wing has offices for the President's military assistants. The Press Rooms are used by TV, radio, and newspaper reporters.

More than a million people tour this famous home every year. If you went on the tour, you could see some of the best-known rooms, such as the East Room, which is the largest room in the White House, and the State Dining Room, which can hold 140 guests.

★ **White House** The building where the President of the United States lives and works

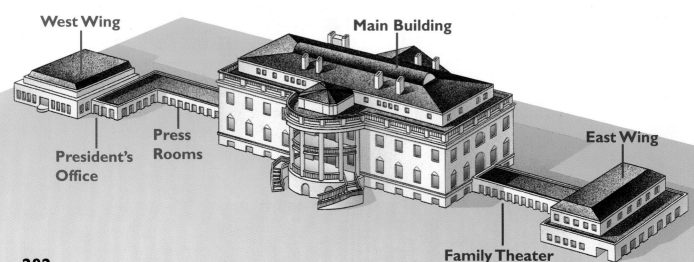

West Wing

Main Building

President's Office

Press Rooms

East Wing

Family Theater

a History

A National Symbol

The White House is more than the place where our President lives and works. It has become a symbol of our country. But it's a symbol that is always changing.

Each new President has brought changes to the White House. President Dwight Eisenhower added a golf putting green, and President Harry Truman added a private balcony. Follow the pictures on the next few pages to see some of the other interesting events in the White House's history.

▲ Abigail Adams, the wife of President John Adams, hung her laundry in the East Room because the White House was stilll being built when they moved in.

▼ Almost everything in the White House was destroyed when parts of Washington, D.C., were set on fire during the War of 1812.

Families in the White House

Many of the families that have lived in the White House have had young children around. Although being the child of a President can be difficult, it can also be fun. James Garfield's two sons had pillow fights while riding bicycles in the East Room. Amy Carter had a treehouse on the White House lawn. The Bush grandchildren often enjoyed the bowling alley, swimming pool, and movie theater.

▲ Eleanor Roosevelt was one of the most active First Ladies. Among the many things she did, she also found time to host picnics on the White House lawn.

▼ Woodrow Wilson let sheep graze on the White House lawn. During World War I (1914–1918) the wool was sold to raise money.

Theodore Roosevelt's six children had many pets at the White House, including this macaw, a black bear, and a kangaroo rat. ▶

284

The leader of Russia gave John F. Kennedy's daughter a puppy whose mother had flown in a space rocket.

Since President Taft weighed more than 300 pounds, he had a special bathtub—big enough to hold four adult men—put in the White House.

REFOCUS

1. Why is the White House an important national symbol?

2. Who is the only President who never lived in the White House?

THINK ABOUT IT

Do you think you would like to grow up in the White House? Why or why not?

WRITE ABOUT IT

Write about the changes you would make if you lived in the White House.

Map Adventure

⭐ **KEY WORD**

monument

A Walk on the

FOCUS *The National Mall in Washington, D.C., is home to many monuments and museums that celebrate our history.*

The National Mall

The National Mall attracts many people each day, but it's not a place to shop. The Mall is a narrow park that stretches for two miles from the Lincoln Memorial to the Capitol building. The Lincoln Memorial, a **monument** to our sixteenth President, is shown below. Today the Mall is lined with many different museums and monuments. But when Washington was first built, the Mall was not the beautiful park that people see today. The land was swampy and muddy, and the Capitol was one of the few buildings there.

⭐ **monument** A building or statue put up to help people remember a special person or event

Mall

Museum Displays

The museums that line the Mall are all part of the Smithsonian Institution. The oldest museum building is the Castle, shown below. The museums hold millions of items in science, art, and history. The National Museum of Natural History has the largest blue diamond and the Insect Zoo. In the National Museum of American History, you can see Ford's Model T and Alexander Graham Bell's original telephone.

The Monuments

The monuments on the Mall honor some of our Presidents. The Washington Monument, named for our first President, is shown at left. It is the highest structure in Washington, D.C.

There are also memorials that help us remember events in our history. One is the Vietnam Veterans Memorial. The part of the memorial you see below is a statue that honors the women who served in this war.

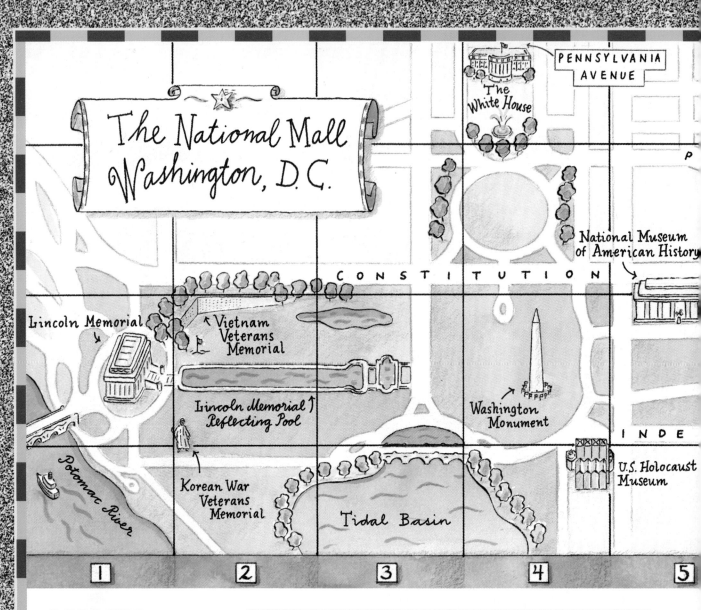

The National Mall
Washington, D.C.

PENNSYLVANIA AVENUE

The White House

National Museum of American History

CONSTITUTION

Lincoln Memorial

← Vietnam Veterans Memorial

Lincoln Memorial Reflecting Pool ↑

Washington Monument

INDE

U.S. Holocaust Museum

Potomac River

Korean War Veterans Memorial

Tidal Basin

1   2   3   4   5

REFOCUS

1. What are some things you can see in the museums of the Smithsonian Institution?

2. What are two monuments on the Mall that honor Presidents of the United States?

Map Index

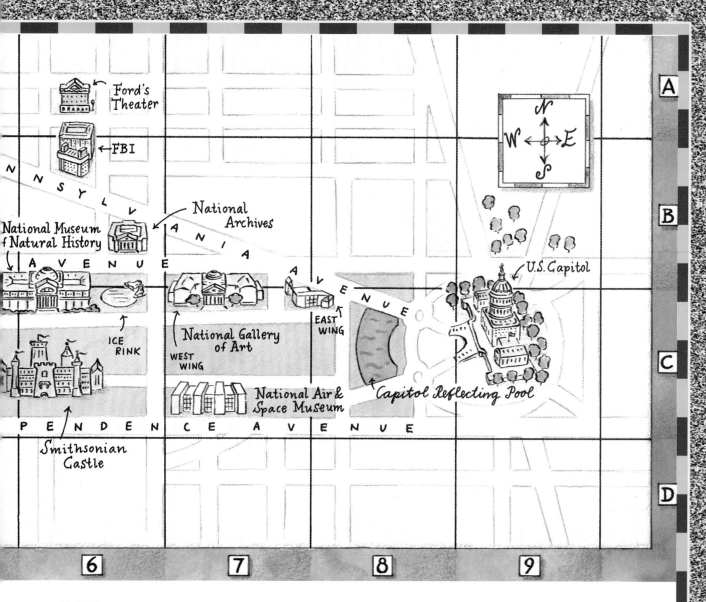

MAP IT

1. The Lincoln Memorial is the first monument you visit. Which box is it in?

2. Use the index to find the Vietnam Veterans Memorial. Is there a shady place nearby where you can have a picnic after you visit the memorial?

3. After riding the elevator to the top of the Washington Monument, you want to visit the White House. In what direction will you need to walk to get to the White House?

4. You want to see the *Spirit of St. Louis*, the airplane in which the first solo flight across the Atlantic Ocean was made. The museum where it is kept is in box C-7. What is the museum's name?

EXPLORE IT

Design a monument to honor someone you think is important. The person does not need to be famous. Choose a spot on the Mall to build your monument.

SUMMING UP

1 DO YOU REMEMBER . . .
COMPREHENSION

1. What is the Constitution of the United States?

2. What is the job of the Supreme Court?

3. Why was the new capital city named Washington, D.C.?

4. Where does the President of the United States live and work?

5. What are three places you could visit on the National Mall?

2 SKILL POWER
READING A GRID MAP

Work with a partner to make a grid map of some place in your community. You might choose your school, a park, or your neighborhood. Put numbers across the top and letters along the side. Make an index for all the places on your map. Then write a list of questions about your map. Exchange maps with another group and try to answer each other's questions.

3 WHAT DO YOU THINK?
CRITICAL THINKING

1. Why is it necessary for our government to have a Vice President?

2. In your opinion, what is the President's most important job?

3. Why, do you think, do people find it important to have a beautiful capital city?

4. Why are there rooms in the White House set aside for the press?

5. What new monuments might be built in Washington, D.C., in the future?

4 SAY IT, WRITE IT, USE IT
VOCABULARY

Write a travel brochure about Washington, D.C. Try to use five of the words below.

Congress	President
Constitution	Supreme Court
district	survey
monument	White House

5 GEOGRAPHY AND YOU
MAP STUDY

Use the map here or on page 276 to answer the following questions.

1. What state is north of Washington, D.C.?

2. What river is Washington, D.C., located on?

3. What building is at the east end of the National Mall?

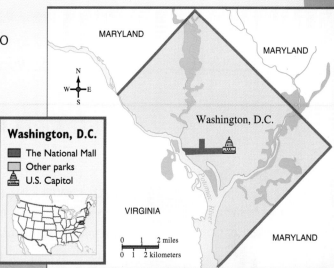

Washington, D.C.
- The National Mall
- Other parks
- U.S. Capitol

MARYLAND
MARYLAND
Washington, D.C.
VIRGINIA
MARYLAND
Potomac River

0 1 2 miles
0 1 2 kilometers

6 TAKE ACTION
CITIZENSHIP

Our government leaders make many important decisions that affect our lives. Yet many citizens do not vote in elections. How might you persuade people to use their right to vote? You might talk to adults about voting or make posters that remind people to vote. Choose one way to convince people to use their right to vote.

7 GET CREATIVE
MUSIC CONNECTION

Some cities have had famous songs written about them. You may have heard "New York, New York" or "I Left My Heart in San Francisco." With a group, write a song about Washington, D.C. Make up your own words. You may borrow a melody from another song.

LOOKING AHEAD

In the next chapter you'll learn about some of our national symbols.

Chapter 12

BRINGING US

People of many backgrounds live in the United States. By learning from each other and working together, we build strong communities and a strong nation.

CONTENTS

▼ What symbol is this girl dressed up as? Find out on page 296.

TOGETHER

These books are about ways people live and work together. Read one that interests you and fill out a book-review form.

READ AND RESEARCH

The Seven Days of Kwanzaa **by Angela Shelf Medearis** (Scholastic, 1994)
On December 26 of every year, African Americans come together for a seven-day celebration of their heritage. Learn about this special time. *(nonfiction)*

Uncle Willie and the Soup Kitchen **by DyAnne DiSalvo-Ryan** (William Morrow & Co., 1991)
A young boy tells about the day he visits a soup kitchen. Read how he helps his Uncle Willie feed more than 100 hungry people. *(fiction)*

Everybody Cooks Rice **by Norah Dooley, illustrations by Peter J. Thornton** (Carolrhoda Books, 1991)
When dinner is ready, Carrie must search the neighborhood to find her brother. Follow Carrie from house to house and discover how families from different backgrounds cook rice. *(fiction)*

Knowing how to use latitude and longitude lines will help you find places on maps.

UNDERSTAND IT

The lines that run across maps and globes are lines of *latitude*. The lines that run up and down are lines of *longitude*.

EXPLORE IT

One line of latitude, the *equator*, is like a belt around the middle of the earth. The other latitudes measure distances in degrees (°) north or south of the equator. The *prime meridian* is a special line of longitude. The other longitude lines measure distances east and west of the prime meridian. New Orleans is located at 30° north latitude and 90° west longitude.

| 150°W | 120°W | 90°W | 60°W | 30°W | 0° | 30°E | 60°E | 90°E | 120°E | 150°E | 180°E |

ARCTIC OCEAN

60°N

NORTH AMERICA

EUROPE

ASIA

ATLANTIC OCEAN

30°N

New Orleans

PACIFIC OCEAN

0° Equator

AFRICA

SOUTH AMERICA

INDIAN OCEAN

PACIFIC OCEAN

30°S

PACIFIC OCEAN

Prime Meridian

AUSTRALIA

60°S

ANTARCTICA

LATITUDE AND LONGITUDE

TRY IT

Play a game using lines of latitude and longitude. Make a game card for each of the seven continents. On one side of each card, write a latitude and longitude location that would fall inside that continent. Two examples are shown below.

Then show your partner the measurements on one of your cards and ask him or her to name the continent. Take turns until you have each used all your cards.

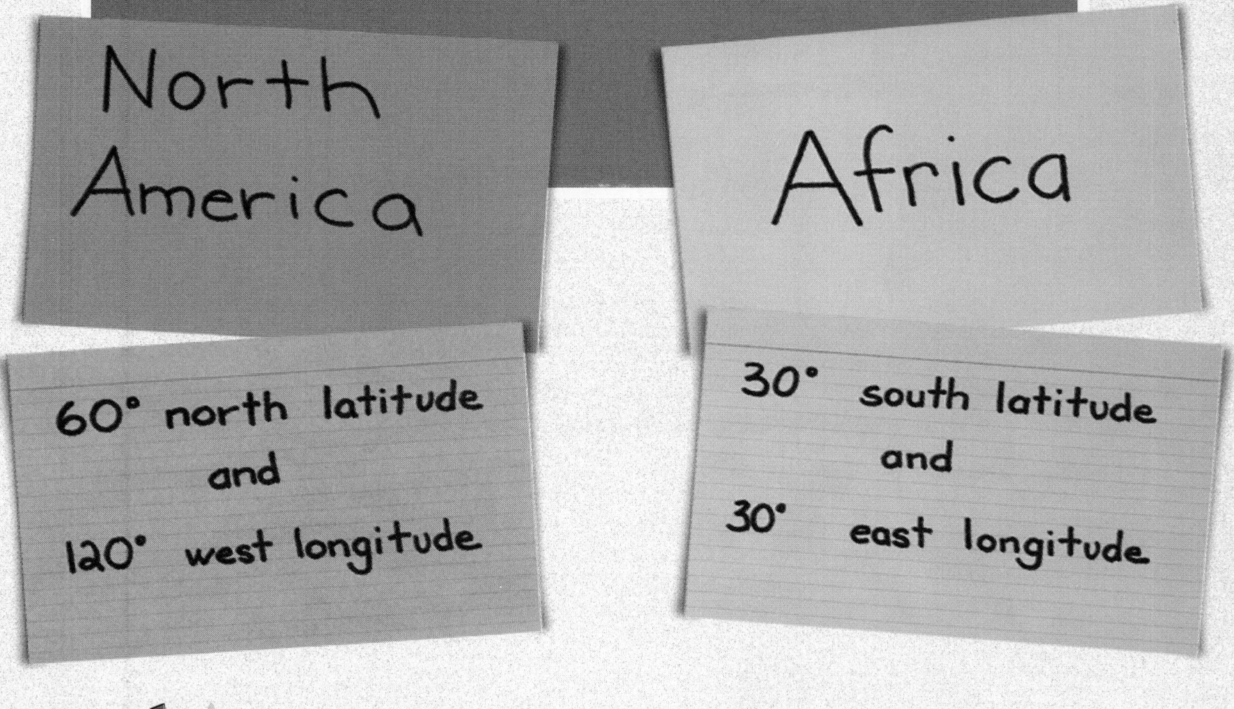

North America

Africa

60° north latitude
and
120° west longitude

30° south latitude
and
30° east longitude

SKILL POWER SEARCH

Look for a map with latitude and longitude lines in this chapter and practice using these lines to help you find different places.

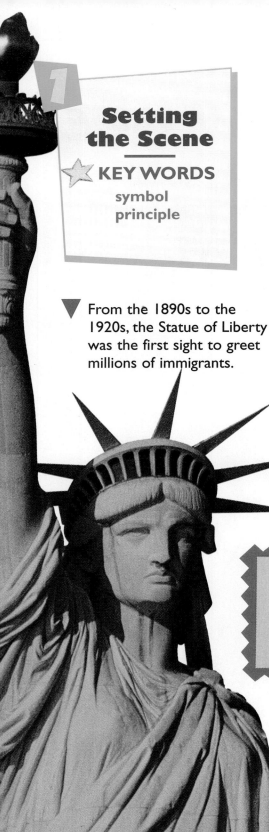

Setting the Scene

⭐ **KEY WORDS**

symbol
principle

One Nation

FOCUS *By sharing our different customs, traditions, and ideas, we make our communities stronger.*

▼ From the 1890s to the 1920s, the Statue of Liberty was the first sight to greet millions of immigrants.

Where Are You From?

If someone asked you where you were from, what would you say? You could answer with the name of your town or state. You could say you were from the United States. But what else could you say? Where did your ancestors come from?

American Indians have been here for thousands of years, but other people in the United States have a much more recent immigrant background.

Since the 1950s about five million immigrants have come from Mexico to the United States. Many came to find jobs.

NORTH
AMERICA

ATLANTIC
OCEAN

PACIFIC
OCEAN

SOUTH
AMERICA

Immigrants From Around the World

160°W 140°W 120°W 100°W 80°W 60°W

From Many

You may not have moved here from another country. Your parents and even your grandparents may not have come from another country. But most likely someone in your family came here from somewhere else.

Why did people come to the United States? Some came hoping to find a better life, some came for adventure, and some had no choice but to come. The map below shows why some groups came to the United States.

In the 1840s and 1850s, about 1 1/2 million Irish immigrants came to the United States. Many came when their potato crop failed.

From the 1840s to the 1880s, about 4 million German immigrants came to the United States. Many were looking for jobs.

Since 1965, thousands of Koreans have come to the United States each year. Many came to get away from crowded cities.

From the 1600s to the 1800s, thousands of Africans from present-day countries such as Nigeria, Ghana, Senegal, Sierra Leone, and Angola were forced to come to the United States as slaves.

EUROPE

ASIA

AFRICA

PACIFIC OCEAN

INDIAN OCEAN

ATLANTIC OCEAN

AUSTRALIA

ANTARCTICA

20°W   0°   20°E   40°E   60°E   80°E   100°E   120°E   140°E   160°E

60°N

20°N

0°

40°S

60°S

80°S

Violins and other instruments were often brought to the United States by immigrants.

Sharing Music

Many immigrants brought their customs and traditions with them. Music was often an important part of their traditions. When immigrants first arrived, many struggled under difficult conditions. They often used music as a way to pass the time and entertain themselves.

Africans who were enslaved were forced to work under the harshest conditions. They often sang songs as they labored in the fields. Many of these songs contained messages of freedom. Enslaved people also made musical instruments such as banjos, shown at left.

Irish immigrants, as well as others, often brought violins with them. As you have learned, many Irish immigrants helped build the transcontinental railroad. They wrote and sang songs about their hard work. Part of one such song is shown at left.

Banjos were based on similar instruments used in Africa.

Paddy Works on the Railway

In eighteen hundred and forty-two
I left the old world for the new,
Oh, spare me the luck that brought me through
To work upon the railway.

298

▲ Lacrosse was first played by Native Americans.

Games and Sports

Many of the games and sports we play today were first developed in other countries. Chess started in India. Pick-up-sticks began in China. Immigrants introduced various sports to the United States. The Dutch brought bowling with them when they came here from the Netherlands in the 1600s. The French brought tennis. Soccer came with the English.

Not all our games and sports came from other places. Native Americans invented lacrosse. Lacrosse is a very fast team sport in which players use a stick with a net at one end to pass a hard rubber ball. Other sports, such as basketball and football, were invented here. These sports are now played all over the world.

Sharing December Holidays

Many Americans celebrate holidays in December. Each holiday has its own traditions, **symbols**, and music.

Christmas is a holiday with many traditions. The tradition of decorating an evergreen tree came from German immigrants. Where do you think the Christmas tree pictured at left is located? The poinsettia is a Mexican plant that has become a symbol of Christmas.

Chanukah (HAH noo kah) is a Jewish holiday that lasts for eight days. It is celebrated with games, gifts, and special foods. Candles are lit each night.

Kwanzaa (KWAHN zuh) is an African American holiday that is celebrated from December 26 to January 1. Each day a different candle is lit. Each candle stands for a **principle** such as unity or creativity.

symbol An object that represents something else
principle A rule used in deciding how to behave

During Chanukah, children may play games with a dreidel (DRAY dul).

This mat is used during Kwanzaa, a time for African Americans to celebrate their culture.

▲ This boy is helping his grandfather prepare for a Tet celebration.

Celebrating the New Year

When do you celebrate New Year's Day? Many observe this holiday on January 1, but others celebrate it on a different date.

Americans who have immigrated from Vietnam may celebrate Tet, a New Year's celebration that falls between January 20 and February 20. Chinese Americans celebrate their new year during the same time period. People who are from India may celebrate Diwali, a New Year's celebration that takes place in late October or early November.

Celebrations from different cultures are alike in some ways. New Year's celebrations are a time for family and friends, for thinking about the old year, and for planning how to make the new year better.

▼ Children make lamps like this one during Diwali celebrations.

SHOW WHAT YOU KNOW!

REFOCUS

1. Name some reasons that immigrants have come to the United States.

2. What are some of the things that immigrants have brought to America?

THINK ABOUT IT

What other traditions or customs do you know about? Share what you know with your classmates.

WRITE ABOUT IT

If you were moving to a new country, what traditions or customs would you take with you? Why?

Citizenship

⭐ **KEY WORD**

settlement
house

Helping One

FOCUS *When we help one another, we may come to know and understand each other better.*

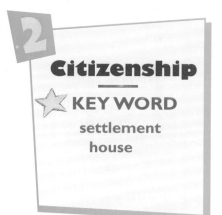

A History of Working Together

Americans have always worked together to solve problems and to help others meet their needs. In 1889, Jane Addams, shown at left, began to help people in a new way. She opened a settlement house called Hull House, in Chicago, to help immigrants build new lives in this country. The people who lived and worked at Hull House, which is shown below, taught English and other subjects to immigrants. They started one of Chicago's first kindergartens and worked to get cleaner streets and better housing in the city.

⭐ **settlement house** A neighborhood center that provides services such as job training and English classes

Another

▲ Whether by cleaning a beach or helping to build a park, children can help their communities in many ways.

Working Together Today

People are still helping one another today, many of them as volunteers. Some volunteers help people learn to read. Others visit and take meals to elderly or sick people who cannot leave their homes. Many volunteers still help new immigrants.

Children also volunteer to help others. Some schools organize teams of students to clean up parks and playgrounds. Some students collect food for people who are hungry.

People who have special needs often work together to help one another. One example is a group in New York City called The Door. This is a group of teenagers and young adults with physical disabilities who work together. They are preparing a display of artwork, photos, and writing samples. The purpose of the display is to teach others about the needs of people with physical disabilities.

Habitat for Humanity

Habitat for Humanity is a group based in Americus, Georgia, that volunteers to build houses for people who need them. Since it was started in 1976, Habitat for Humanity has built more than 40,000 houses in the United States and in other countries.

People are able to buy Habitat for Humanity houses for a very low price. House prices are low because homeowners agree to spend many hours helping to build their own houses. They also agree to help build houses for other people who need them. Volunteers from the community donate their time and labor, and many people give money and building materials.

Habitat for Humanity is an example of how people can help themselves at the same time they help others.

▼ These women in Austin, Texas, are building a house for Habitat for Humanity.

Helping the World Community

Many Americans work to help people in other countries. Taking part in a CROP Walk is one way to do that. CROP, a relief agency, raises money to help people who are hungry. The money raised by CROP walks is used to buy food. It is also used to buy farm tools and to train people to grow healthy food crops. Helping people raise their own food is a good way to prevent hunger.

Another way that people help others in our world community is by raising money for the United Nations Children's Fund, known as UNICEF. UNICEF helps millions of children around the world. Many children collect money for UNICEF. The money is used to pay for food, medical care, and education for children in many countries.

SHOW WHAT YOU KNOW!

REFOCUS

1. What was Hull House?

2. What are some of the things that a volunteer might do?

THINK ABOUT IT

Why is it important for people to work together in communities?

COMMUNITY CHECK

Make a list of ways that children can volunteer in your school or in your community.

Computer

FOCUS *Ever-changing technology brings us closer to people all around the world.*

Our Shrinking World

In the past it was often difficult to stay in touch with people who lived far away. It could take weeks for a letter to be delivered across the country. But today you can communicate almost immediately by using a computer.

Computers can help you in many other ways as well. They can help you find and share information. There are special **networks**, such as the Internet, which make the sharing of information possible.

⭐ **network** A system for connecting computers

Computer Facts

Many computer chips are no larger than a fingernail.

The smallest computer chip can fit through the eye of a needle.

Connections

Getting Information

The Internet and other networks use **modems** and telephone lines to connect millions of computers all over the world. These networks are part of the information superhighway. But instead of being a highway that has cars and trucks, this highway carries information to and from colleges, businesses, government offices, and other places.

Lots of useful information is available on the Internet. With an adult you can use the Internet to visit a science lab, check on sports scores, read a book, or even find out what the President is doing.

modem A device that lets information be sent over telephone lines

Then and Now

The first computer weighed over 30 tons and filled an entire room.

Today, computers may weigh only a few pounds and can fit on your lap.

307

Computer Communities

There are many reasons that people use computers. Sometimes computers can help people meet other people and form new communities. Some schools use computer networks to connect students with senior citizens. The students can teach the seniors how to use the computers, and the seniors can help the students with their homework.

Many schools around the world use Kid's Network, a program made by the people who publish *National Geographic* magazine. In this program, schools from around the world are linked together, so students can share information and work on projects together. Using these programs, children learn new things and meet students from faraway places.

Children at Mount Sinai Medical Center use a computer to play with other kids.

REFOCUS

1. What is the Internet?

2. How do computer networks help build new communities?

THINK ABOUT IT

Why is it important for children in the hospital to keep in touch with other children?

WRITE ABOUT IT

What would you ask a child in another country if your classrooms were linked by a computer network?

Helping People

Computer networks are also being used in a very special way by some hospitals. There is one network that lets children who are sick play with other children in hospitals across the country.

Children use the network to meet other kids, play games, or solve problems. They can use animated characters, such as E.T., to help them move through the computer games. The photo at the top of the page shows what the computer screen looks like. This program has helped many children deal with the difficulties of being sick.

Our Country

Citizenship

⭐ KEY WORDS

liberty
national
anthem

FOCUS *The national symbols we share bring us together as a community.*

Sharing Symbols

Although Americans come from different places and have different traditions, we have many things in common. Some of the things we share are our national symbols. These symbols help unite us as one community.

The Liberty Bell

Our country was started because people wanted liberty, or freedom. When the colonies declared their independence from Great Britain in 1776, they rang the Liberty Bell to celebrate. The bell was rung almost every July after that until 1835, when it cracked. Workers tried to fix the crack, but could not. And ringing the bell made the crack deepen. So since 1846, the bell has been silent. But even in its silence, the Liberty Bell remains one of our symbols of freedom.

⭐ **liberty** The condition of being free from the control of others

United

The Bald Eagle

Another symbol of our freedom is the bald eagle. The eagle isn't really bald—it just looks that way from a distance. There are actually white feathers all over the eagle's head.

In 1782 the bald eagle was named our national bird. It was chosen because the bald eagle lives only in North America. And since bald eagles are very strong and fly high and free in the sky, they are also a symbol of strength and freedom.

The Great Seal

The bald eagle can be seen on the Great Seal of the United States. This seal is used on important official papers as well as on our money.

The bald eagle is only one symbol on the Great Seal. The arrows are a symbol of war, and the olive branch is a symbol of peace. The eagle is facing the olive branch to show that the United States wants peace but will be ready in case of war. Can you find other symbols on the seal? Try counting the number of arrows, or the number of leaves on the olive branch.

The American Flag

The American flag is another symbol we share. It represents our nation as one made up of many states. Count the stripes on the American flag. The number of stripes stands for the number of states there were when the country first began. Today there are 50 stars on the flag—one for each of the 50 states.

In 1777 the United States passed a law that said that the flag would have 13 stripes and 13 stars. The colors would be red, white, and blue. The pictures below show some of the changes the American flag has gone through. What has changed? What has stayed the same?

1775–1777 **1795** **1818** **1912–1959**

The Star-Spangled Banner

Our flag is more than a symbol. It is also the story behind "The Star-Spangled Banner," our national anthem. The words to this song were written in 1814 by Francis Scott Key, who is shown below.

In 1814 the United States was at war with Great Britain. When the British attacked Fort McHenry, which protected the city of Baltimore, Key watched the battle all night. He saw "the bombs bursting in air." He wondered if the fort would be captured. In "the dawn's early light," Key found out. The "flag was still there" at Fort McHenry. The fort had held. Baltimore was safe!

Francis Scott Key was so happy that he wrote a poem to celebrate. The first verse is shown below. Soon the poem was set to music, and in 1931 it became our national anthem, "The Star-Spangled Banner."

★ **national anthem** The official song of a country

The Star-Spangled Banner

Oh, say! can you see, by the dawn's early light,
What so proudly we hailed at the twilight's last gleaming,
Whose broad stripes and bright stars, through the perilous fight,
O'er the ramparts we watched were so gallantly streaming?
And the rockets' red glare, the bombs bursting in air,
Gave proof through the night that our flag was still there.
Oh, say, does that Star-Spangled Banner yet wave
O'er the land of the free and the home of the brave?

The Pledge of Allegiance

I pledge allegiance
to the flag of the
United States of America
and to the Republic
for which it stands,
one Nation under God,
indivisible, with liberty
and justice for all.

The Pledge

The year 1892 was the 400th anniversary of Columbus's arrival in America. A man named Francis Bellamy, from Boston, Massachusetts, helped plan a celebration for Columbus Day. Children raised new flags and recited a short pledge written by Bellamy. The pledge had been printed in a magazine and sent to children all over the country. This became known as the Pledge of Allegiance.

When we say the Pledge of Allegiance, we are making a promise. We are promising to be loyal to our flag and to our country.

Holidays We Share

The table below shows some of the holidays we share. These are special days to honor important people and events from our nation's past.

Americans come from all different places, and we each bring something to our country. The holidays, symbols, and traditions we share bring us together as one community.

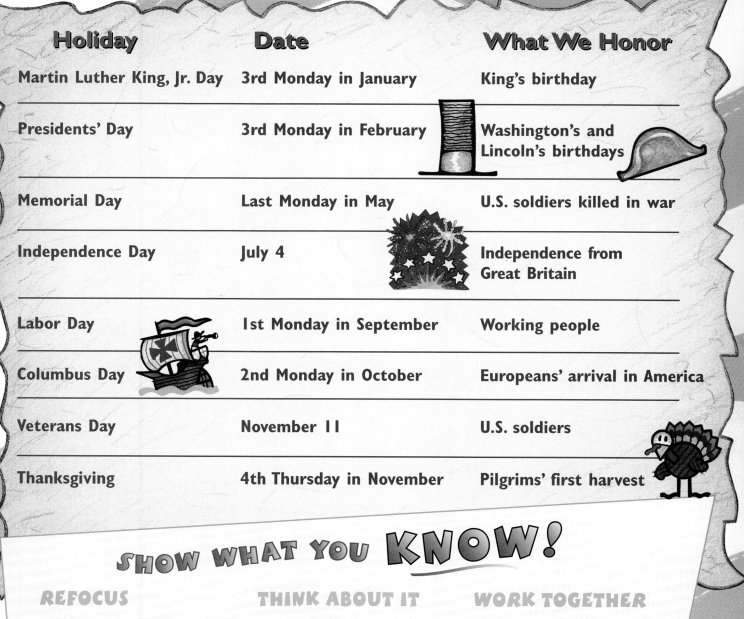

Holiday	Date	What We Honor
Martin Luther King, Jr. Day	3rd Monday in January	King's birthday
Presidents' Day	3rd Monday in February	Washington's and Lincoln's birthdays
Memorial Day	Last Monday in May	U.S. soldiers killed in war
Independence Day	July 4	Independence from Great Britain
Labor Day	1st Monday in September	Working people
Columbus Day	2nd Monday in October	Europeans' arrival in America
Veterans Day	November 11	U.S. soldiers
Thanksgiving	4th Thursday in November	Pilgrims' first harvest

SHOW WHAT YOU KNOW!

REFOCUS

1. What is our national anthem?

2. What do the stars and stripes on our flag stand for?

THINK ABOUT IT

If you could choose any animal to be a symbol of our country, what would you choose? Explain your choice.

WORK TOGETHER

With a small group, write your own anthem for our country. You can use the tune from another song.

SUMMING UP

1 DO YOU REMEMBER . . .
COMPREHENSION

1. What are three holidays people may celebrate in December?

2. What are some ways people celebrate a new year?

3. What is a volunteer?

4. How can computers help people get information?

5. Why are there 13 stripes and 50 stars on the American flag?

2 SKILL POWER
LATITUDE AND LONGITUDE

Where in the world are you? To find out, use the map of the United States in the Atlas on pages 320–321. Find where your state is located. Which latitude line or lines are closest to your state? Which longitude line or lines are closest?

3 WHAT DO YOU THINK?
CRITICAL THINKING

1. Why was the holiday of Kwanzaa created?

2. How might immigrants have felt when they first saw the Statue of Liberty?

3. Why does Habitat for Humanity require people to help build their own houses?

4. How can computer networks help people become better educated?

5. Choose two symbols of the United States. Tell how they are alike and how they are different.

4 SAY IT, WRITE IT, USE IT
VOCABULARY

Think about what it's like to be an immigrant to the United States. Write a skit describing the trip to America and the first week living here. Use as many of the words below as possible.

liberty   principle
modem   settlement house
national anthem   symbol
network

5 GEOGRAPHY AND YOU
MAP STUDY

Use the maps in this chapter to answer these questions.

1. What continent would you be in if you were at the equator and 60 degrees west longitude?

2. From what country in North America have about five million people immigrated to the United States?

6 TAKE ACTION
CITIZENSHIP

Americans are known for their willingness to volunteer to help others. You can volunteer, too. Make a list of five things you can do in your school or in your neighborhood. Your list might include bringing in the mail for an elderly person or picking up litter near your school.

7 GET CREATIVE
SCIENCE CONNECTION

The bald eagle, one of our national symbols, has been considered an endangered or threatened animal since the 1960s. Hunters, pollution, and the loss of wilderness have all had harmful effects on bald eagles. With a small group, find out about some of the ways in which groups are working to help bald eagles. Make a poster to show what these groups are doing.

LOOKING BACK

Look back at all of the different kinds of communities you've learned about this past year.

REFERENCE

CONTENTS

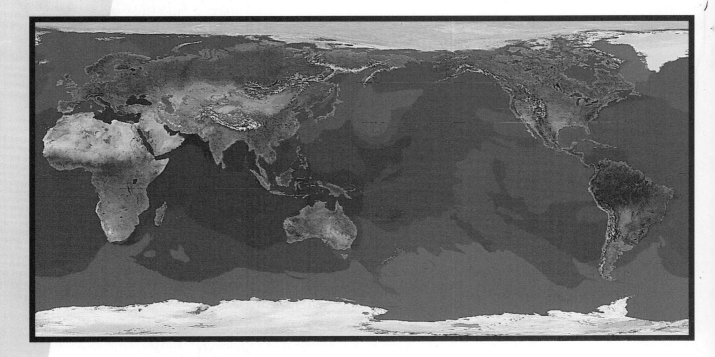

SECTION

RESEARCH AND REFERENCE

If you want to find out where the people and places you are studying about are located, you can use the atlas shown here. If you want to make your own maps or understand the meaning of geography words, these books will help you.

Maps and Mapping: Geography Facts and Experiments by Barbara Taylor (Kingfisher, 1993)

If you wanted to create a map of your room, how would you do it? Discover how to make all different kinds of maps using colors, scales, and symbols.

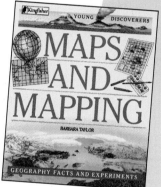

Geography From A to Z: A Picture Glossary by Jack Knowlton, illustrated by Harriett Barton (HarperCollins Publishers, 1988)

From archipelagos to zones, you will learn about the geographical features of our earth. Colorful drawings will show you what these features look like and where they are found.

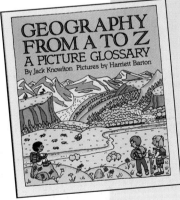

My First Atlas by Bill Boyle, illustrated by Dave Hopkins (Dorling Kindersley, 1994)

This atlas will help you learn about the different parts of the world. You will enjoy seeing where the people live and the work they do.

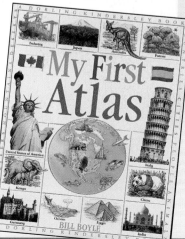

ATLAS

140°W 130°W 125°W 120°W 115°W 110°W 105°W 100°W

• Seattle
Olympia ★   • Spokane
Washington
Columbia River
Portland •
★ Salem
• Eugene
Oregon

Great Falls •   *Missouri River*
Montana
Helena ★
• Billings

North Dakota
Bismarck ★

Idaho
• Boise
Snake River
Pocatello • • Idaho Falls
• Victor
Wyoming
Casper •

South Dakota
• Pierre ★
Rapid City •

Laramie •   • Cheyenne ★
Nebraska
Grand Island •
Platte River

• Reno
★ Carson City
Nevada

Great Salt Lake
West Valley • ★ • Salt Lake City
• Provo
Utah

Denver • ★ • Aurora
Colorado
Colorado Springs •
Arkansas River
Kansas

Sacramento ★
San Francisco • • Oakland
• San Jose
• Fresno
California

• Las Vegas

Colorado River

Anaheim •
Los Angeles • • Riverside
Long Beach • • Santa Ana
• San Diego

Arizona
Phoenix ★
• Mesa
• Tucson

Santa Fe ★
• Albuquerque
New Mexico
• Roswell
Las Cruces •
El Paso •

• Lawton

Texas
San Antonio •

PACIFIC OCEAN

Rio Grande

MEXICO

RUSSIA
Bering Strait
ARCTIC OCEAN
70°N

Bering Sea

Alaska
• Fairbanks
CANADA

Anchorage •
60°N
Gulf of Alaska
Juneau ★

ALEUTIAN ISLANDS
160°W 150°W 140°W

0   300   600 miles
0   300   600 kilometers

Kauai   22°N
Niihau
Kailua • *Oahu*
Pearl City • ★ Honolulu *Molokai*
Lanai   *Maui*
Hawaii *Kahoolawe*

PACIFIC OCEAN
0   50   100 miles
0   50   100 kilometers
160°W 158°W 156°W
20°N

Hawaii

CANADA

nd Forks

argo

Duluth

Minnesota

Minneapolis ● ★ St. Paul

ioux Falls

Lake Superior

Michigan

Green Bay ●

Wisconsin

Madison ★

Milwaukee ●

Cedar Rapids ●

Iowa

Davenport ●

Des Moines ●

Omaha ●

Lincoln

nsas City ● Kansas City ●

eka ★

Jefferson ★

City

Missouri

ichita

Isa

lahoma

ity

lahoma

Little Rock ●

Fort

Smith ●

Arkansas

North ● Little Rock

rlington ●

Dallas ●

ort Worth ●

Shreveport ●

Jackson ★

Mississippi

Louisiana

Baton Rouge ★

stin

Houston ●

Corpus

Christi

Red River

Lake Michigan

Grand ●

Rapids

Lansing ★ ●

Rockford ●

Chicago ●

Illinois

Springfield ★ ●

Louisville ●

Frankfort ★

Lexington ●

Kentucky

Knoxville ●

Nashville ★

Tennessee

Memphis ●

Meridian ●

Alabama

Biloxi ●

Mobile ●

New Orleans ●

Gulf of Mexico

Lake Huron

Detroit ●

Gary ●

Fort Wayne ●

Indiana

Indianapolis ★

Cincinnati ●

Toledo ●

Cleveland ●

Akron ●

Ohio

Columbus ★ ●

Pittsburgh ●

West

Virginia

Charleston ★

Huntington ●

Birmingham ●

Atlanta ●

Columbus ●

Montgomery ★

Lake Ontario

Rochester ●

Buffalo ●

Waterloo ●

New

York

Pennsylvania

Harrisburg ★

Wheeling ●

Rockville ●

Washington, D.C. ⊛

Ohio River

Lake Erie

St. Lawrence River

Maine

Augusta ★

Vermont

Lewiston ●

Burlington ● Portland ●

Montpelier ★ New

Rutland ● Hampshire

Concord ★ Nashua ●

Manchester ●

Albany ★ Worcester ● Boston ★

Springfield ● Pawtucket ●

Hartford ★ Providence ★

New Haven ● Warwick ●

Bridgeport ●

Jersey City ● New York City

Newark

Trenton ★

Philadelphia ●

Wilmington ●

Newark ●

Dover ★

Massachusetts

Rhode Island

Connecticut

New Jersey

Delaware

ATLANTIC

OCEAN

Annapolis ★

Maryland

Baltimore ●

Virginia

Richmond ★

Norfolk ● Virginia Beach ●

Greensboro ●

Raleigh ★

North Carolina

Charlotte ●

South

Carolina

Columbia ★

North Charleston ● Charleston ●

Georgia

Savannah ●

Jacksonville ●

Tallahassee ★

Florida

St. Petersburg ● Tampa ●

Miami ●

BAHAMAS

Tropic of Cancer

CUBA

N

W ✦ E

S

UNITED STATES
POLITICAL

— Rivers

⊛ National capital

★ State capitals

● Other cities

0   150   300 miles

0   150   300 kilometers

321

THE UNITED STATES AT NIGHT FROM SPACE

This composite view of the United States was taken in 1991 on three moonless, cloudless nights. The images were taken by United States Air Force Defense Mapping Satellites orbiting Earth at an altitude of 450 miles.

ARCTIC OCEAN

Arctic Circle

Greenland (Den.)

Alaska (U.S.)

ALEUTIAN IS. (U.S.)

CANADA

NORTH

AMERICA

UNITED STATES

See inset below

Bermuda (U.K.)

ATLANTIC OCEAN

AZORES (Port.)

MEXICO

Caribbean Sea

CAPE VERDE

Midway I. (U.S.)

Tropic of Cancer

HAWAII (U.S.)

VENEZUELA

GUYANA
SURINAME
French Guiana (Fr.)

COLOMBIA

Equator

GALÁPAGOS IS. (Ecuador)

SOUTH

ECUADOR

AMERICA

BRAZIL

WESTERN SAMOA

AMERICAN SAMOA (U.S.)

PACIFIC OCEAN

FRENCH POLYNESIA (Fr.)

PERU

TONGA

BOLIVIA

PARAGUAY

COOK IS. (N.Z.)

Pitcairn I. (U.K.)

Tropic of Capricorn

CHILE

URUGUAY

Easter I. (Chile)

ARGENTINA

International Date Line

FALKLAND IS. (U.K.)

Antarctic Circle

WEST INDIES AND
CENTRAL AMERICA

0   150   300 miles
0   150   300 kilometers

UNITED STATES

30°N

N
W   E
S

ATLANTIC OCEAN

Gulf of Mexico

25°N

B
A
H
A
M
A
S

Tropic of Cancer

CUBA

20°N

TURKS AND CAICOS IS. (U.K.)

BR. VIRGIN IS. (U.K.)

MEXICO

CAYMAN ISLANDS (U.K.)

Hispaniola

GREATER ANTILLES

HAITI

DOMINICAN REPUBLIC

Puerto Rico (U.S.)

ANTIGUA AND BARBUDA

BELIZE

JAMAICA

VIRGIN ISLANDS (U.S.)

Guadeloupe (Fr.)

GUATEMALA

ST. KITTS AND NEVIS

DOMINICA

Caribbean Sea

Martinique (Fr.)

HONDURAS

ST. LUCIA

EL SALVADOR

NICARAGUA

NETH. ANTILLES (Neth.)
ARUBA

ST. VINCENT AND THE GRENADINES

BARBADOS

GRENADA

LESSER ANTILLES

COSTA RICA

TRINIDAD AND TOBAGO

PANAMA

COLOMBIA

VENEZUELA

90°W   85°W   80°W   75°W   70°W   65°W   60°W

North Pole

SVALBARD
(Nor.)

CELAND

See inset below

EUROPE

RUSSIA

ASIA

20°W   0°   20°E   40°E   60°E   80°E   100°E   120°E   140°E   160°E

KAZAKSTAN

MONGOLIA

N. KOREA
JAPAN
S. KOREA

GEORGIA
ARMENIA
TURKEY
MALTA CYPRUS   SYRIA
TUNISIA
LEBANON
ISRAEL
West Bank
and Gaza Strip

AZERBAIJAN
TAJIKISTAN
KYRGYZSTAN

CHINA

PACIFIC OCEAN

IRAQ
IRAN
JORDAN   KUWAIT
QATAR
BAHRAIN
SAUDI
ARABIA   U.A.E.

AFGHANISTAN

PAKISTAN

NEPAL

BHUTAN

TAIWAN

Hong Kong
Macao (Port.)

Wake I. (U.S.)

MOROCCO
ALGERIA
LIBYA

Western
Sahara
(Mor.)

AFRICA

EGYPT

INDIA

MYANMAR
(BURMA)

VIETNAM

NORTHERN
MARIANA IS. (U.S.)

MAURITANIA
MALI
NIGER
CHAD

ERITREA

BANGLA-
DESH

THAILAND

Guam
(U.S.)

MARSHALL IS.

SENEGAL
GAMBIA
GUINEA-BISSAU
GUINEA
SIERRA
LEONE
COTE
D'IVOIRE
GHANA
TOGO
BENIN
LIBERIA
EQUATORIAL
GUINEA
SÃO TOMÉ
AND PRÍNCIPE
Cabinda
(Angola)

BURKINA
FASO
NIGERIA

CENTRAL
AFRICAN
REP.
CAMEROON
GABON

SUDAN

ETHIOPIA

UGANDA
ZAIRE
RWANDA
BURUNDI

KENYA

TANZANIA

YEMEN OMAN

DJIBOUTI

SRI
LANKA

MALDIVES

CAMBODIA
BRUNEI
MALAYSIA

SINGAPORE

PALAU

FEDERATED STATES
OF MICRONESIA

PHILIPPINES

NAURU

KIRIBATI
TUVALU

SEYCHELLES

INDONESIA

PAPUA
NEW GUINEA

SOLOMON IS.

VANUATU

ANGOLA
ZAMBIA
ZIMBABWE

MALAWI

COMOROS

MADAGASCAR

Réunion (Fr.)

FIJI

New Caledonia (Fr.)

NAMIBIA
BOTSWANA

SWAZILAND
SOUTH
AFRICA
LESOTHO

MAURITIUS

INDIAN OCEAN

AUSTRALIA

WORLD POLITICAL

0   1,000   2,000 miles

0   1,000   2,000 kilometers

NEW
ZEALAND

ANTARCTICA

South Pole

Prime Meridian

EUROPE

0   200   400 miles
0   400 kilometers

30°E
20°E

10°E

Arctic Circle

N
W   E
S

60°N

FINLAND

0°

10°W

NORWAY

SWEDEN

ESTONIA
LATVIA
LITHUANIA
RUSSIA

RUSSIA

North Sea

UNITED
KINGDOM
IRELAND

DENMARK

NETHERLANDS

POLAND

BELARUS

50°N

ATLANTIC
OCEAN

GERMANY
BELGIUM
LUX.

CZECH
REP.
SLOVAKIA

UKRAINE

MOLDOVA

FRANCE

LIECH.
SWITZ.   AUSTRIA
SLOVENIA
MONACO   SAN
MARINO

HUNGARY
ROMANIA
CROATIA
BOSNIA-
HERZ. YUGO.
BULGARIA

Black Sea

40°N

ANDORRA

PORTUGAL

SPAIN

Corsica (Fr.)
Sardinia (It.)

BALEARIC IS. (Sp.)

Gibraltar (U.K.)

ITALY

MACEDONIA
ALBANIA
GREECE

TURKEY

Mediterranean Sea

Sicily (It.)

325

NORTH AMERICA POLITICAL

- ⊛ National capitals
- ◉ Cities with populations over one million
- • Major cities
- ⎯ National boundaries
- ⎯ State boundaries

0   300   600 miles

0   300   600 kilometers

ASIA

EUROPE

Bering Sea

Bering Strait

Barrow

ARCTIC OCEAN

Alaska (U.S.)

Anchorage

Beaufort Sea

Greenland (Kalaalit Nunaat) (Den.)

Baffin Bay

Gulf of Alaska

Whitehorse

Juneau

Yukon R.

Arctic Circle

Mackenzie R.

Great Bear Lake

Yellowknife

Great Slave Lake

Nuuk

Iqaluit

Labrador Sea

PACIFIC OCEAN

Edmonton

Victoria   Vancouver

CANADA

Churchill

Hudson Bay

Goose Bay

Seattle

Calgary

Saskatoon

Sept-Îles

Gander

St. John's

Portland

Spokane

Regina

Lake Winnipeg

Winnipeg

ST. PIERRE-MIQUELON (Fr.)

Columbia R.

Missouri R.

Great Lakes

Quebec

St. John

San Francisco

Great Salt Lake

Salt Lake City

Minneapolis

St. Paul

Montreal

Ottawa

Halifax

Colorado R.

Denver

Omaha

Milwaukee

Toronto

Detroit

Buffalo

Boston

Los Angeles

San Diego

Phoenix

Arkansas R.

Kansas City

Chicago

Cleveland

Pittsburgh

Cincinnati

New York

Philadelphia

Washington, D.C.

UNITED STATES

St. Louis

Ohio R.

Norfolk

ATLANTIC OCEAN

El Paso

Dallas

Memphis

Tropic of Cancer

Rio Grande

Atlanta

Bermuda (U.K.)

San Antonio

Monterrey

Houston

New Orleans

MEXICO

Gulf of Mexico

Miami

BAHAMAS

Guadalajara

Nassau

N

W   E

S

Mexico City

Orizaba

Havana

CUBA

DOMINICAN REPUBLIC

CAYMAN ISLANDS (U.K.)

Santiago

HAITI

Puerto Rico (U.S.)

VIRGIN IS. (U.S.-U.K.)

ANTIGUA AND BARBUDA

Belmopan

BELIZE

Port-au-Prince

Santo Domingo

Guadeloupe (Fr.)

GUATEMALA

Guatemala

JAMAICA

Kingston

ST. KITTS AND NEVIS

DOMINICA

MARTINIQUE (Fr.)

HONDURAS

San Salvador

Tegucigalpa

Caribbean Sea

ST. LUCIA

BARBADOS

EL SALVADOR

NICARAGUA

NETH. ANTILLES (Neth.)

ST. VINCENT AND THE GRENADINES

ARUBA

GRENADA

Managua

Panama Canal

TRINIDAD AND TOBAGO

San José

PANAMA

COSTA RICA

Panama

SOUTH AMERICA

Caribbean Sea

Barranquilla
Cartagena
Maracaibo
Valencia   Caracas
Barquisimeto
GUYANA   SURINAME

Cúcuta
San   VENEZUELA
Cristóbal
French Guiana
(Fr.)

Bucaramanga
Medellín
Bogotá
Orinoco R.
Georgetown
Paramaribo
Cayenne
ATLANTIC OCEAN

Cali
COLOMBIA

Quito   Belém
Equator   Manaus   Amazon R.
GALÁPAGOS IS.   ECUADOR   São Luís
(Ecuador)
Guayaquil   Fortaleza
Iquitos

Madeira R.
B R A Z I L
Xingu R.
Tocantins R.
Trujillo   Recife
PERU   Maceió
Araguaia R.
São Francisco R.

Lima   Cuzco
Callao   Salvador
L. Titicaca   Brasília

Arequipa   La Paz   BOLIVIA
Sucre
Belo
Horizonte

N

Chuquicamata
PARAGUAY
Paraná R.
Rio de Janeiro
São Paulo   Niterói
Santos
W   E

Tropic of Capricorn
Antofagasta
Paraguay R.
Asunción
Curitiba
S

San Felix I.   San Ambrosio I.
(Chile)   (Chile)
Tucumán
Uruguay R.
Pôrto Alegre

CHILE   Córdoba
Santa Fe
URUGUAY
ATLANTIC OCEAN

Valparaíso   Rosario   Paraná
Santiago   Buenos Aires   Montevideo
Juan Fernández Is.
(Chile)   La Plata
Concepción   ARGENTINA
Mar del Plata
Bahía Blanca

SOUTH AMERICA POLITICAL

⊛   National capitals

◎   Cities with populations over one million

•   Other cities

International boundaries

0   400   800 miles

0   400   800 kilometers

PACIFIC OCEAN

Strait of
Magellan
Punta Arenas   FALKLAND IS. (U.K.)
(MALVINAS IS.)

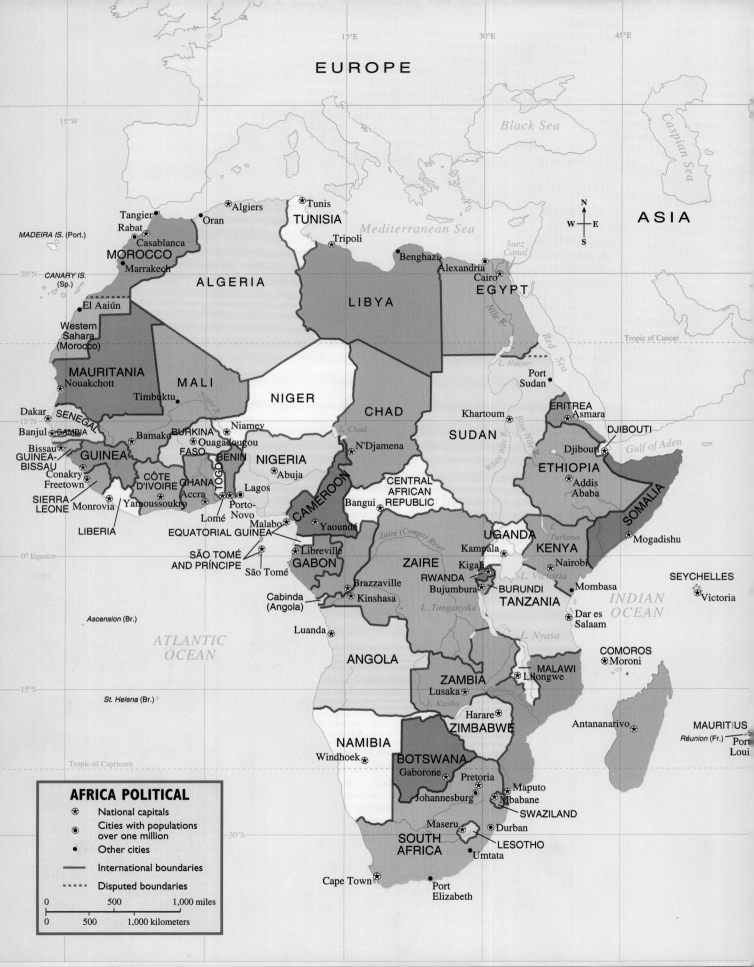

AFRICA POLITICAL

- ✪ National capitals
- ◉ Cities with populations over one million
- • Other cities
- ── International boundaries
- ┈┈┈ Disputed boundaries

0   500   1,000 miles

0   500   1,000 kilometers

EUROPE

ASIA

Black Sea

Caspian Sea

N
W   E
S

Mediterranean Sea

Suez Canal

MADEIRA IS. (Port.)

Tangier
Rabat
Casablanca
MOROCCO
Marrakech

Algiers
Oran
Tunis
TUNISIA
Tripoli
Benghazi
Alexandria
Cairo
EGYPT

CANARY IS. (Sp.)

30°N

El Aaiún

ALGERIA

LIBYA

Nile R.

L. Nasser

Tropic of Cancer

Western Sahara (Morocco)

Port Sudan

Red Sea

MAURITANIA
Nouakchott

MALI

Timbuktu

Niger R.

NIGER

CHAD

Khartoum

SUDAN

Blue Nile R.

ERITREA
Asmara
DJIBOUTI
Djibouti

15°N

Dakar
SENEGAL
Banjul
GAMBIA
Bissau
GUINEA-BISSAU
Conakry
Freetown

Bamako

Niamey

BURKINA FASO
Ouagadougou

BENIN

N'Djamena

NIGERIA
Abuja

L. Chad

CENTRAL AFRICAN REPUBLIC

Gulf of Aden

White Nile R.

ETHIOPIA
Addis Ababa

SOMALIA

GUINEA

SIERRA LEONE
Monrovia

CÔTE D'IVOIRE
Yamoussoukro

GHANA
Accra

TOGO

Lagos

Lomé
Porto-Novo

LIBERIA

EQUATORIAL GUINEA
Malabo
CAMEROON
Yaoundé

Bangui

Mogadishu

SÃO TOMÉ AND PRÍNCIPE
São Tomé

Libreville
GABON

ZAIRE

Zaire (Congo) River

Kampala
UGANDA
KENYA

L. Turkana

Nairobi

Mombasa

SEYCHELLES
Victoria

0° Equator

Cabinda (Angola)

Brazzaville
Kinshasa

RWANDA
Kigali
Bujumbura
BURUNDI
TANZANIA

L. Victoria

Dar es Salaam

INDIAN OCEAN

Ascension (Br.)

Luanda

L. Tanganyika

COMOROS
Moroni

ATLANTIC OCEAN

ANGOLA

L. Nyasa

St. Helena (Br.)

15°S

ZAMBIA
Lusaka

MALAWI
Lilongwe

Zambezi River

L. Kariba

Harare
ZIMBABWE

Antananarivo

MAURITIUS
Réunion (Fr.)
Port Loui

NAMIBIA

Windhoek

BOTSWANA
Gaborone

Pretoria
Johannesburg

Maputo
Mbabane
SWAZILAND

Tropic of Capricorn

30°S

Maseru
LESOTHO
Durban

SOUTH AFRICA
Umtata

Cape Town

Port Elizabeth

15°W   15°E   30°E   45°E

EUROPE POLITICAL

- ⊛ National capitals
- ⊙ Cities with populations over one million
- • Other cities
- ⌇ International boundaries

0 — 250 — 500 miles
0 — 250 — 500 kilometers

ATLANTIC OCEAN

ICELAND
Reykjavík
Kópavogur

Barents Sea

Murmansk

Arkhangel'sk

White Sea

L. Onega

L. Ladoga

Norwegian Sea

Narvik

FINLAND
Tampere

Helsinki

Trondheim

Bergen

NORWAY
Oslo

SWEDEN
Göteborg

Stockholm

St. Petersburg

Volga R.

Yaroslavl

RUSSIA

Moscow

Tula

ESTONIA
Tallinn

Riga **LATVIA**

LITHUANIA
Vilnius

RUSSIA
Kaliningrad

BELARUS
Minsk

DENMARK
Aarhus

Copenhagen

Baltic Sea

Gdańsk

POLAND
Poznań
Warsaw
Łódź
Wrocław
Kraków

North Sea

UNITED KINGDOM
Glasgow
Belfast
Leeds
Liverpool
Sheffield
Manchester

IRELAND
Dublin
Cork

Birmingham

London

Thames R.

English Channel

NETHERLANDS
Amsterdam
The Hague
Rotterdam
Antwerp
Ghent
Brussels
BELGIUM

Hamburg
Bremen
Hannover

GERMANY
Berlin
Cologne Leipzig
Dresden

Elbe R.
Oder R.

Ostrava
Prague
CZECH REP

Kiev

Kharkiv

UKRAINE
Lviv
Kirovograd
Dnepropetrovsk
Zaporizhzhya

Dnieper R.
Dniester R.

Kryvyy Rog

MOLDOVA
Chişinău

Odesa

LUXEMBOURG
Luxembourg

Frankfurt
Stuttgart

Rhine R.
Danube R.

LIECHTENSTEIN
Vaduz

Munich

Vienna

SLOVAKIA
Bratislava

Miskolc
Budapest

HUNGARY

Cluj

ROMANIA
Timişoara

Bucharest

FRANCE
Paris

Loire R.
Seine R.

Bordeaux

SWITZERLAND
Bern
Zürich

AUSTRIA
Graz

Lyon

ITALY
Milan
Turin
Genoa

Po R.

San Marino

Florence

SLOVENIA
Ljubljana

CROATIA
Zagreb

BOSNIA-HERZEGOVINA
Sarajevo

Belgrade

YUGOSLAVIA

Durrës

BULGARIA
Sofia
Plovdiv

Danube R.

Black Sea

Bay of Biscay

Toulouse

ANDORRA
Andorra-La Vella

MONACO
Monaco

Marseille
Nice

SAN MARINO

VATICAN CITY

Rome
Naples

Adriatic Sea

Tiranë
ALBANIA

Skopje
MACEDONIA

Thessaloníki

Istanbul

TURKEY
Ankara

ASIA

PORTUGAL
Oporto

SPAIN
Madrid
Saragossa
Barcelona

Valencia

Seville

Lisbon

Duero R.
Ebro R.
Tagus R.

AFRICA

Strait of Gibraltar

Gibraltar (U.K.)

Mediterranean Sea

Palermo

MALTA
Valletta

GREECE
Athens

Aegean Sea

ARCTIC OCEAN

Barents Sea

NEW SIBERIAN IS.

Novaya Zemlya

Laptev Sea

Kara Sea

EUROPE

RUSSIA

Ob R.

Lena R.

Angara R.

Lower Tunguska R.

⊛ Yekaterinburg

Samara ⊛

⊛ Chelyabinsk

⊛ Tomsk

Yenisey R.

⊛ Krasnoyarsk

Orenburg ⊛

⊛ Magnitogorsk

⊙ Omsk

Ishim R.

⊙ Novosibirsk

⊛ Irkutsk

Shilka R.

L. Baikal

⊛ Izmir

■ Krasnodar

Black Sea

⊙ Ankara

TURKEY

GEORGIA

⊛ Tbilisi

⊛ Yerevan

ARMENIA

⊛ Baku

Aral Sea

Ural R.

KAZAKSTAN

L. Balqash

⊛ Ulaanbaat

Mediterranean Sea

Nicosia ⊛
CYPRUS

AZERBAIJAN

Caspian Sea

TURKMENISTAN

UZBEKISTAN

⊛ Tashkent

⊛ Almaty

MONGOLIA

West Bank &
Gaza Strip
⊛ Beirut ⊛ LEBANON
SYRIA
Damascus ⊛
Suez Canal
Jerusalem
⊛ ISRAEL ⊛ Amman
EGYPT *SINAI PEN.*
JORDAN

IRAQ

⊛ Baghdad

Euphrates R.

Tigris R.

⊛ Ashgabat

Amu Darya

Syr Darya

⊙ Bishkek
KYRGYZSTAN

⊛ Ürümqi

⊛ Tehran

Dushanbe ⊛ TAJIKISTAN

Xinjiang

Great Wall

Basra ■
KUWAIT

● Abadan

Kuwait

IRAN

Kabul ⊛

AFGHANISTAN

⊛ Kashmir

Islamabad ⊛

Huang (Yellow R.)

⊛ Lanzhou

CHINA

AFRICA

Mecca ⊛

Riyadh ⊛

⊛ Manama

BAHRAIN

QATAR

Doha ⊛

UNITED ARAB EMIRATES

OMAN

Abu Dhabi ⊛

Persian Gulf

Lahore ⊛

PAKISTAN

Indus R.

Sutlej R.

⊛ Delhi

New Delhi ⊛

Tibet

⊛ Lhasa

Kathmandu ⊛
NEPAL

Thimphu ⊛
BHUTAN

Chengdu ⊙

Chongqing ⊙

Red Sea

SAUDI
ARABIA

Muscat ⊛

Gulf of Oman

Karachi ●

Hyderabad ⊛

Changjiang (Yangzi R.)

⊛ San'a

YEMEN

OMAN

Aden ●

Gulf of Aden

Arabian Sea

⊙ Ahmadabad

INDIA

Ganges R.

Dhaka ⊛
BANGLADESH

Calcutta ●

Brahmaputra R.

Mandalay ●

⊛ Kunming

Hanoi ⊛
LAOS

Socotra (Yemen)

Bombay ●

Hyderabad ⊙

MYANMAR
(BURMA)

Irrawaddy R.

Salween R.

Vientiane ⊛

INDIAN
OCEAN

Madras ●

Bay of Bengal

Yangon ⊛
(Rangoon)

THAILAND

Bangkok ⊛

ANDAMAN IS.
(India)

Andaman Sea

CAMBOD

Phnom Penh ⊛

Ho Chi Minh C

Gulf of Thailand

LAKSHADWEEP
(India)

NICOBAR IS.
(India)

Colombo ⊛
SRI
LANKA

MA

MALDIVES

⊛ Male

Kuala
Lump

Medan ●
Singapore ●
SINGAPOR

N

W ✦ E

S

Sumatra

Palembang

ASIA POLITICAL

⊛ National capitals

◉ Cities with populations over one million

• Other cities

── International boundaries

┈┈ Disputed boundary

| 0 | 250 | 500 | 750 | 1,000 miles |

| 0 | 500 | 1,000 kilometers |

PACIFIC OCEAN

Magadan

KAMCHATKA PENINSULA

Sea of Okhotsk

Aldan R.

Amur R.

Sakhalin I. (Russia)

KURIL IS. (Russia)

Khabarovsk

Sapporo

Vladivostok

Harbin

Inner Mongolia

Sea of Japan

Fushun

Shenyang

NORTH KOREA

P'yongyang

Beijing Dalian

Seoul

Tianjin

SOUTH KOREA

Pusan

Qingdao

Tokyo

Yokohama

Kyoto Nagoya

Kobe

Osaka

JAPAN

Kitakyushu

Yellow Sea

East China Sea

Nanjing

Shanghai

Wuhan

RYUKYU IS. (Japan)

Taipei

TAIWAN

Xijiang (West R.)

Luzon Strait

Guangzhou

Macao (Port.)

Hong Kong

South China Sea

Da Nang

VIETNAM

Tropic of Cancer

MARSHALL ISLANDS

Majuro

KIRIBATI

Bairiki

NORTHERN MARIANA IS. (U.S.)

Palikir

Yaren

NAURU

TUVALU

Funifuti

Philippine Sea

FEDERATED STATES OF MICRONESIA

Guam (U.S.)

FIJI

Suva

Manila

Koror

PALAU

Davao

Equator

SOLOMON ISLANDS

Honiara

VANUATU

Port-Vila

Bandar Seri Begawan

BRUNEI

AYSIA

Celebes Sea

Manado

Jayapura

Irian Jaya

New Guinea

PAPUA NEW GUINEA

Lae

Port Moresby

New Caledonia (Fr.)

I N D O N E S I A

Samarinda

Pontianak

Borneo

Celebes

Banjarmasin

Ujung Pandang

Banda Sea

Arafura Sea

Coral Sea

Jakarta

Java

Surabaya

Bandung

East Timor (Indo.)

Timor

AUSTRALIA

120°E   140°E   160°E

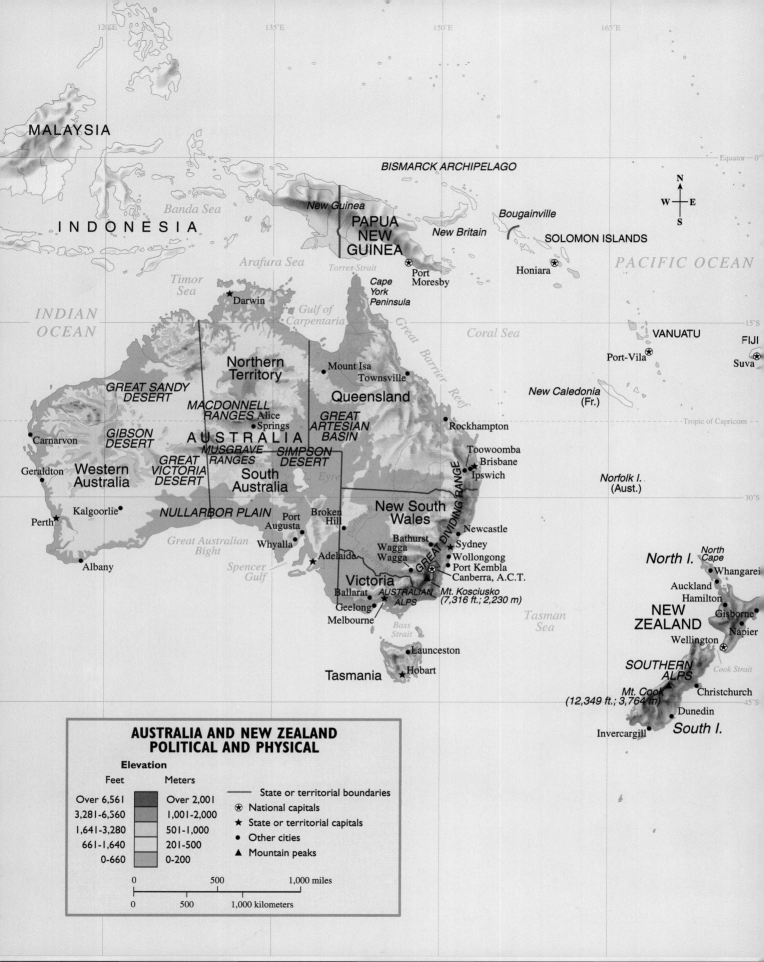

AUSTRALIA AND NEW ZEALAND POLITICAL AND PHYSICAL

Elevation

Feet	Meters
Over 6,561	Over 2,001
3,281-6,560	1,001-2,000
1,641-3,280	501-1,000
661-1,640	201-500
0-660	0-200

— State or territorial boundaries
⊛ National capitals
★ State or territorial capitals
• Other cities
▲ Mountain peaks

0   500   1,000 miles
0   500   1,000 kilometers

MALAYSIA

INDONESIA

Banda Sea

Arafura Sea

Timor Sea

INDIAN OCEAN

BISMARCK ARCHIPELAGO

New Guinea

PAPUA NEW GUINEA

⊛ Port Moresby

Torres Strait

Bougainville

New Britain

SOLOMON ISLANDS

⊛ Honiara

PACIFIC OCEAN

N
W   E
S

Cape York Peninsula

Gulf of Carpentaria

★ Darwin

Northern Territory

GREAT SANDY DESERT

MACDONNELL RANGES • Alice Springs

GIBSON DESERT

• Carnarvon

AUSTRALIA

MUSGRAVE RANGES

GREAT VICTORIA DESERT

Western Australia

• Geraldton

South Australia

• Mount Isa
• Townsville

Queensland

GREAT ARTESIAN BASIN

Coral Sea

Great Barrier Reef

• Rockhampton

VANUATU
Port-Vila ⊛

FIJI
Suva ⊛

New Caledonia (Fr.)

Tropic of Capricorn

Toowoomba •
Brisbane •
★ Ipswich

Norfolk I. (Aust.)

NULLARBOR PLAIN

• Kalgoorlie

★ Perth

L. Eyre

SIMPSON DESERT

Port Augusta •
Whyalla •

Broken Hill •

New South Wales

GREAT DIVIDING RANGE

Bathurst •
Wagga Wagga •

Newcastle •
★ Sydney
• Wollongong
• Port Kembla
⊛ Canberra, A.C.T.

Great Australian Bight

Spencer Gulf

★ Adelaide

• Albany

Victoria

Ballarat •
Geelong •
★ Melbourne

AUSTRALIAN ALPS

Mt. Kosciusko (7,316 ft.; 2,230 m)

Tasman Sea

North I.

North Cape

• Whangarei

Auckland •
Hamilton •

NEW ZEALAND

• Gisborne
• Napier

Wellington ⊛

Bass Strait

• Launceston

Tasmania

★ Hobart

SOUTHERN ALPS

Cook Strait

Mt. Cook (12,349 ft.; 3,764 m)

• Christchurch

• Dunedin

South I.

Invercargill •

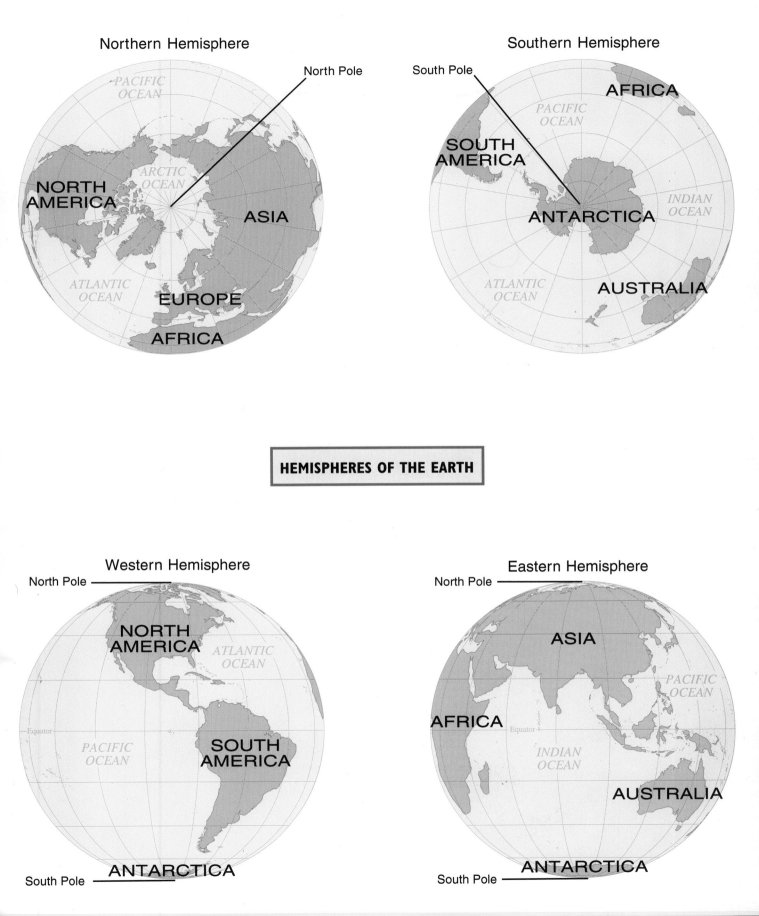

Northern Hemisphere

North Pole

PACIFIC OCEAN

ARCTIC OCEAN

NORTH AMERICA

ASIA

ATLANTIC OCEAN

EUROPE

AFRICA

Southern Hemisphere

South Pole

AFRICA

PACIFIC OCEAN

SOUTH AMERICA

ANTARCTICA

INDIAN OCEAN

ATLANTIC OCEAN

AUSTRALIA

HEMISPHERES OF THE EARTH

Western Hemisphere

North Pole

NORTH AMERICA

ATLANTIC OCEAN

Equator

PACIFIC OCEAN

SOUTH AMERICA

ANTARCTICA

South Pole

Eastern Hemisphere

North Pole

ASIA

PACIFIC OCEAN

AFRICA

Equator

INDIAN OCEAN

AUSTRALIA

ANTARCTICA

South Pole

PACIFIC
OCEAN

Olympia ★ Washington
Salem ★
        Oregon
Sacramento ★
California
Carson City ★
        Nevada
Salt Lake
City ★
        Utah
Phoenix ★
Arizona

Montana
Helena ★
        Idaho
Boise ★
        Wyoming
        Cheyenne ★
        Denver ★
Colorado
Santa Fe ★
New
Mexico

North
Dakota
Bismarck ★
South
Dakota
Pierre ★
Nebraska
Lincoln ★
Kansas
        Topeka ★
Oklahoma
Oklahoma
City ★

Minnesota
St. Paul ★
Iowa
Des Moines ★
Missouri
Jefferson
City ★
Arkansas
Little Rock ★

Texas
Austin ★
Louisiana

PACIFIC
OCEAN

Alaska

Juneau ★

PACIFIC
OCEAN

Honolulu ★

Hawaii

39
26
24
48
7
9
2
17
14
16
31
10
45
44
18
37
8
3
47
33
22

U.S. Places of Interest

⊛ National capital

★ State capitals

Key

1. Assateague Island National Seashore, MD
2. Badlands National Park, SD
3. Carlsbad Caverns National Park, NM
4. Chesapeake Wildlife Refuge, DE
5. Churchill Downs, Louisville, KY
6. Circus World Museum, Baraboo, WI
7. Crater Lake National Park, OR
8. Crater of Diamonds State Park, Little Rock, AR
9. Craters of the Moon National Monument, ID
10. Desert National Wildlife Refuge, NV
11. Etowah Mound, GA
12. Fort Gaines, Dauphin Island, AL
13. Fort Sumter Historic Park, Charleston, SC
14. Frontier Days Rodeo, Cheyenne, WY
15. Gateway Arch, St. Louis, MO
16. Golden Gate Bridge, San Francisco, CA
17. Golden Spike Nat'l Historic Site, Promontory, UT
18. Grand Canyon National Park, AZ
19. Grand Ole Opry, Nashville, TN
20. Green Mountains National Forest, VT
21. Harpers Ferry, WV
22. Hawaii Volcanoes National Park, HI
23. Henry Ford Museum, Dearborn, MI
24. Hockey Hall of Fame, Eveleth, MN
25. Indy 500, Indianapolis, IN
26. International Peace Park, ND
27. Iowa Arts Festival, Iowa City, IA
28. John F. Kennedy Space Center, Cape Canaveral, FL
29. Liberty Bell, Philadelphia, PA
30. Lincoln Monument and Tomb, Springfield, IL
31. Mile High Stadium, Denver, CO
32. Morristown National Historical Park, NJ
33. Denali National Park, AK
34. Mount Vernon, VA
35. Mystic Seaport, Mystic, CT
36. Natchez Museum of African American History and Culture, Biloxi, MS
37. National Cowboy Hall of Fame and Western Heritage Center, Oklahoma City, OK
38. Old Ironsides, Boston, MA
39. Olympic National Park, WA
40. Portland Head Light, ME
41. Rock and Roll Hall of Fame, Cleveland, OH
42. Slater Mill, Pawtucket, RI
43. Statue of Liberty, New York Harbor, NY
44. Strategic Air Command Museum, NE
45. Strong City Annual Rodeo, Strong City, KS
46. Superdome, New Orleans, LA
47. The Alamo, San Antonio, TX
48. Virginia City Ghost Town, Virginia City, MT
49. White Mountains National Forest, NH
50. Wright Brothers National Memorial, NC

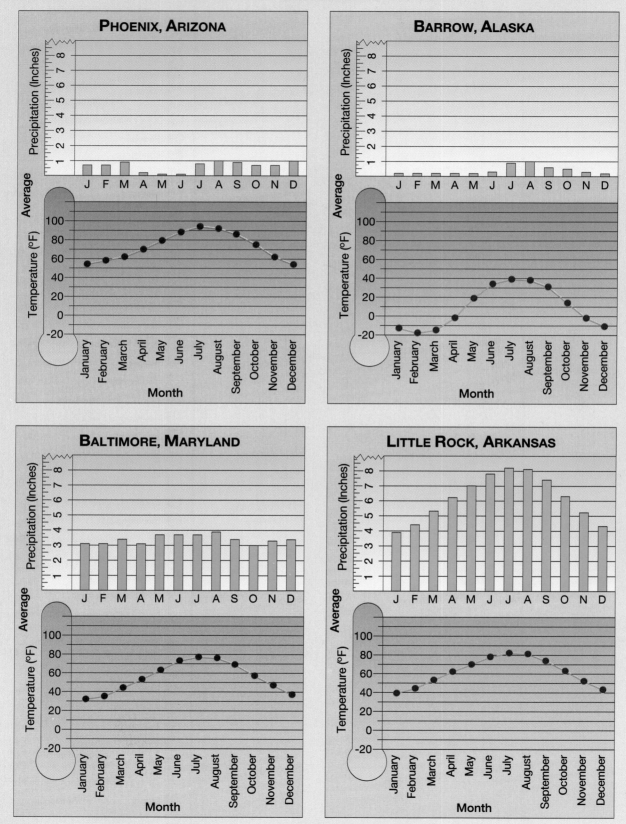

GLOSSARY

Some words in this book may be new to you or difficult to pronounce. Those words have been spelled phonetically in parentheses. The syllable that receives stress in a word is shown in small capital letters.

For example: Chicago (shuh KAH goh)

Most phonetic spellings are easy to read. In the following Pronunciation Key, you can see how letters are used to show different sounds.

PRONUNCIATION KEY

a	after	(AF tur)		yoo	few	(fyoo)
ah	father	(FAH thhur)		u	taken	(TAYK un)
ai	care	(kair)			matter	(MAT ur)
aw	dog	(dawg)		uh	ago	(uh GOH)
ay	paper	(PAY pur)				
e	letter	(LET ur)		ch	chicken	(CHIHK un)
ee	eat	(eet)		g	game	(gaym)
				ing	coming	(KUM ing)
ih	trip	(trihp)		j	job	(jahb)
eye	idea	(eye DEE uh)		k	came	(kaym)
y	hide	(hyd)		ng	long	(lawng)
ye	lie	(lye)		s	city	(SIHT ee)
				sh	ship	(shihp)
oh	flow	(floh)		th	thin	(thihn)
oi	boy	(boi)		thh	feather	(FETHH ur)
oo	rule	(rool)		y	yard	(yahrd)
or	horse	(hors)		z	size	(syz)
ou	cow	(kou)		zh	division	(duh VIHZH un)

A

abbreviation (uh bree vee AY shun)   A shortened form of a word. p. M13.

adapt (uh DAPT)   To change in order to fit new conditions. p. 165.

adobe (uh DOH bee)   A clay brick that has dried in the sun. p. 219.

ancestor (AN ses tur)   A person from whom one is descended. p. 165.

artifact (AHRT uh fakt)   An object, often old, made by humans. p. 107.

assembly line (uh SEM blee lyn)   A row of people working in a line to put together a product. p. 120.

B

barge (bahrj)   A large flat boat used for carrying goods along a river. p. 38.

bar graph (bahr graf)   A graph that uses bars to show information. p. 72.

bee (bee)   A meeting of people to work together or compete. p. 225.

blacksmith (BLAK smihth)   A person who shapes iron to make things, such as horseshoes. p. 200.

boom town (boom toun)   A town that starts suddenly. p. 44.

budget (BUJ iht)   A plan for using money. p. 256.

C

canyon (KAN yun)   A deep, narrow valley with steep sides. p. M16.

capital (KAP ut ul)   A city in which laws and plans for a state or nation are made. p. 23.

caravan (KAR uh van)   A group of people traveling together. p. 149.

chore (chor)   A task that has to be done on a regular basis. p. 200.

citizen (SIHT uh zun)   A person who is a member of a nation. p. 248.

clan (klan)   A group of people who are related to a common ancestor. p. 173.

climate (KLYE mut)   The kind of weather a place has over a long period of time. p. 9.

coast (kohst)   Land that borders on the sea or ocean. pp. M16, 80.

colony (KAHL uh nee)   A place that is settled by people from another country and ruled by that country. p. 191.

combine (KAHM byn)   A machine used to cut grain. p. 51.

community (kuh MYOO nuh tee)   A group of people who share a place, or a place where people live, work, and play. p. 6.

commute (kuh MYOOT)   To travel regularly between two places. p. 117.

compass rose (KUM pus rohz)   A drawing that shows where north, south, east, and west are on a map. p. M10.

Congress (KAHNG grus)   The group of elected people that makes our country's laws. p. 272.

Constitution (kahn stuh TOO shun)   The set of laws by which the United States is governed. p. 271.

continent (KAHN tuh nunt)   A large body of land on the earth. The seven continents are North America, South America, Asia, Africa, Europe, Australia, and Antarctica. p. M6.

council (KOUN sul)   A group of people that works for a community or city government. p. 252.

county (KOUNT ee)   A part of a state that may contain one or more communities. p. 247.

covered wagon (KUV urd WAG un)   A large wagon with an arched canvas cover. p. 142.

cradleboard (KRAYD ul bord)   A carrier for babies, made from leather, wood, and other natural materials. p. 178.

crew (kroo)   All the people who work on a ship. p. 206.

culture (KUL chur)   A way of life. p. 101.

custom (KUS tum)   Something that has been done a certain way for a long time. p. 205.

D

dairy cow (DAIR ee kou)   A cow that produces milk. p. 71.

dam (dam)   A wall built to hold back the flow of water. p. 48.

debate (dee BAYT)   To discuss different sides of a question. p. 258.

district (DIHS trihkt)   An area set aside for a special purpose. p. 277.

E

elder (EL dur)   An older person who is respected in a community. p. 183.

equator (ee KWAYT ur)   An imaginary line drawn around the earth on maps and globes. It is halfway between the North Pole and the South Pole. The equator divides the earth into the Northern and Southern Hemispheres. pp. M5, 294.

explorer (ek SPLOR ur)   A person who travels to unknown places. p. 48.

F

fact (fakt)   A statement that is true and can be proved. p. 244.

factory (FAK tuh ree)   A building where products are made, especially by people using machines. p. 18.

ferry (FER ee)   A boat used for taking people or cars across a body of water. p. 131.

forest (FOR ihst)   A thick growth of trees that covers a large area. p. M16.

G

geography (jee AHG ruh fee)   The study of the earth and the way people use it. p. 23.

globe (glohb)   A model of the earth. p. M4.

goods (goodz)   Products that can be bought and sold. p. 19.

government (GUV urn munt)   Group of people who make laws and provide services. p. 246.

governor (GUV ur nur)   The leader of a state government. p. 260.

H

habitat (HAB ih tat)   The place where an animal or plant usually lives. p. 128.

harbor (HAHR bur)   A sheltered coastal place where ships can dock. pp. M16, 95.

harpoon (hahr POON)   A spear with a sharp point at one end and a cord attached to the other end. p. 170.

harvest (HAHR vihst)   A gathering of ripe crops from the land on which they were grown. p. 51.

hatchery (HACH ur ee)   A place for hatching eggs. p. 65.

hemisphere (HEM ih sfeer)   A half of the earth. p. M5.

herder (HURD ur)   A person who takes care of a herd, or group, of moving animals. p. 152.

heritage (HER ih tihj)   Something that is handed down from one's ancestors or the past. p. 230.

hill (hihl)   Raised land that is lower and more rounded than a mountain. p. M16.

history (HIHS tuh ree)   The story of the past. p. 23.

hogan (HOH gun)   A house made of logs covered with mud. p. 173.

I

immigrant (IHM uh grunt)   A person who comes to settle in a new country. p. 221.

inset map (IHN set map)   A small map connected to a larger one. p. M12.

irrigate (IHR uh gayt)   To supply water to an area through the use of ditches, canals, and pipes. p. 69.

island (EYE lund)   An area that is surrounded by water. p. M16.

K

key (kee)　A part of a map that shows what symbols are used on the map. p. M3.

L

lake (layk)　A body of water that is sometimes surrounded by land. pp. M17, 340.

landform (LAND form)　The shape of the land's surface. p. 32.

latitude (LAT uh tood)　A distance, measured in degrees, north or south of the equator. p. 294.

law (law)　A written rule that everyone must follow. p. 17.

legend (LEJ und)　A story that is handed down through the years among a people. p. 167.

legislature (LEJ ihs lay chur)　A group of people that makes laws. p. 260.

liberty (LIHB ur tee)　The condition of being free from the control of others. p. 310.

line graph (lyn graf)　A graph using lines which shows changes over time. p. 162.

longitude (LAHN juh tood)　A distance, measured in degrees, east or west of the prime meridian. p. 294.

M

map (map)　A drawing that represents all or part of the earth's surface. p. M2.

mayor (MAY ur)　The leader of a town or city. p. 252.

mesa (MAY suh)　A flat-topped hill or mountain with steep sides. p. 172.

mine (myn)　A hole dug in the earth to dig out natural resources, such as gold. p. 44.

mission (MIHSH un)　A small church and settlement where people were taught Christianity. p. 94.

mobile home (MOH bul hohm)　A large movable home that is parked for a long time in one location. p. 146.

moccasin (MAHK uh sun)　A shoe made of soft leather. p. 178.

model (MAH dul)　A small copy of a real thing. p. M4.

modem (MOH dum)　A device that converts information to be sent over telephone lines. p. 307.

monument (MAHN yoo munt)　A building or statue erected to help people remember a special person or an event. p. 286.

mountain (MOUNT un)　A steep, high land area. p. M17.

mouth (of a river) (mouth)　The place where a river flows into a larger body of water. p. M17.

N

national anthem (NASH uh nul AN thum)　The official song of a country. "The Star-Spangled Banner" is the national anthem of the United States. p. 313.

national park (NASH uh nul pahrk)　Land cared for and protected by the national government. p. 149.

natural resource (NACH ur ul REE sors)　Something found in nature that is useful to people, such as a mineral or a body of water. p. 32.

network (NET wurk) A system for connecting computers. p. 306.

Northern Hemisphere (NOR thhurn HEM-ih sfeer) The northern half of the earth. p. M5.

O

ocean (OH shun) A very large body of salt water that covers almost three-fourths of the earth's surface. p. M6.

opinion (uh PIHN yun) A statement that tells what a person feels or believes. p. 244.

P

participate (pahr TIHS uh payt) To take part in something with other people. p. 13.

pasture (PAS chur) A grassland where animals eat. p. 71.

peninsula (puh NIHN suh luh) A piece of land that is bordered by water on three sides. p. M17.

pie graph (pye graf) A kind of graph drawn in the shape of a circle. p. 67.

Pilgrim (PIHL grum) One of the group of people who settled in Plymouth, Massachusetts, in 1620. p. 191.

pioneer (pye uh NEER) A person who goes before, opening the way for others to follow. p. 142.

plain (playn) A broad stretch of level, or nearly level, land. p. M17.

planned community (pland kuh MYOO-nuh tee) A community in which the location of buildings and streets is decided on before building begins. p. 124.

plateau (pla TOH) A raised, level piece of land that covers a large area. p. 77.

pollution (puh LOO shun) The act of letting out wastes or poisonous substances into the environment. The unclean state of air, land, or water. p. 121.

population (pahp yoo LAY shun) The number of people living in a certain place. p. 89.

port (port) A place where ships load and unload products. p. 88.

powwow (POU wou) A celebration of Native American culture that includes traditional dances, songs, and traditional dress. p. 181.

precipitation (pree sihp uh TAY shun) Rain, snow, or any other moisture that falls from the sky. p. 168.

President (PREZ uh dunt) The elected leader of the United States. p. 271.

prime meridian (prym muh RIHD ee un) The line of longitude from which other lines of longitude are measured. p. 294.

principle (PRIHN suh pul) A rule or truth used to guide behavior. p. 300.

profit (PRAHF iht) The money gained in a business after expenses have been subtracted. p. 68.

public transportation (PUB lihk trans pur-TAY shun) Transportation, often run by a local government, that anyone can pay to use. p. 96.

R

rally (RAL ee) A large meeting held for a particular purpose. p. 149.

ranch (ranch)   A large farm where cattle, sheep, or horses are raised. p. 76.

reindeer (RAYN deer)   A large deer found in northern regions. p. 152.

representative (rep ruh ZEN tuh tihv)   A person who acts or speaks for others. p. 249.

reservation (rez ur VAY shun)   Land set aside for a particular use. Some Native Americans live on reservations in the United States. Many Native American reservations are located in the West. p. 140.

responsibility (rih spahn suh BIHL uh tee)   Something a person is expected to do or take care of. p. 16.

river (RIHV ur)   A long, flowing body of water. p. M17.

rural area (ROOR ul AIR ee uh)   An uncrowded place where towns are far apart and surrounded by open land, such as fields, or forests. p. 62.

S

scale (skayl)   A measurement on a map that shows the distances between places. p. M9.

seine (sayn)   A net that is used to catch fish near the surface of the water. p. 81.

services (SUR vihs ihz)   Work that is done for others, rather than work in which a product is made. p. 19.

settlement house (SET ul munt hous)   A neighborhood center that provides services, such as job training and English classes. p. 302.

settler (SET lur)   A person who makes his or her home in a new place. p. 197.

site (syt)   A piece of land to be used for a special purpose. p. 183.

skyscraper (SKYE skray pur)   A very tall building. p. 89.

slate (slayt)   A thin piece of smooth rock that is used as a chalkboard. p. 227.

sod (sahd)   The top layer of earth containing grass with its roots. p. 224.

solar energy (SOH lur EN ur jee)   Energy that comes from the sun. p. 36.

source (of a river) (sors)   The place where a river begins. p. M17.

Southern Hemisphere (SUTHH urn HEM-ih sfeer)   The southern half of the earth. p. M5.

special-purpose (map) (SPESH ul PUR pus)   A map that shows a special type of information, such as amounts of rainfall. p. M14.

suburb (SUB urb)   A community located near a city. p. 114.

subway (SUB way)   A train that runs underground. p. 97.

Supreme Court (suh PREEM kort)   The highest court in the United States, made up of nine judges who decide whether laws are fair. p. 272.

survey (sur VAY)   To measure and mark the boundaries of a piece of land. p. 277.

symbol (SIHM bul) A sign used on a map to stand for real things and places. p. M3.

An object that represents something else. p. 300.

T

tax (taks)   Money collected by a government. p. 250.

taxi (TAK see)   An automobile that carries passengers for money. p. 96.

technology (tek NAHL uh jee)   The use of science to make tasks easier in industry and everyday life. p. 67.

tipi (TEE pee)   A cone-shaped tent made of animal skins or other materials. p. 139.

tornado (tor NAY doh)   A column of air that whirls very fast and often causes destruction. p. 223.

totem pole (TOHT um pohl)   A wooden post carved and painted with animals and other natural objects that tells a story or legend. p. 169.

tourism (TOR ihz um)   The business of serving people who travel. p. 105.

trade (trayd)   The buying and selling of products. p. 39.

tradition (truh DIHSH un)   A set of very old beliefs and ways of doing things. p. 140.

transcontinental (tranz kahn tuh NENT ul) That which goes from one side of a continent to the other. p. 234.

trawl (trawl)   A fishing net that is dragged along the ocean floor. p. 81.

V

valley (VAL ee)   A long, low area of land, usually situated between mountains or hills. p. M17.

vaquero (vah KER oh)   A person hired to care for cattle. p. 218.

volunteer (vahl un TEER)   A person who chooses to do work and is not paid for it. p. 101.

vote (voht)   To express one's choice in an election. p. 248.

W

wagon train (WAG un trayn)   A group or line of wagons traveling together. p. 144.

weather (WETHH ur)   The condition of the air at a certain time. p. 9.

White House (wyt hous)   The building in which the President of the United States lives and works. p. 282.

wigwam (WIHG wahm)   A traditional Native American home, sometimes shaped as a dome. p. 203.

INDEX

Page numbers in italics indicate illustrations.

ACKNOWLEDGEMENTS

Special thanks are given to the following: Acorn Hall, Morristown; American Sheep Industry Association, Englewood, CO; Chicago Transit Authority, Chicago, IL; The Children's Museum, Boston, MA; Department of Water Resources, State of California, Sacramento, CA; Greater Houston Convention Bureau, Houston, TX; Historical Society, Morristown, NJ; Houston International Festival, Houston, TX; Houston Livestock and Rodeo Show, Houston, TX; Levittown Historical Society, Levittown, NY; Mount Sinai Medical Center, New York, NY; Museum of Early Trades and Crafts, Madison, NJ; National Agricultural Statistics Service, U.S. Department of Agriculture, Washington, D.C.; National Museum of the American Indian, Smithsonian Institution, New York, NY; National Parks Service Office of Public Affairs, U.S. Department of the Interior, Washington, D.C.; New Jersey Agricultural Museum, North Brunswick, NJ; North Dakota Historical Society, State Archives and Historical Research Library, Bismarck, ND; North Dakota State Library, Bismarck, ND; Oregon-California Trails Association, Independence, MO; Plimoth Plantation, Plymouth, MA; Texas Medical Center, Houston, TX; Wool Bureau, Inc., U.S. Branch, International Wool Secretariat, New York, NY.

Grateful acknowledgment is made to the following publishers, authors, and agents for their permission to reprint copyrighted material. Every effort has been made to locate all copyright proprietors; any errors or omissions in copyright notice are inadvertent and will be corrected in future printings as they are discovered.

from *Across the Wide Dark Sea* by Jean Van Leeuwen. Text copyright ©1995 by Jean Van Leeuwen. Cover illustration copyright ©1995 by Thomas B. Allen. Used by permission of Dial Books for Young Readers, a division of Penguin Books USA Inc.

from *Family Farm* by Thomas Locker. Copyright ©1988 by Thomas Locker. Used by permission of Dial Books, a division of Penguin Books USA Inc.

from *If You're Not from the Prairie...* by David Bouchard. Text copyright ©1995 by David Bouchard. Cover illustration copyright ©1995 by Henry Ripplinger. Reprinted with the permission of Atheneum Books for Young Readers, an imprint of Simon & Schuster, and of Raincoast Books Distribution Limited.

from *Look Out, Washington D.C.!* by Patricia Reilly Giff. Text copyright ©1995 by Patricia Reilly Giff. Cover illustration copyright ©1995 by Blanche Sims. Used by permission of Delacorte Press, a division of Bantam Doubleday Dell Publishing Group, Inc.

from *Paul Bunyan and Babe the Blue Ox* by Jan Gleiter and Kathleen Thompson. Copyright ©1985 by Raintree Publishers Limited Partnership. Reprinted by permission of Steck-Vaughn Company.

from *Round and Round the Money Goes* by Melvin and Gilda Berger. Text copyright ©1993 by Melvin and Gilda Berger. Cover illustration copyright ©1993 by Jane McCreary. Reprinted by permission of Ideals Children's Books, an imprint of Hambleton-Hill Publishing, Inc.

CREDITS

Front Cover *Design, Art Direction, and Production:* Design Five, NYC; *Photo:* Dana Sigall. *Details:* Ann Duncan/Tom Stack & Associates; Comstock; R. Garnett/Visual Contact; Terry Donnelly/Tom Stack & Associates; Don & Pat Valenti/DRK Photo; Greg Ryan & Sally Beyer/Positive Reflections.

Maps Ortelius Design
Atlas Maps Mapping Specialists Limited, except 334: Ortelius Design

All photographs by Silver Burdett Ginn (SBG) unless otherwise noted.

Photographs 8: William M. Horowitz/The Image Bank. 8–9: Walter Bibikow/The Image Bank. 9: Alvis Upitis/The Image Bank. 10: *t.l.* R. Thompson/Picture Perfect USA ; *t.r.* Picture Perfect USA; *b.l.* Kul Bhatia/Picture Perfect USA. 11: *t.* Picture Perfect USA; *b.* Jean S. Buldain/Picture Perfect USA. 12: Reid Miles for SBG. 13: *t.* Jose Carrillo/PhotoEdit; *b.* Deborah Davis/PhotoEdit. 17: Nancy Sheehan/PhotoEdit. 19: *t., m.r.* Earl Fansler Photographers, Inc.; *b.* Myrleen Ferguson/PhotoEdit. 22–23: ChromoSohm/Sohm/Unicorn Stock Photos. 23: Tom Brakefield/The Stock Market. 32: *t.* Larry Aiuppy/FPG International. 34: *t.* Tom Bean/DRK Photo; *b.* S. Nielsen/DRK Photo. 34–35: Rod Planck/Tom Stack & Associates. 35: *t.l.* Robert Knight/Tony Stone Images; *t.r.* Buff & Gerald Corsi/Tom Stack & Associates; *b.* Greg Ryan & Sally Beyer/Positive Reflections. 36: *l.* Gary Yeowell/Tony Stone Images; *r.* John Cancalosi/Tom Stack & Associates. 38: The Granger Collection, New York. 38–39: © David R. Frazier/Photo Researchers, Inc. 40: Dwight B. Miller. 41: *l.* Randall Hyman; *r.* Charles Schmidt/Unicorn Stock Photos. 42–43: Dwight B. Miller. 43: John Warden/Tony Stone Images. 44: *t.* Colorado Historical Society; *m.* Denver Public Library, Western History Department; *b.* James Balog/Tony Stone Images. 45: *t.* Aaron Strong/Liaison International; *b.* Bob Thomason/Tony Stone Images. 46–47: Tom Bean. 47: MP Kahl/DRK Photo. 48: *t.* The Heard Museum, Phoenix, Arizona; *b.* Superstock. 48––49: *bkgd.* Randy A. Prentice. 50–51: R. Garnett/Visual Contact. 52–53: Thomas Kitchen/Tom Stack & Associates. 56–57: Abbe Boon for SBG. 62–63: Larry Lefever from Grant Heilman. 64: *t.* David Conklin/PhotoEdit; *b.l.* Inga Spence/Tom Stack & Associates. 65: *bkgd.* Byron Augustin/Tom Stack & Associates; *l.* Garry McMichael from Grant Heilman; *r.* Runk/Schoenberger from Grant Heilman. 66–67: Grant Heilman. 68: *t.* Gary J. Benson. 73: *t.l.* John Colwell from Grant Heilman; *t.r.* Larry Lefever from Grant Heilman; *b.l.* Larry Lefever from Grant Heilman. 74–75: *bkgd.* Grant Heilman. 76–77: Barrie Rokeach/The Image Bank. 78: *t.* Linda Dufurrena from Grant Heilman; *b.* Midwestock. 89: Hiroyuki Matsumoto/Tony Stone Images. 91: Michael Yamashita/Westlight. 92: Frances M. Roberts. 93: Michael Kingsford/Envision. 94: The Bettmann Archive. 96: *l.* Peter Pearson/Tony Stone Images; *r.* Barry Durand/Odyssey Productions. 101: *t.* Courtesy, Sarah King; *m.* Archive Photos; *b.* Ron Litt/TexStock. 102–103: Texas Medical Center. 104: Nigel Atherton/Tony Stone Images. 106: *t.* Robert Frerck/Odyssey Productions. 107: Robert Frerck/Tony Stone Images. 114–115: © 1995 Alex S. MacLean/Landslides. 116–117: Ken Karp for SBG. 118–119: Don Smetzer/Tony Stone Images. 120: *t.* Steve Proehl/The Image Bank; *b.* Ford Motor Company. 121: *t.* Ted Horowitz/The Stock Market; *b.* William McCoy/Rainbow. 124: Bernard Hoffman/LIFE Magazine/© TIME, Inc. 126: *t.* E.R. Degginger/Color-Pic, Inc.; *b.* Joe McDonald/Bruce Coleman. 127: *t.*